Law, Force and Diplomacy
at Sea

To my parents

Law, Force and Diplomacy at Sea

Ken Booth

University College of Wales, Aberystwyth

London
GEORGE ALLEN & UNWIN
Boston   Sydney

George Allen & Unwin (Publishers) Ltd,
40 Museum Street, London WC1A 1LU, UK

George Allen & Unwin (Publishers) Ltd,
Park Lane, Hemel Hempstead, Herts HP2 4TE, UK

Allen & Unwin, Inc.,
Fifty Cross Street, Winchester, Mass. 01890, USA

George Allen & Unwin Australia Pty Ltd,
8 Napier Street, North Sydney, NSW 2060, Australia

First published in 1985.

British Library Cataloguing in Publication Data

Booth, Ken
    Law, force and diplomacy at sea.
1. Maritime law
I. Title
    341.4'5   JX4411
ISBN 0-04-341027-8
ISBN 0-04-341028-6 Pbk

Library of Congress Cataloging in Publication Data

Booth, Ken
    Law, force and diplomacy at sea.
    Bibliography: p.
    Includes index.
    1. Maritime law.   2. Naval law.   3. Naval strategy.
I. Title.
JX4411.B66 1985   341.4'5   84-9381
ISBN 0-04-341027-8 (alk. paper)
ISBN 0-03-341028-6 (pbk. : alk. paper)

Set in 10 on 11½ point Palatino by Lathams Typesetting, Dunstable
and printed in Great Britain
by Butler and Tanner Ltd., Frome and London.

Contents

Maps

ix

Preface

I once heard a story about a poor woman from the industrial north of England who was taken to the seaside. She had never seen the ocean before. Thrilled, she walked across the sand and stood in the water. For the first time in her life, she said with wonder, she had finally seen something of which there was enough for everybody.

Two generations later, this story seems like ancient history. Today, the oceans are used and abused, and claimed and occupied at an unprecedented rate. Even the seven seas cannot now match human need, and greed. Were the poor northern woman to retrace her steps across the same beach today, she would probably look out, with her feet smeared with tar and with an oil rig spoiling her view, and immediately realize that there is no longer enough ocean for every-body — unless wisdom and sensible management are allowed to prevail.

In the rapidly changing maritime environment of the last decade, management and control have been the logical responses to the heavy pressures on the use of the sea. These pressures and responses inevitably have long- and short-term implications for those accustomed to use the seas in traditional ways. Navies, obviously, cannot be un-affected. And it is this confrontation between the desire of most states for greater national control over adjacent parts of the ocean and a 'fairer' distribution of the maritime resources beyond, and the contin-uing desire of the traditional naval powers to be free to use the sea to the maximum of their naval and economic ability, which has pro-duced the tension that provides the setting for this book. Clearly, there are serious implications for naval strategy in the growing trend towards national and international jurisdiction over larger parts of the troubled maritime common.

Since the early 1970s the attention of the major navies has been drawn to an unusual extent to the subject of the changing law of the sea — a subject whose own evolution has been one of the clearest indicators of the rapidly evolving maritime scene. The focus of this attention has been the Third United Nations Conference on the Law of the Sea (UNCLOS III), and it is the purpose of this book to examine the naval dimension of the work of the conference, and to speculate about its implications for the future of naval power. The future cannot be ignored, since it will be argued that UNCLOS III represents a beginning more than an end: the international politics of the sea will never be the same again.

Law, Force and Diplomacy at Sea is directed to three groups of readers. First, it attempts to explain to students of naval strategy the present state of play regarding the relevant provisions of the law of the sea, and to speculate about future trends which might affect naval strategy. Secondly, it attempts to indicate to those international lawyers with an interest in the law of the sea the most relevant aspects of contemporary naval developments. And finally it is hoped that the book might direct the attention of students of defence policy and international affairs generally towards the important security questions concerning that watery element which covers approximately two-thirds of the earth's surface.

In seeking to interest these three groups, this book is intended to contribute to the debate taking place about the signature and ratification of the UN Convention On The Law Of The Sea, which was first opened for signature in December 1982. By analysing the naval dimension of the problem in detail, we should be able to see more clearly what would be achieved by a widely supported Convention, and what risks are being jeopardized by the non-adherence of several major powers. Nevertheless, it is important to note that many of the arguments which follow will remain valid regardless of the fate of the 1982 Convention; this is because some of its main provisions, notably the legitimizing of the exclusive economic zone (EEZ), have already become established features of the maritime scene as a result of the development of customary international law. As well as participating in the current debate about the Convention, it is also hoped that the book will contribute to the drawing up of the agenda for the discussion of the relationship between naval strategy and the law of the sea in the post-UNCLOS III world.

This book grew out of a paper which I presented to the Annual Conference of the Law of the Sea Institute (LSI) at The Hague in 1978. My thanks are due initially to Professor Gary Knight, for inviting me to that conference, and then to the Director of the LSI, Dr John Craven, for granting me permission to expand and revise material subsequently published in the proceedings of the conference. The original paper was published in *The Law of the Sea: Neglected Issues,* edited by J. K. Gamble, Jr. Five years later, stimulation to look back at UNCLOS III and finish off the book was provided by an invitation by Professor Douglas Johnston to present a paper at the LSI's 1983 Conference in Oslo. The proceedings of that conference, *The 1982 Convention on the Law of the Sea,* are being edited by Albert Koers and Bernard H. Oxman.

I wish to record my gratitude to Jane Davis, a selfless research

Preface

assistant, for her help during the preparation of the original paper; and to Dr Barry Buzan and Dr Barry D. Hunt for their detailed comments on it. For typing the manuscript I thank Mrs D. Hamer, Mrs E. Jenkins and Mrs M. Weston; and for drawing the maps Mr M. Gelly Jones. In addition to the LSI, the following granted me permission to reprint material: the *International Journal*, for paragraphs first published in my article 'Naval strategy and the spread of psycho-legal boundaries at sea' (from vol. 38, no. 3); the *San Diego Law Review*, for the appendix (from vol. 20, no. 3); and *Time* magazine, for the map printed on page 131 (from the issue of 11 July 1983). Finally, it would be churlish not to express my gratitude to Michael Holdsworth and John Whitehead of George Allen & Unwin, for showing me a degree of patience which was as encouraging as it was surprising.

This book would not have been written if, in the first place, officers of the LSI had not encouraged me to try to confront the military issues of the law of the sea — a subject I had previously avoided. By such encouragement, these individuals were fulfilling the Institute's mandate to provide a forum for the exchange of information and ideas concerning the uses of the sea and its resources. The Institute stimulates debate and disseminates knowledge, and long may it succeed in its task. Such efforts are the foundation-stones for the sane management of the oceans. As we face a future in which there is no longer enough sea for everybody, the sharing of relevant ideas and knowledge is at a premium. It is one of our most precious renewable resources.

KEN BOOTH

Abbreviations

ABM	anti-ballistic missile(s)
ASW	anti-submarine warfare
EEZ	exclusive economic zone
EFZ	exclusive fishery zone
ICBM	inter-continental ballistic missile(s)
IMO	International Maritime Organization
LOS	law of the sea
MEZ	maritime exclusion zone
NATO	North Atlantic Treaty Organization
OAU	Organization of African Unity
SALT	Strategic Arms Limitation Talks
SLBM	submarine-launched ballistic missile(s)
SSBN	ballistic missile firing submarine
START	Strategic Arms Reduction Talks
TEZ	total exclusion zone
UNCLOS	United Nations Conference on the Law of the Sea
UNCTAD	United Nations Conference Trade and Development

PART ONE

The Context

1

Between Law and War:
The Problem

Naval strategy and the law of the sea have always been connected. But never has the character of the relationship, or its implications, been as complex as it promises to be in the years and decades ahead. International politics have entered, many of us believe, an era of manifold interaction and multicrisis, in which global problems and national assertiveness threaten to rip the fabric of order. Struggle will be the norm and some states will collapse under the strain. In such a setting the variables and issues which are the stuff of international politics promise to be more complicated and confused than ever before. This will be the case in maritime affairs, as elsewhere, and it is against these unsettled and unsettling prospects that speculation must take place about the future relationship between the changing law of the sea and the changing character of naval strategy.

The Neglected Military Dimension

Through the six years of preparation,[1] eight years of negotiation and eleven sessions which led up to the signing and in some cases the non-signing of the UN Convention On The Law Of The Sea at Montego Bay, Jamaica, on 10 December 1982, the public discussion of the changing law of the sea was sometimes akin to watching *Hamlet* without the Prince. The naval factor was crucial to the positions of some states, but it was not at centre stage — or did not seem to be. To the superficial observer, an essential part of the plot seemed to be missing. It has therefore been entirely appropriate to classify the military dimension of the changing law of the sea as a 'neglected issue'.[2]

The apparent neglect of the military dimension in the public deliberations of UNCLOS III should be no surprise to close observers of the United Nations. On-stage performances in that organization often fail to hold up a mirror to the real world of affairs. The United Nations has some of the characteristics of a church, as well as all the characteristics of a debating chamber. The ritual incantations of this peculiar but indispensable forum are usually most evident when its members deal with disarmament. Consequently, it would have been difficult for UNCLOS III to have completely escaped the organization's normal habits. As a result, UNCLOS III seemed to treat military considerations rather like Victorians in Britain treated sex, that is, as 'an inexplicable incursion which must occasionally be indulged, but which should always be ignored'.[3]

The fact that the naval dimension did not seem to play its full part in UNCLOS III does not mean that everybody concerned thought the matter to be unimportant. Such an impression would be mistaken. It should not be forgotten that while reticent Victorian patriarchs might have ignored the subject of sex in the drawing room, elsewhere they took the opportunity to father many offspring. Similarly, while the naval dimension of the changing law of the sea was generally neglected in public UN forums, the subject did receive appropriate attention from naval establishments, and particularly those of the traditional naval powers.[4] Through the 1970s the changing law of the sea was of some strategic concern to all those governments with an interest in deploying warships at some distance from their own coastlines.

There was therefore a 'backroom' quality to the diplomatic treatment of the military dimension of the changing law of the sea. But the subject was neglected in another sense by those groups which in the 1970s wrote at greatest length about the law of the sea, namely, international lawyers and those who might be called politico-ecologists. The neglect of these groups took the form of neglectful analysis. The politico-ecologists rejected thinking in military terms, or tried to cope with complex reality by reducing it to a few simple propositions and moral standpoints. As a result, nobody much listened to them: this was sometimes a pity. Among the few international lawyers who devoted time to thinking as opposed simply to talking about military strategy, some were decidely conservative, if not hawkish. As a result, they tended to gain the ear of officials: this was not always undesirable.

Despite the saturation of the market-place of ideas on general law of the sea issues, there is still a need for a comprehensive analysis of its military dimension, particularly if it is informed by strategic rather than legalistic or idealistic thinking, and if at the same time it goes beyond the generally narrow confines of most writing about the subject. Since the future of the law of the sea still remains to be settled, even after the arrival of the 1982 Convention, this need will remain for some while to come.

Falling between Stools

Strategists and international lawyers usually make strange bed-fellows. Exponents in law and in the application of reason over power do not easily snuggle up to brokers in disorder and international conflict. There is a mutual coolness. Consequently, the issues which lie between them usually fail to get the attention they deserve.

In areas where strategists and international lawyers should have overlapping interests, such as the military implications of the changing law of the sea, both groups tend either to ignore the other's area of expertise entirely, or embrace its 'conventional convictions' with enthusiasm and some relief, but perhaps with less than full understanding. As a result, issues of mutual interest have not attracted an appropriate standard of commentary. The military implications of the law of the sea is one impoverished subject straddling the boundary between law and strategy, and the laws of war are another. Only the surface of these subjects tends to be examined. This was certainly the case for a long time with the strategic dimensions of the law of the sea. For many years there was little subtle analysis and few new ideas. One still does not need to read much on this subject before one finds oneself digesting the same material. The record suggests that the changing law of the sea is too serious to be left to international lawyers.

Both strategists and international lawyers have suffered from what Anatol Rapoport has called the 'blindness of involvement', the tendency of any profession to focus so narrowly on its own area of expertise that it ignores the extent to which knowledge is a seamless web (Rapoport, 1960, ch. 16). In addition to this familiar habit, there is an extra element involved in the present case resulting from the almost quasi-ideological professional antipathy between the relevant professions. Strategists, on the one hand, tend to regard international law as inconsequential in the world of power and force, and they see international lawyers as unworldly pedants. In contrast, international lawyers tend to regard strategists and their subject matter as being not quite respectable, and rather crude. Each profession regards the other's area of expertise as too specialized or technical, and therefore something best left to the strange experts interested in such matters. Knowledge, in consequence, becomes highly compartmentalized. Specialists rarely read each other's professional journals, and rarely does specialist speak unto specialist. The drawbacks are obvious. The world is full of problems which are made worse for the want of shared information and ideas.

It is therefore important to resist the tendency to compartmentalization. Instead we should stress the unity of law and strategy. After all, they are not utterly distinct activities. Both the law of the sea and

5

naval strategy have their roots in and are concerned with the national interests of states in using the oceans in desired ways, and in preventing their being used in an adverse fashion. Both areas of expertise seek to cope with problems which arise in the international market-place of power and influence. In short, both law and war are continuations of politics by other means.

In recent years talking about the law of the sea has become one of those growth industries so characteristic of modern academic life. At first such industries flourish in response to events in the world of affairs. After a time the industry often develops a momentum of its own, and the relevent specialists talk largely to themselves. Writing and talking tends to expand to fill the time which the experts have to develop their ideas, which over the prolonged history of UNCLOS III has been a great deal. Despite this, the military dimension of the law of the sea has nevertheless remained neglected. In part this was a reflection of the proclivities of the law of the sea 'community' and the distractions of naval establishments.

Through the 1970s, while the law of the sea industry flourished, Western naval strategists were for the most part preoccupied by a variety of more immediate concerns; this prevented them from thinking too much about what many of them saw as the UN talk-shop and its academic baggage-train. For each of the major naval establishments, the technical, political and economic perplexities involved in maintaining or enhancing the utility of naval forces in an increasingly hostile environment meant that law of the sea matters only forced their way in through the cracks. Furthermore, devising strategies for, and then fighting budgetary battles at home also took up an inordinate amount of time, energy and intellectual throw-weight. (It is not usually appreciated that the most troublesome day-to-day worry for naval establishments is not the strategic development of their potential wartime adversary, but the resource-hunger and hence budgetary ambitions of their own national armies and air forces.)

While the major naval establishments were distracted by more pressing concerns, the attention of the law of the sea community was dominated by the commercial and resource problems and prospects relating to the management of the oceans. This emphasis on resource rather than strategic questions accorded with the immediate interests of most of the countries involved in the changing maritime environment. In a broader sense it also seemed to be in line with the belief in the 1970s that international politics should be more concerned with economic, environmental and social issues than with the narrowly military concerns which had traditionally dominated national agendas. In the 1970s security and order came to be understood to rest on more than merely a balance of firepower. Ideas flourished about a 'North—South dialogue' and a 'New International Economic Order'.

But at the start of the 1980s the perspectives of many observers changed almost overnight. Realism came back into fashion. For the industrialized world immediate concerns about national economic stability elbowed out ideas about a new international economic order, and traditonal military anxieties rose to the top of many national agendas. For some, including the United States of Ronald Reagan and the Britain of Margaret Thatcher, this meant that narrower 'defence' problems replaced wider 'security' issues — a change which had loud echoes in the law of the sea negotiations.

In the relatively stable 1970s it was appropriate that military concerns were low on the agenda for many states: but in the more complex 1980s, when feelings about international insecurity have intensified dramatically, it is equally appropriate that military concerns are given more attention. Several countries see themselves at a strategic crossroads. Even so, the strategic problems of most countries are not primarily naval, since few have the capability or will to use warships at great distances from their own shores. Consequently, to date, their interest in the development of the law of the sea has been affected more by economic than by military considerations. So far, defence policy has not been a dominant factor in the national policies of most countries towards the law of the sea: but for a fistful of the most powerful states, strategy has been a major determinant, and this will remain so for the foreseeable future.

While naval strategy has not been the determining factor in the maritime policies of most countries, the law of the sea has not been a major determinant in the evolution of naval strategy. Naval strategy has been and will be shaped by threat perceptions, economic considerations and technological innovations rather than by changes in the legal regime at sea. Consequently we would expect naval strategy to change in the years ahead regardless of whether and how the legal regime at sea develops. Naval strategy cannot stand still, and remain effective. It has always to adjust to the material and psychological 'realities' of its time. That said, it is evident that developments in the law of the sea will affect the course of future naval strategy, though in the medium term — say, twenty years — it will be a matter of fine tuning rather than basic change. No international legal regime at sea which is likely in that time-span will fundamentally affect the exercise of naval power, though it will later be argued that this will not necessarily be the case thereafter. For the immediate future naval strategy can be conceived as a canoe being propelled downstream by an irresistible current. Developments in the law of the sea represent the paddle. The canoe has to 'go' with the current (the technical, political and economic changes) but the paddle will enable it to veer marginally to one side or the other, as usefully and successfully as the sense and strength of the occupants permit. Good navigation depends upon the judicious alignment of canoe, paddle and current, just as an effective policy depends upon the judicious alignment of strategy, tactics and the flow of events.

Approaches and Assumptions

From these introductory remarks, it should be evident that the problem we face is a complex one. Consequently, in thinking about such a diverse and unsettled set of interrelationships as those involved in the future military uses of the sea, it is sensible to avoid highly pin-pointed prediction. Here, as elsewhere in international relations, any attempt to produce accurate prediction for more than a short time ahead (the time will vary with the subject matter) is an activity which cannot be taken seriously. The aim in this study is therefore modest. Instead of offering pin-pointed prediction, it is exercise in conjecture or speculation (Knorr and Morgenstern, 1968); it attempts to think ahead with what relevant evidence is available in order to identify types of legal and strategic developments and interrelationships which might arise out of likely trends in the maritime environment.

Confidence in the unpredictability of the future is entirely justified by the nature of the subject matter. Strategic doctrines that have been thought 'timeless' one year have dropped out of sight a few years later, and in a throwaway era of rapid research and development, military technology is often obsolete before the first rust-spot appears on the bodywork. Ten years can be a long time in international politics. In the 1970s, for example, some national attitudes on law of the sea matters changed almost overnight, as with the Afro-Asian 'discovery' of the sea or the rapid switch of attitude by the traditional maritime powers on the EEZ concept. Uncertainty about the future is further compounded by the fact that the outcome of several international conflicts, including some with a maritime dimension, is dependent upon the impact of the 'contingent and unforeseen', and on the dynamic interaction of various unpredictable developments. The maritime environment is an uncertain medium in more ways than one, and any attempt to make precise predictions is not only likely to turn out a failure, but is also likely to be dangerous or wasteful or both if specific policy decisions are taken on the basis of those predictions.

In addition to rejecting highly pin-pointed prediction, the student of this subject should also recognize that it is less meaningful than ever to conceive 'naval strategy' as a discrete segment of military affairs. Accordingly, in the discussion which follows it is to be understood that naval strategy no longer simply means warships. Not only is it increasingly important to stress the interconnectedness of land, sea and air forces, but more than ever 'naval strategy' has come to be concerned with the projection of military power or force against the shore. The idea that warships exist simply to fight warships has had its day, and the concept of naval strategy has had to expand to meet this change. Our concern is with the use of the sea in so far as it has military implications. These will mainly be 'naval', but by no means exclusively so.

Naval strategists, like other strategists, have a long tradition of being incurious about other nations (Booth, 1979a). Because of this, they have a poor record of being able to see how their own behaviour and ideas have appeared to others, and they have a poor record when it comes to understanding the hopes and fears of other nations. This in part explains why threat analysis and strategic forecasting have generally been done so badly. The profound and misleading ethnocentrism which characterizes much thinking about international relations extends to the issue of the law of the sea. It means, for example, that the literature which exists on the military implications of the law of the sea is dominated by Western and especially US hopes and fear. The present study hopes to suggest some different perspectives, and at least indicate possible implications for the navies of small and medium powers, as well as those of the superpowers and the other major powers. Unfortunately, however, it must be admitted that there is relatively little material available to help detailed speculation about these other navies. It is therefore hoped that the lacuna of this study will provoke and encourage area specialists to do the necessary work on regional naval developments. In a world of better communications (but not necessarily better communication), increased interaction (but not necessarily better understanding of it), and with the rise of new regional powers, it is more important than ever to have a global perspective when contemplating strategic developments.

While the variety of national outlooks which focus on the subject matter of this study is recognized, the main emphasis throughout will be on the problems and prospects for the major naval powers ('naval powers' being loosely defined through this book as those with an interest in deploying warships at some distance from their own coastlines, and not simply in contiguous waters). The emphasis on the major naval powers is easily justified since the major naval powers will be most affected by, and therefore have most interest in, the strategic implications of the changing law of the sea. Consequently this book will be of most interest to readers in North America and Great Britain.

It is widely expected that the 1980s and beyond will be a grim period in international affairs. Interdependence and violence will rub together closely, and produce an era of multicrisis. War and intervention seem to be back in season, and this must form part of the backdrop to any contemplation of the future of strategy. However, although this book is concerned with the threat and use of force, there will be little about nuclear war, the ultimate use of force. Nuclear war is possible, and in the long term even probable, but it cannot be regarded as a continuation of politics in any commonsense meaning of Clausewitz's famous aphorism: any war which is as destructive as nuclear war promises to be can only be regarded as a failure of politics and the antithesis of reasonable strategic thinking. Because this book is about likely rather than unlikely contingencies, and is about strategy rather than the abnegation of strategy, it will therefore concentrate on the business of navies in less catastrophic circumstances − in those circumstances we in the West complacently call 'peace'.

After the years of negotiation involved in UNCLOS III there has been a strong tendency to suppose that the signing of the Convention marked the end of the road. But it is only now, after the signing, that we can really begin to appreciate all the details and dimensions of the problem before us. The ceremony at Montego Bay in Jamaica in December 1982 was analogous to a childbirth which follows a long and difficult pregnancy. Those who thought that the difficulties would end have found themselves mistaken. As with the birth of a baby − any baby − the trouble was only just beginning.

Notes Chapter 1

1 UNCLOS III began its main work at Caracas in 1974, but earlier discussion had taken place in the Ad Hoc Committee on Peaceful Uses of the Seabed and Ocean Floor beyond National Jurisdiction. On the preparatory stages leading up to the session at Caracas, see Hollick, 1981, chs 7 and 8.
2 Hence it was included among the other assorted important and unimportant 'neglected issues' at the Twelfth Annual Conference of the LSI held at The Hague in 1978 (Gamble, 1979).
3 This was originally said by Geoffrey Vickers about the English attitude to the use of force in general (quoted by Garnett, 1976, p. 137).
4 For example, the *United States Naval Institute Proceedings* provided a number of generally brief articles on this subject over the years, and some were of a very high standard. Among the more recent note particularly Clingan, 1980, Swayze, 1980, and Neutze, 1983.

2

Between Past and Future: UNCLOS III

Since the early 1970s thinking about the changing law of the sea has virtually been synonymous with thinking about the evolution of UNCLOS III. The history of this conference reminds one of a glacier slowly, very slowly, grinding down towards the ocean from mountain tops whose highest reaches were always in the clouds. In the course of its journey this remarkable phenomenon was examined by an ex-panding group of air-tripping conference-watchers. This group des-cribed and analysed changes in the conference with all the interest, to the public at large, that the minute changes of a large body of ice have to non-glaciologists. After a decade, this glacier-conference came to an end, but it hung at the brink of the ocean rather than becoming part of it. If it does proceed, years will pass before its effects will be fully absorbed and diffused throughout the whole maritime environment. It may not even move forward: the changing climate might yet cause it miserably to shrink.

The Law of the Sea: Where Have We Been?

Before we can usefully speculate about the implications of this great event in the history of the law of the sea it is necessary to refer to the past, albeit briefly, since our views about the past, whether we realize it or not, always shape our speculation about the future. If we cannot read the past accurately, about which so much is known, what hope can we have of reading the future with any success?

Western ideas about the history of the law of the sea have been dominated by a long-established Anglo-American navalist perspec-tive. This body of ideas was and is the product of a more confident and less complex era, and one which was characterized by maritime supre-

11

macy. Although the circumstances have changed significantly, navalist verities remain part of the folk memory of the Anglo-Saxon world. This memory includes a set of assumptions and an associated baggage of historical 'lessons', ideas and myths which are still with us.

History is neither objective nor neutral. We write and think about the past in the light of the present, and hence the axiom of historians that all history is, in a sense, contemporary history. If we approach the evolution of the law of the sea with this in mind, we might choose to emphasize a number of different 'lessons' and ideas than those which have formed the backbone of the established Western literature. Instead of the order and self-confidence seen by traditionalists, it might be more helpful to stress other characteristics of the history of the law of the sea, that is, those elements which seem more pertinent from the perspective of an increasingly confusing world full of complex interrelationships and highly politicized issues. If an uncertainty of outlook about the future is allowed to fertilize our thinking about the law of the sea in the past, we will be bound to ask whether its evolution was as orderly and whether its results were as reasonable as they are invariably thought to have been. As a result, we might choose to emphasize a set of different features about the law of the sea than those which characterize international law textbooks. In particular, our own fractured situation might encourage us to stress that the law of the sea has always been a ball in the political arena, that ocean regime development has always followed a pendulum pattern, and that the evolution of the law of the sea has always been untidy.

'Policy-oriented jurisprudence' is a new phrase but an old idea.[1] The political character of the development of the law of the sea was evident in the very origin of the modern doctrine of the 'freedom of the seas'. The legal argument for this doctrine was originally and most famously put by the Dutchman Hugo Grotius in 1609. It was subsequently expanded into his notable book *Mare Liberum*, published in 1618, which became the basis of the later doctrine of the freedom of the seas. Grotius's motive was political. He was writing in order to uphold the right of the Dutch to navigation and commerce with the East Indies in spite of the Portuguese claims to monopoly. From the outset, therefore, the doctrine of the freedom of the seas was politically inspired. And so it has remained. But like anything with 'freedom' in its title, it has taken on moral overtones.

'Freedom' is a beguiling word, but a slippery concept. It causes trouble because of its bifurcated nature: are we talking about freedom *from* or freedom *to*? 'Freedom from' is the hope of the have-nots, the disadvantaged and the egalitarians. 'Freedom to', on the other hand, is the hope of the haves, the powerful and the individualists. When these differences are projected on to the concept of the 'freedom of the seas', it becomes clear that this historic doctrine was not all it seems to have been. For the powerful, the 'freedom of the seas' was a permissive doctrine, which enabled them to use the seas to further their interests to the limits of their will and capability. For the weak, however, it was a doctrine which allowed unpleasant things to be done to them: it was a means of oppression, not an expression of freedom.

In the nineteenth century the *Pax Britannica* was characterized by a long period of stability at sea which coincided with and partly contributed to a remarkable period of international order and economic development. But this stable maritime regime provided more than predictability and peaceful (or not very violent) change: it also created the conditions in which British political and economic supremacy could be exercized through large parts of the world, and recognized through even more. The doctrine of the 'freedom of the seas' meant that the sea was equally 'free' for all nations to use. It just happened that Britain, as the greatest seapower of the period, was able to use it best to further its own national interests.

One aspect of Britain's ability to use the sea was the doctrine of belligerent's rights (O'Connell, 1975, pp. 101–3, 116–28). This again was hard national interest dressed up as legal doctrine. Against the British insistence on belligerent's rights, the neutrals in wartime earnestly argued in favour of the pure freedom of the seas: they wished to continue using the sea for trading purposes. All sides dressed up their national interest in legal doctrine. It was a case of law being a continuation of politics by other means. Thus, although the British were the great profiteers from the doctrine of the freedom of the seas, they sometimes had it used against them. The British tried to juggle both doctrines in the air, the freedom of the seas and belligerent's rights, and for this reason they resisted attempts at the codification of these ideas. In principle, the British wished to use the sea 'freely', but since blockade and the other strategies of trade warfare represented one of their major options during conflict, they also wanted special rights. This inconsistency in law (if not in national interest) led to the jibe that 'In peace Britain ruled the waves: in war Britain waived the rules'.

Since the Second World War the peoples who were the historic targets of Western maritime supremacy have become independent, at least in some sense. They have developed their own ideas about security and prosperity, and order and justice. Spokesmen of the traditional naval powers have found it difficult to appreciate the extent to which these peoples could have seen the doctrine of the freedom of the seas as a hostile political, economic and strategic instrument.

Objectively speaking, the 'freedom of the seas' simply represented an expression of power. It did not represent a self-evidently 'superior' legal order. To see the traditional doctrine in such a light should not mean that Westerners need feel guilty about their imperial past. The

13

past was the doing of our ancestors. Furthermore, imperialism has never been the monopoly of the industrialized Western world, as the existence of the present Soviet Russian empire testifies, while the imperial regimes of some Western nations have by no means been the worst expressions of man's inhumanity to man, as is evident from some of the blood-thirsty regimes which presently give much of the Third World a bad reputation. The doctrine of the freedom of the seas was merely a symptom of the fact that nations attempt to further their interests by whatever instruments they have at their disposal, be they military or economic, diplomatic or legal.

It sometimes happens that legal doctrines take on the 'superior' morality of the status quo. When this happens, it is obviously more difficult to change attitudes. In the case of the British, the traditional guardians of the doctrine of the freedom of the seas, changing attitudes on such matters flies in the face of the national habit of investing any workable tradition with moral authority. There is a national tendency to believe that if something has lasted a long time then it must be good. And this habit is further strengthened by the widespread assumption that support for the status quo is somehow 'apolitical', and that change is always for the worse. Given such attitudes it is hardly surprising that the doctrine of the freedom of the seas sometimes seems to be cant in the mouths of Western navalists.

In addition to appearing to be 'good', as well as useful, the traditional maritime regime has also generally been perceived to have had a permanence and stability which did not always exist in practice. As it happens, ocean regime development across the centuries has followed a pendulum character; and, as with just about everything else, the period since 1945 has seen a quickening in the pace of change, and often not for the better from the Western viewpoint. Historically, ocean regime development has swung between pressure for the enclosure of parts of the sea on the one hand, and the desire for freedom of navigation on the other. Consequently, the present is not the first time when the society of states has seemed to be heading in the direction of enclosure. In the distant past, the Romans favoured some controls following the free navigation practices of the Greeks. Later, extensive claims were made to the 'Sovereignty of the Seas' by Norman Kings. Wardens were appointed of the sea as well as of provinces in the regions, and as is happening today, responsibility for the maintenance of rights, equity and peace crept out from the land and extended out to sea (Laughton, 1866, pp. 721–5; Colombos, 1967, pp. 48–9). It was the seventeenth century, however, which witnessed the classical debate about the freedom of the seas. The arguments then employed were 'strikingly similar' to those of the 1970s, and the nature of the whole debate appeared to be 'surprisingly contemporary in its character' (O'Connell, 1978, p. 11).

14

After the case for *mare liberum* had been championed by Grotius, the pendulum swung quickly the other way, with the arguments of the Englishman John Selden for a 'closed sea'. In *Mare Clausum*, first published in 1635, Selden argued that the seas, just like the land, could become the exclusive property of nations. Like that of Grotius, his doctrine had a political impetus: Selden was seeking to justify the restriction of foreign fishing off British coasts. Once again, in relations between nations, the law was following politics: law between nations is the servant of power, rarely its master. There are times when maritime powers want freedom of navigation, and there are times when coastal states wish to claim exclusive ownership over parts or the whole of the oceans. The legal outcome depends upon *who* dominates *whom*.

The next important development in the law of the sea came from another Dutchman, Cornelius van Bynkershoek. In *De Domino Maris*, published in 1702, he suggested that a state's dominion over the sea should be restricted to the range over which its power extended from the adjacent land. This was taken to be the maximum range of a cannon. Except in Scandinavia, the distance agreed was 3 miles. With this rule, the Grotius-Selden-Bynkershoek framework established the terms of the debate about the law of the sea for the centuries following.

Law of the sea doctrines have swung according to the contemporary constellation of military and political power and to beliefs about the exhaustibility of the ocean's resources. The era of the *Pax Britannica*, for example, now appears to many to have been a golden age in which both freedom and order seemed to be at the maximum of what was humanly possible. But the *Pax Britannica* was only one, admittedly long, period in the evolution of the law of the sea. It was an important stage, but it should not be taken to have been the 'norm', historically speaking. It was only one extreme in the swing of the politico-legal pendulum.

Those whose minds are fixed on the image of maritime order under British and then US naval supremacy are apt to underestimate the extent to which the detailed character of the evolution of the law of the sea has been the subject of dispute; and they are apt to overlook the fact that universal formal agreements about the law of the sea have been the exception rather than the rule. In the nineteenth and twentieth centuries, for example, the freedom of the seas was based on a mixture of Anglo-American naval power and customary international law. It was not the outcome of a comprehensive treaty following a grand conference between all the interested powers.

The society of states has never found it easy to draw up a universally acceptable law of the sea. Leaving aside the grinding history of UNCLOS III, we should not forget the '100 years of hullabaloo over innocent passage' (O'Connell, 1978, p. 17), the failure in 1930 to codify the law of the sea (including a failure to achieve a consensus on the breadth of the territorial sea), the nine-year preparation for the first UN Conference on the Law of the Sea which was held at Geneva in 1958, the failures at Geneva in UNCLOS I and II in 1958 and 1960 over the territorial sea and other matters, and the limited number of ratifications of the Conventions which were adopted. The history of the law of the sea suggests that it is sometimes more prudent to accept a tolerable untidiness than to press for universal agreement.

Alongside the difficulties facing the codification of the law there has been a growing trend towards 'unilateralism' in maritime claims. Ironically, this development was sparked off by the US government, which subsequently became the major opponent of unilateral claims to the oceans. The catalytic event was the issuing of the Truman Proclamation in 1945, in which the United States claimed jurisdiction and control over the natural resources of its contiguous continental shelf (Hollick, 1981, ch. 2). This Proclamation was quickly followed by a series of unilateral claims in the late 1940s by various South American states. Mexico issued claims over its continental shelf and the establishment of a fishery conservation zone. Argentina and Panama issued claims over the resources of their adjacent shelves and superjacent waters. Chile and Peru issued claims of sovereignty over the resources of the sea to a distance of 200 miles. Then, in 1952, came the Santiago Declaration, in which Chile, Ecuador and Peru claimed sovereignty to 200 miles.[2] The next twenty years saw a number of other claims, which resulted in a series of disputes and conflicts over a wide range of interests in ocean space. It might also be mentioned that during this recent period in the history of the law of the sea there were several major changes of national policy. In addition to those mentioned, the most notable was the collapse of Anglo-American hostility to the idea of extending national rights to 200 miles.

If one takes a half-century perspective on the history of the law of the sea, it is evident that it has been an untidy business, strewn with difficulties and disagreements. This background should give some pause to those who either expect too much from UNCLOS III in its attempt to codify a universal agreement, or to those who believe that a failure to produce a universal agreement will automatically lead to the spread of turmoil at sea. Even if, at present, the future law of the sea is not as clear-cut and regularized as many would have hoped, it should never be forgotten that the past was not as clear-cut and regularized as many of us tend to imagine. But it worked. Whatever the fate of the 1982 Convention, we can take some comfort from the fact that recent history suggests that legal untidiness and political chaos are not synonymous in the development of the law of the sea.

The lessons to be drawn from these brief points about the past are mainly relevant for the traditional naval powers. At the risk of oversimplifying, we can look at the past in two ways. On the one hand we can visualize it as a golden age now cracking up, a period of history which represented a remarkable degree of order in at least one area of international life. On the other hand the old order can be equated with British naval supremacy and the age of imperialism. From this latter perspective the 'golden age' was at the expense of the weak. The recent history of the law of the sea can therefore be interpreted not so much as a slide from a golden age into a period of instability, but as an attempt to evolve from a structure of injustice to a more generally acceptable regime, one which is both more equitable and better suited to deal with the changed character of world politics.

It is imperative to recognize and accept the political nature of the law of the sea. Shared perceptions in this regard are vital because if the eventual outcome of UNCLOS III is not satisfactory to important powers or numerous weaker actors in the system, then the foundations for the new rules will be shaky. A stable system requires consent. It has to meet the aspirations of those who see the traditional maritime regime as being out of touch with the present needs and desires of many members of the international community. But it also has to be acceptable to the interests of the major powers. Without their support, any new system will be uncertain: this is why the numerically powerful smaller states must exercise restraint in their claims. So far they have generally done this.

The proponents of conflicting law of the sea ideologies — which can be expressed simply as 'freedom of the seas' versus 'common heritage' — must accept that their doctrines are essentially political instruments. Moralizing is therefore best avoided. When self-interest becomes dressed up in too much moral rectitude, trouble is bound to occur. Those who see law of the sea issues as theology rather than politics will cling to positions with more determination than objective interests might dictate. In addition, differing viewpoints will tend to be dismissed as illegitimate, and their holders seen as evil, rather than simply different. We are merely fellow competitors in the games that nations play. It is therefore important to divest our thinking of maritime theologies. This is easier said than done, for the mighty tend to dress up their interests in ideological garb, as indeed do the meek. In the light of the past, present and future advantages which the freedom of the seas doctrine offers them, the position of the traditional naval powers is easily understood. But if that political interest is infused with ideological passion, the notion of the 'freedom of the seas' will become an icon, and this will only complicate the issue. The 'freedom of the seas' will become what Sir Julian Corbett said it was at the beginning of this century, namely, one of those 'ringing phrases which haunts the ear and continues to confuse the judgement' (Gretton, 1965, p. 61).

The Characteristics of UNCLOS III

If we wipe our eyes free of our folk history illusions and professional predispositions about the law of the sea, it should be evident that the past is not what it was. The history of the law of the sea has been chequered and politicized; and even the classical period of *mare liberum* can now be seen to have been a 'golden age' only for some. More scepticism about the past might have tempered some of the excessive expectations about UNCLOS III.

As was indicated earlier, UNCLOS III grew out of converging economic, technological and political pressures in the late 1960s. The Grotian framework as a whole was under strain, while particular aspects of the old regime were breaking down. Like the poor woman referred to in the Preface, Hugo Grotius could not have imagined that the seas might one day be exhausted, just as he could not have imagined that land-based resources such as forests might one day be depleted. Since an overused sea was inconceivable to Grotius, it does not follow that he would have remained 'Grotian' in outlook had he been writing today. Instead, he might well have accepted that in circumstances of stress absolute freedom has to be rejected in favour of reasonable use; and that reasonable use requires agreed rules and careful management. Reasonable use cannot be guaranteed by permissive rights, with each government the arbiter of its own actions.

The aspect of the law of the sea which was in most immediate disarray in the late 1960s was the territorial sea. At that time only 22 per cent of the international community still adhered to the traditional three-mile limit.[3] The United States and the Soviet Union, because of their concern about the expansion of claims, favoured convening a new UN conference, to tidy up the unsatisfactory situation left over by UNCLOS I and II. At roughly the same time, a number of other nations were also turning their attention seawards, but in their case it was to the promise of the seabed rather than to the problems of the surface: the maritime appetites of numerous countries, particularly in the less developed world, had been stimulated by the historic declaration in 1967 by Ambassador Arvid Pardo of Malta that the minerals of the deep seabed should be regarded as the 'common heritage of mankind'. This principle was subsequently endorsed by the General Assembly of the United Nations.

Albeit from different perspectives, both the superpowers and the developing world saw an interest in convening a third UNCLOS. Planning began on the back of the Ad Hoc Committee on Peaceful Uses of the Seabed and Ocean Floor Beyond National Jurisdiction, and substantive work began at Caracas, Venezuela, in 1974. The glacier of UNCLOS III had begun to leave the mountain tops. This is not the place to provide a detailed history of UNCLOS III. Such a formidable task requires an energetic historian at once at home with diplomacy, international law and economics, as well as all the highly technical subjects concerned with maritime affairs. For the moment, a few comments on its general characteristics will suffice.

From the outset UNCLOS III was a lawyer's dream. It was an attempt to apply reason and rules to over two-thirds of the earth's surface. Complete success was impossible, since global quick-fixes seem bound to fail in a world of sovereign states. But what is remarkable is the extent to which UNCLOS III nearly succeeded in bringing a universally agreed set of rules to such a complex of issues. Of course, the Convention which was eventually produced by the conference contained ambiguities and problems, and the solution of one difficulty often produced only another, but the size of the achievement of UNCLOS III should be measured against the 'impossibility' of the original task.

During the course of UNCLOS III some of its supporters invested it with more than merely law of the sea significance. It came to be seen as a major event in the history of international politics in general (Mann Borgese, 1982, pp. 698–718). In particular UNCLOS III came to be seen as the first attempt at a comprehensive implementation of the idea of a New International Economic Order. And in turn its Convention came to be seen as a possible blueprint for further ventures in global welfare management. Those governments with traditionalist outlooks naturally became concerned about the very innovations and precedents which were welcomed so enthusiastically by the revisionists.

As a set of negotiations, UNCLOS III took much too long for its own good. Like the almost contemporaneous SALT II negotiations in arms control, the slow process of law of the sea codification could not bear the changes in the world outside. National and international politics never stand still, and neither SALT nor UNCLOS could outlast the pace of international change, not to mention four US Presidents. The passage of time obviously allowed some deadlocks to be broken, but the main effect of longevity seemed to be in creating the opportunity for new problems to be thrown up. In the case of SALT II the prolonged interplay of competing national interests dashed the high hopes about arms control which had set the process in motion in the late 1960s. It remains to be seen if this will also be the fate of UNCLOS III.

During the substantive years of the UNCLOS III negotiations between 1974 and 1982, there were periods when the conference was trapped in sterile debate of a procedural and legalistic kind. But such periods were more than matched by constructive sessions characterized by new ideas, compromise and progress. Over the years the major areas of disagreement fluctuated – now it was straits, now the seabed – but in every case, until the very end, the disagreement was resolved. The final disagreement over the future of the deep seabed regime continues to cast a shadow over the fate of the Convention.

In addition to the substantive achievements of UNCLOS III, which will be discussed in detail below, many participants and observers derived considerable satisfaction from the new processes which it pioneered. These alone helped to make the conference a singular episode in international relations, whatever the fate of the Convention. UNCLOS III proceeded on the basis of three main principles. First, there was the idea of a package deal. This meant that the Convention was to be regarded as a whole, in order to encourage a spirit of give-and-take. Secondly, there was the notion of consensus. This encouraged progress in the talks by avoiding the deadlocks which are apt to arise in international organizations when movement depends upon majority voting, or, worse still, unanimity. Finally, there was the gentleman's agreement that voting would nevertheless take place in the last resort if consensus broke down. This helped governments to overcome their doubts, and put their trust in the consensus principle. In the event, these three principles interacted effectively, and for the most part produced a spirit of give-and-take. The principles were both the product and the creator of a particular UNCLOS III atmosphere. There was a strong sense that the processes of international law-making were being developed, as well as the substance of the law of the sea (Pardo, 1983, p. 491). To some participants UNCLOS III almost became a way of life. At the eleventh hour, however, the consensus broke down as a result of a major policy shift by the Reagan administration. As a result, the fate of the Convention now rests not on the consensus principle, which enabled it to get so far, but upon national decisions relating to signing and ratification.

Throughout UNCLOS III, national decisions depended upon the balance between domestic bureaucratic and political groupings. The Washington hot-house, as ever, was the object of most interest and scrutiny, and in this case at least one is tempted to say that the bargaining in domestic politics was every bit as intense as that between the governments involved. Between governments, important alignments were formed. One of the most important was the Third World grouping, the so-called Group of 77 (which eventually increased its membership to approximately 120). But like most other alignments, the Group of 77 was not always a coherent body. This was also the case with the Western industrialized world, though not on security issues: in this area it even shared a strong identity of interests with the Soviet bloc, which, as ever, was the most united. Some groups had more problems than others: the land-locked and geographically disadvanted states (Appendix: Table 7) faced an uphill struggle in all directions. Given this background, the complexity of the issues involved and the number and variety of participants, it is not surprising that UNCLOS III was condemned to be one of the longest multilateral conferences ever. Although the Mutual Force Reduction talks in Vienna, for one, outdistance it, in view of the larger number of participants involved, UNCLOS III must nevertheless hold some record in terms of diplomat-hours committed.

The effort invested in UNCLOS III produced a Convention which bears all the signs and scars of nine years of multilateral negotiation. It is a package deal, the product of compromises between all manner of states and conflicting interests. In this sense it represents a pragmatic and political achievement; it is not a lawyer's dream made flesh. Confronted by a succession of difficult problems, the participants reached compromises and showed a general desire to move ahead. Real trouble came only at the final stage, when new faces and beliefs in Washington after 1980 resulted in a drastic change of policy. Following the new Reagan administration's review of all aspects of ex-President Carter's policy, its participation in the eleventh session of UNCLOS III early in 1982 was uncompromising. This was followed by an announcement on 9 July 1982 by President Reagan that the United States would not sign the Draft Convention of UNCLOS III. Reagan acknowledged that many US national interests would benefit from the Convention, but he asserted that his administration's objection to the Convention's seabed mining provisions were decisive (Richardson, 1983, p. 505). A handful of like-minded governments rallied to Reagan's side. Determinedly, the rest of the participants attempted to limit the damage and get the Convention back on course. In December 1982 they trooped in droves to the signing ceremony at Montego Bay to affirm their faith in the Convention. But they did so with a strong sense of disappointment, a feeling of having come so near yet . . .

The Convention which was opened for signature at Montego Bay offered a comprehensive set of rules for the management of the many interrelated matters concerning the oceans. So expressed, it is no wonder that observers are sometimes tempted to be carried away by its achievements (Mann Borgese, 1982, pp. 698–718). Without doubt, the 1982 Convention is significant: but the important question concerns the exact nature and extent of that significance. Obviously, different individuals and interests will tend to emphasize different aspects of the 1982 United Nations Convention On The Law Of The Sea (U.N.Doc. A/CONF. 62/122). But all are likely to agree that it is a formidable document, consisting as it does of a Preamble, seventeen Parts, 320 Articles and nine Annexes — the whole amounting to 194 pages. What follows is a list of the text's major achievements. By no means all the provisions listed have direct military implications. This dimension will be taken up in detail in Chapter 4. For the moment the aim is to establish the nature of the Convention in order to see it in historical perspective. In the list which follows no weighting as to the relative importance of particular provisions will be given; the order followed is simply that of the Convention itself.

The Major Achievements of the 1982 UN Convention

PART II   TERRITORIAL SEA AND CONTIGUOUS ZONE

Articles 3—16. These helped to tidy up the situation relating to the limits of the territorial sea. It was agreed that coastal states would exercise sovereignty to a distance of 12 miles, and foreign ships would have the right of innocent passage through these waters (for territorial sea claims, see Appendix: Table 1).

Article 19. Some progress was made in clarifying the concept of 'innocent passage'.

PART III   STRAITS USED FOR INTERNATIONAL NAVIGATION

Articles 37—44. The 'transit passage' concept was created for international straits. It permits warship passage, submarine transit and aircraft overflight.

PART IV   ARCHIPELAGIC STATES

Article 49. The concept of archipelagic water was legitimized. This allows island nations to exercise considerable authority over seas defined as theirs (Appendix: Table 5).

PART V   EXCLUSIVE ECONOMIC ZONE

Articles 55—75. The concept of a 200-mile exclusive economic zone was introduced, in which the coastal state would have the exclusive right to manage the living and non-living resources of the sea (Appendix: Table 2; and endpaper maps). Other states would have freedom of navigation and overflight, and the right to lay submarine cables and pipelines. Land-locked and geographically disadvantaged states would have certain fishing rights.

PART VI   CONTINENTAL SHELF

Article 76. This involved a change in the definition of the continental shelf. Coastal states were given a shelf of at least 200 miles, and in some cases 350 miles or beyond.

Articles 77—8. The coastal state was granted the exclusive right to manage the living and non-living resources of the continental shelf.

The legal status of the superjacent waters and air space would not be affected.

Article 87. The traditional freedoms in the high seas were confirmed, but additional rights were granted concerning scientific research and the construction of artificial islands.

Article 118. It was agreed that states should co-operate in the conservation and management of living resources in the high seas.

Articles 136−7. The 'Area' and its resources were deemed to be 'the common heritage of mankind', that is, outside the scope of national jurisdiction. No state (or other 'national or judicial person') shall claim or exercise sovereignty or sovereign rights over any part of the Area. The 'Area' was defined as the seabed and its subsoil beyond zones of national jurisdiction.

Article 150. The activities of the Area shall be carried out in such a manner as to foster the 'healthy development' of the world economy, the 'balanced growth' of international trade and the promotion of international co-operation for the 'over-all development of all countries, especially developing States'.

Article 156. An international Sea-Bed Authority was established to manage the mineral resources of the deep seabed for the benefit of all mankind.

Article 1970. 'The enterprise' was established as the Authority's commercial organ, to carry out the mining, processing and marketing of minerals in the Area.

Articles 186−91. A comprehensive dispute settlement system was created for seabed problems.

Articles 192−237. A comprehensive legal system for international maritime environmental protection was established,. obliging all states to protect and preserve the marine environment and to control all pollution.

Articles 238−65. A broad system of marine scientific research was established, including an obligation on the parties to co-operate in the development and transfer of marine science. Research is to be for peaceful purposes.

PART XVI   DEVELOPMENT AND TRANSFER OF MARINE TECHNOLOGY

Articles 266—78. While granting due regard to the legitimate interests of the suppliers, states are obliged to promote the development and transfer of marine technology.

PART XV   SETTLEMENT OF DISPUTES

Articles 279—99. A comprehensive and binding system of disputes settlement was established. This obliges states to settle by peaceful means their disputes over the interpretation or application of the Convention.

Whatever one thinks about the 1982 Convention — whether one is 'for', 'against', or 'undecided' — all should be able to agree with one of its enthusiastic supporters that 'There never has been a document like this' (Mann Borgese, 1982, p. 708). The Convention deals with all matters relating to the law of the sea. It seeks to balance national rights and duties. It attempts to achieve an effective compromise between the interests of all types of states. In some respects it adjusts what was the established law to a rapidly changing environment; and in other respects it is an experiment in international co-operation. It is wide ranging, technical, problem-meeting and problem-creating. Sometimes it is realistic, and sometimes it is hopelessly idealistic; occasionally it is rhetorical and doctrinaire and at other times pragmatic and sensible. In short, in the way it invites adjectives, the Convention is a uniquely Thesaurus-tempting document. The law of the sea will never be the same again.

The Outstanding Problems: Where Are We Going?

While most governments and most observers greatly welcomed the Convention, the final stages of UNCLOS III were pervaded by a strong sense of disappointment as a result of the Reagan administration's decision to reject the document which successive US governments had helped to create. With the opposition of such a pivotal country, the Convention's future was placed in jeopardy. The fact that the new administration of President Reagan had every right to review its policy and change its mind did not impress the many idealistic supporters of the Convention: they naturally felt robbed. Realists who were friends of the United States and supporters of the Convention simply believed that a serious miscalculation had been made.

The change in US policy meant that the international consensus on the changing law of the sea had broken down. Instead of a long-awaited and universally signed Convention, the international community in 1982 was faced by a string of questions. Was there any possibility that the US government would change its mind? Which other states would be encouraged to stand outside the Convention? Would enough states ratify the Convention to bring it into operation? Would non-signing and non-ratifying states be bound by the Convention, or would they simply be able to choose those bits and pieces they supported? What could be done to make the Convention more acceptable to reluctant governments? Was there an acceptable alternative to the existing Convention? If the world's major maritime power did not accede to the Convention, would it be worth having? Accepting that the law of the sea would not be the same again after 1982, what in fact would it look like? Such a series of questions was the only rational response to the big question, 'Where are we going?' Unfortunately, there are still few clear answers to any of these questions, and by the time there are, it might be too late.

As a result of UNCLOS III's eleventh-hour disappointment because of the change in US policy, the signing ceremony at Montego Bay was much more restrained than it might have been. Nevertheless, a brave face was shown, and on 10 December 1982 a greater number of states than had been expected did sign. In all, 119 governments put their name to the Convention, and they were representative of all groups and all interests. According to Bernado Zuleta, the Special Representative of the UN Secretary General at UNCLOS III,

> Never in the history of treaty-making has such a large and varied number of countries signed a convention on the day it was opened for signature. The number of signatories exceeded the most optimistic expectations and surprised those who had predicted that it would be difficult to obtain on the first day the fifty signatures that were required to convene the Preparatory Commission for the International Sea-Bed Authority and for the International Tribunal for the Law of the Sea. The Montego Bay meeting was remarkable also because of the level of representation and the substance of the statements made by 21 delegations. (1983, p. 476)

This degree of support was impressive, but numbers do not count for everything in international politics. Observers were at least as conscious of the minority of countries which did not sign as they were of the majority which flourished their pens.

Earlier, on 30 April 1982, when UNCLOS III had adopted the text of its Draft Convention, four states had rejected it and seventeen had abstained. The four rejectionist states were Israel, Turkey, the United States and Venezuela. They did not change their minds in the next seven months. Most of the abstaining states, on the other hand, did subsequently sign the Convention at Montego Bay. The exceptions, still ostensibly making up their minds, were Belgium, the Federal Republic of Germany, Italy, Luxemburg, Spain and the United Kingdom. This was also the position of the eleven states which had supported the text in April but which decided not to sign in December: of these the most important was Japan.

The collection of an impressive number of signatories in favour of the Convention was only a beginning in the process of bringing it to life. The amount of support indicated the positive attitude of most members of the international community, and of their eventual intention to ratify and adhere to the Convention. But the history of treaty-making shows that there is many a slip between cup and lip, especially between signing and ratification. This was the experience of both the 1958 Geneva Law of the Sea Conventions and of the 1979 SALT II agreements. The provisions of the 1982 Convention will become law for the parties one year after sixty states have ratified it. In the short term the signs are hopeful, and the supporters of the Convention remain optimistic. By mid-1983 a handful of additional states had signed the Convention, pushing the total of signatories to 125. This meant that the non-signatories now amounted to only about one-fifth of the signatories. Almost all the Third World had signed the Convention, and all the Soviet bloc; and although a significant number of states still have not signed, only a handful of governments have definitely come out against signing, notably the United States. The rest of the non-signatories are in various stages of making up their minds.[4]

While the states which are definitely opposed to the Convention, or are still abstaining, are not significant in terms of voting power at the United Nations, they are significant in terms of the more important indices of international power, namely, economic, political and military strength. President Reagan reminded UNCLOS-watchers of this in July 1982, when he noted that the seventeen states which were then abstaining from the Draft Convention produced more than 60 per cent of the world's gross national product and provided more than 60 per cent of the contributions to the running of the United Nations (Robertson and Vasaturo, 1983, p. 693). Despite such muscle-flexing by the Reagan administration, and its continued opposition to UNCLOS III's ideas about seabed mining, the supporters of the Convention still hope for a change of policy by the United States and its 'like-minded' supporters in other countries. Whether or not this happens, the belief was strong in the months following the Montego Bay ceremony that there would still be enough nations willing to support the Convention to ensure that the requisite number of ratifications would be achieved; those who held this belief hoped the Convention could come into force by 1987-8 at the latest (Richardson, 1983, p. 506). By mid-1983, however, less than ten states had actually ratified.

US policy is clearly the key to the immediate future of the Convention, just as it was to the final sessions of UNCLOS III (Robertson and Vasaturo, 1983, pp. 679–711). The main features of this policy therefore require a brief examination. This is not easily done, for nowhere was the law of the sea such a complex policy issue as in the United States, where its technical and other aspects were tossed about by the powerful tides, waves and currents – not forgetting the cross-currents – of US domestic politics and bureaucratic mega-activity. By 1980 the flow of events in Washington was against the Convention, and it remains to be seen whether it will ever regain its former course.

When, in April 1982, President Reagan announced his administration's rejection of the Draft Convention, it did not come as a complete surprise. The possibility of change had already been signalled by the administration's antipathy towards President Carter's more accommodating attitude towards the Third World, by the Republican Party's criticism of the Convention during the 1979 election campaign, and by the susceptibility of the Reagan White House to those US business and mining interests which for some years had been lobbying against the Convention (Hollick, 1981, *passim*, provides the most comprehensive account of this complicated story). As the possibility of US rejection became increasingly likely, the hostility of the Third World could not be hidden. Third World delegates voiced their fears that the United States was 'sabotaging' the Convention, and undermining the 'common heritage' principle for the sake of 'greedy private corporations' (Rosen, 1981; Robertson and Vasaturo, 1983, p. 686). At the same time they pressed the governments supporting the United States, or abstaining, to accept the Convention on existing terms, whether or not the United States signed: 'If not, we'll go on without them' said one Asian delegate (Guest, 1981).

On 29 January 1982 President Reagan announced six necessary objectives in an 'acceptable' law of the sea treaty. These focused on issues concerning the operation and decision-making of the deep seabed regime, the prevention of undesirable precedents for international organizations and the problem of Senate approval (Robertson and Vasaturo, 1983, pp. 681–2). Significantly, President Reagan took no exception to any of the provisions of the Draft Convention which had military implications. But the US change of policy and muscle-flexing did not deflect the supporters of the Draft Convention from their chosen path. All the modifications desired by Reagan were not made during the eleventh and final session of UNCLOS III in March and April 1982. Consequently, the United States voted against the Draft Convention on 30 April; and on 9 July 1982 President Reagan announced that the United States would not accede to the Convention when it was opened for signature in December.

According to Elliot Richardson, a distinguished Republican and the

Chairman of the US Delegation to UNCLOS III between 1977 and 1980,

> The President's statement acknowledges that the Covention
> would benefit a wide array of United States interests – the mobi-
> lity of air and naval forces, commercial navigation, fisheries,
> environmental protection, scientific research, the conservation of
> marine mammals, dispute settlement, and more. The admini-
> stration objected to only one of the Convention's seventeen parts
> – that dealing with deep seabed mining. Within that part, the
> incompatibility with free-market principles of some of its provi-
> sions, particularly those on technology transfer and the limitation
> of seabed mineral production, was viewed as fatal to the whole
> Convention. (1983, pp. 506–7)

The essence of the problem, simply, was that a handful of provisions
in the Convention were unacceptable to the free enterprise principles
of the Reagan administration and some of its supporters, and that
these principles were determined to be the paramount US interest in
the issue. In addition to the matter of free enterprise principles, US
opposition was also stirred by its superpower unease at what it saw as
giving away more commercial and political power than was really
necessary: in particular there was anxiety about the strengthening of
the Third World interest in general and international organizations in
particular. But not all US businessmen agreed with the President's
ordering of priorities; nor did the majority of law of the sea specialists,
strategists and officials with maritime interests.

The fears of the Reagan administration about some of the far-
reaching implications of the Convention were bound to be fed by
some of the more effusive assessments of the achievements of
UNCLOS III. Note the following, included in a list of concepts adopted
by the Convention which one observer claimed offered 'a new plat-
form from which to launch a new international order':

> The concept of a public international institution (the Seabed
> Authority) that is operational, capable of generating revenue,
> imposing international taxation, bringing multinational com-
> panies into a structured relationship; responsible for resource
> planning on a global scale, as well as for the protection and
> conservation of the marine environment and scientific research.
> An institution linking politics, economics and science in new
> ways – a model, potentially, for international organisations in the
> twenty-first century. (Mann Borgese, 1982, p. 708)

With such internationalism apparently on the march, no wonder a
conservative superpower shuddered. Would the same principles and

procedures be applied to Antarctica, or outer space? If so where next? The irony of the matter, however, is that there is a not insignificant body of opinion which believes that it is unlikely that the Convention's seabed regime will in fact come into operation (Richardson, 1983, p. 506). Some supporters of the Convention were more concerned than others that this might be the case. Some saw the limited progress of the Convention towards a fuller implementation of a New International Economic Order as an argument to use to encourage the Americans to change their minds. Others were gravely disappointed at the limited progress. The latter was the case with Arvid Pardo, the progenitor of the 'common heritage' doctrine. His sad conclusion was that the 'common heritage regime established for the international seabed area is little short of a disaster' (Pardo, 1983, p. 499).

The Reagan administration's belief that the Convention promised bad business and bad precedents led it to reverse the direction of policy of three previous US administrations. The attitude of the President and his backers was buttressed by their confidence in US power and by their growing commitment to a belief that US maritime interests could generally be served by the development of customary international law. Where this was not possible it was expected that specific treaties could be negotiated.[5] Chaos and confusion in the law of the sea, it was argued, would not be the inevitable consequence of a failure to implement a universal Convention. Some observers argued (*The Economist*, 4 April 1982) that Reagan's rethink would at least have the effect of injecting more realism into the proceedings of UNCLOS III, by reminding all participants of the interests and importance of the seabed mining companies on whose efforts the 'common heritage' regime would depend. But could any of the participants really have had any doubt at that stage about the importance of the United States or the seabed miners of the industrial world? What mattered to most participants then was the upholding of the principle of the 'common heritage'. They believed that they had made concessions in the past, and now they looked to the Reagan administration to reciprocate. They still wait.

The interests of the deep seabed mining companies and their supporters are obvious. Nor is it difficult to understand the fears of those in the US government worried about precedents being established for 'new' political and economic orders in international politics. Nevertheless, few disinterested observers agreed with the Reagan administration's assessment of the balance of US interests. The pro-Convention viewpoint has been clearly expressed within US policy-making circles by Elliot Richardson. He has written:

The range of our [US] oceanic interests is wider and deeper than that of any other country. We would also gain more from the convention than any other country. As time goes on it will become increasingly clear that even our deep seabed mining interests will be hurt, not helped, by our staying out. And since our other oceanic interests will also suffer, it seems inevitable that a more realistic assessment of the costs will in due course bring about a reversal of President Reagan's decision. (1983, p. 506)

In his last remark Richardson was allowing the wish to be the father to the thought, for realistic assessments can never be assumed to be 'inevitable' in minds ruled by ideology; and so far in the 1980s, ironically, ideology has proved to be more powerful in the Western governments of Reagan and Thatcher than in the Soviet regimes of Brezhnev and Andropov. Indeed there is a double irony. We see the conservative 'radicals' of the Soviet Russian empire justifying their increasingly pragmatic actions with reference to ideological principles, while the radical conservatives of the Anglo-Saxon world justify their ideologically determined actions with reference to pragmatism and national interest. International politics are rarely what they seem.

The Reagan administration's rethink on the law of the sea was yet another manifestation of the every-man-for-himself attitude which has characterized the tough new conservatism of the West in the 1980s. Interests are defined narrowly, and positions are not conceded unless it is believed to be absolutely necessary. 'Security'is seen to be synonymous with 'defence', and defence means military building. There is a smack of 'might is right' running through such thinking. The every-man-for-himself attitude has brought considerable disappointment to many of the friends of the United States; and the situation has been made worse by the inability of an unprecedented number of US policy-makers to see their own country through the eyes of others. The resounding pro-Convention vote in UNCLOS III in April 1982, subsequently confirmed by the procession of signatures in December, was undoubtedly a massive censure of US foreign policy: but to the ideologues in Washington, the hostile votes of 'irresponsible' small states and the clients of an 'evil Empire' were taken as proof of the rightness of the administration's course, not the opposite. The national self-image treasured by many Americans, especially those on the political 'right', and the image of America presently in the minds of many outsiders, including friends, would probably not recognize each other if they passed in the street.

One particularly troublesome aspect of recent US policy-making, which has been witnessed in NATO affairs as well as the law of the sea, has been the administration's insistence on having its own way. Some, but too few, Americans have recognized the effect this has had on the country's international relationships (Richardson, 1983, p. 512).

Such an attitude is always likely to be counter-productive in a complex world with diffused power relationships. In the law of the sea, as in NATO, the community of democratic nations look for US leadership to be characterized by negotiation and consultation, not by fiat or loyalty tests. Power is not synonymous with intelligence; nor are loyalty tests coterminous with the evolution of rational policy.

If the US government does not reverse its policy, it will have a debilitating effect on the Convention. This will particularly be the case with respect to its provisions on deep seabed mining, which represent the Convention's ideological heart. But there will be costs for the United States, as well as for the Convention. If the majority of the international community remain committed to press on regardless, then the United States will deprive itself of the opportunity to contribute to the development of novel procedures in the law of the sea; there will also be problems regarding its position vis-à-vis the Convention's acceptable provisions. Can the United States simply choose those bits it likes? The disagreements resulting from these matters could cost the United States dearly in terms of its reputation as a constructive and moderate member of the maritime community. Once again, Elliot Richardson has expressed the point bluntly but eloquently from the viewpoint of a committed American insider:

> At the Economic Summit held in Paris on June 6, 1982, President Reagan agreed that the United States would participate in a "global dialogue" on economic issues. Having turned our back on the most comprehensive global dialogue thus far conducted, we will have crippled our capacity to play a leading role in the next rounds. Where shaping the multilateral institutions of the future is concerned, we cannot insist on having everything our own way and still expect to be taken seriously. (1983, pp. 511–12)

It is not too late to change. Soviet observers might claim that the Reagan administration's 1982 decision was 'not accidental', meaning that it was the inevitable outcome of a systemic US arrogance and lack of commitment to international peace and security. But most of us, on the other hand, would prefer to see that decision, which changed the policy of three previous administrations, as an 'accident', in all senses except the fact that US foreign policy is always at the mercy of a four-yearly reappraisal. This means that the pendulum could swing the other way at the next election; or the one afterwards. It depends upon the lottery of US domestic politics. Foreign supporters of the Convention in the months and years ahead should do what they can to help pro-Convention forces in the United States bring about the desired change of policy. In this respect, the work of the Convention's Preparatory Commission will be important in trying to 'perfect' the new

31

regime, by showing that it can work and that its rules can be acceptable to non-parties.[6] A strong pro-Convention constituency does exist in the United States, and includes former Presidents, Secretaries of State, Secretaries of Defense, Chairmen of the Joint Chiefs of Staff, law of the sea experts, officials, and others. It is not too late for a change, and with such a body of positive opinion, nor is such a development impossible. But so much of what happens in the future, as in the past, will be at the mercy of US domestic politics.

When the Reagan administration changed US policy, a number of 'like-minded' governments took the opportunity to indulge their own free enterprise ideas. And it is with these supporters that the Reagan administration has attempted to co-ordinate its minority position. A leading supporter of the United States, the Thatcher government in Britain, also announced that it could not ratify the Convention unless the provisions for deep seabed mining were revised in a satisfactory manner. As they stood, these provisions were said to be based on 'undesirable regulatory principles'; in addition, it was feared that they could constitute 'unsatisfactory precedents'. The British government's announcement — which earned the taunt from the chief Opposition spokesman on foreign affairs that it was 'behaving as President Reagan's poodle' — amounted to a decision not to make a decision. It was argued that since the Convention would be open for signature for two years, there was 'ample time for revision' before making a final decision (*The Times*, 3 December 1982). As with the Reagan administration, there is an underlying assumption in the British government's case that it must be the other side which changes its stance (Webly, 1982, is a characteristic expression of the anti-Convention case in Britain). Similarly, the Thatcher government shared the White House's tendency to give more weight to the lobbying of a small sector of the business community than to the opinion of those concerned with foreign affairs, trade, transport, defence and the environment (Watt, 1982).

Mrs Thatcher's decision to follow the United States naturally attracted criticism from the Third World. There was a sharp attack from Nigeria, for example, which pointed out that Britain was the only member of the Commonwealth which did not become a party to the Convention at Montego Bay (*The Times*, 10 December 1982). The Thatcher government's decision was also widely regretted in Britain. Many close observers of the matter believed that the Convention served British interests with respect to its rights in its EEZ, the control of pollution, the navigation of warships, the activities of the nation's merchant fleet, and probably with respect to deep seabed mining also. As with the United States, there is still time for Britain to sign the Convention, and perhaps there is slightly more likelihood of its so doing. Other industrial states which made decisions not to make decisions in December 1982 included Belgium, the Federal Republic of Germany, Italy and Japan. But not all Western industrial states opposed the Convention, or abstained. Australia, Canada, Denmark, France and Norway signed the Convention. Several commentators have expressed the view that in the end most industrial states will sign and ratify the Convention in order to obtain its many benefits and to preserve good relations with Third World countries (Robertson and Vasaturo, 1983, pp. 703–4).

As a result of the turmoil brought about by Reagan's reversal of US policy, the future of UNCLOS III is not what it was. There are four broad possibilities for the law of the sea. First, there could be no change in the law of the sea. This now seems inconceivable, for reasons which have been indicated earlier, and which will be elaborated in the next chapter. Secondly, there could be disintegration, chaos and confusion in maritime affairs. This seems to be an unduly alarmist prospect. Mutual interest in order at sea is simply too strong to allow this to happen. Furthermore, the most powerful maritime nations are also the ones with the biggest stake in order. Nobody with the will to bring about widespread chaos would have the power to do so. Thirdly, there could be an all-encompassing universally ratified treaty. This was the hope of many participants at UNCLOS III, and it was not wildly idealistic. The hope came very close to fulfilment: UNCLOS III was the story of a President too far. The final possibility, and the generally held expectation in the months following Montego Bay, is that the Convention will receive sufficient ratifications to come into operation by 1986 or so, but that there will be a sizeable body of non-parties, including some of the major industrial powers. From this perspective the Convention serves to give the international community a comprehensive future agenda on law of the sea issues. It will provide a framework for attempts to manage the 'troubled common' which developed at sea through the 1960s and 1970s (Booth, 1977, pp. 274–81). Order will generally prevail at sea, but nobody will get everything, and the possibility of disputes and conflict will be present.

Although UNCLOS III provides a new framework for approaching the troubled politics of the sea, it has done little to ease the problem of the future relationship between signatories and non-signatories of the Convention. What will be the law of the sea for non-signatories? The legal aspects of this question are complex, and are certain to produce considerable discussion. But what happens in practice will largely be the result of the political decision of governments, based on their conceptions (and misconceptions) of their interests. It may be that the non-signatories will decide that they will pick and choose which parts of the Convention they will follow; this has been the attitude, in effect, of the Reagan administration. But others quickly stated their opposi-

tion to such an attitude: they stressed that the Convention was negotiated as a package and should be accepted as a package. In particular
they argued that the 'common heritage' principle is opposed to individual states and their seabed miners staking out claims in the ocean
beyond the areas of national jurisdiction. Against such arguments the
non-party position is that since they have not signed the Convention,
they need not be tied by it. Furthermore, they claim that those provisions which they are willing to accept are norms of customary international law. The outcome will depend upon which grouping has
most political power. In the words of two thoughtful reviewers,

> A treaty that "limps into force" will probably mean that the more
> general provisions of the treaty such as the 200-mile EEZ, will
> become customary international law, while more controversial
> areas, such as seabed exploration, will remain unresolved. With
> only this minimal support, the impact of the treaty on non-
> signing nations could be negligible. Conversely, if most nations
> adopt the treaty, perhaps 140 or more, it would be more likely that
> the treaty as a whole would become binding on all States as
> customary international law. (Robertson and Vasaturo, 1983, p.
> 701)

The issue is wide open, and will cause much discussion in maritime
circles in the years ahead.

The stance of the US delegation on the future status of the Convention in the later stages of UNCLOS III was clear. US delegates argued
that most provisions of the Convention, including those parts dealing
with navigation and overflight, reflected prevailing international
practice; that being the case, the substance of those provisions could
be invoked by non-parties as representing new customary international law (Zuleta, pp. 477–8). This view did not command broad
support at Montego Bay. The last President of UNCLOS III,
Ambassador Koh of Singapore, said:

> Although the Convention consists of a series of compromises,
> they form an integral whole. This is why the Convention does not
> provide for reservations. It is therefore not possible for States to
> pick what they like and disregard what they do not like. In inter-
> national law, as in domestic law, rights and duties go hand in
> hand. It is therefore legally impermissible to claim rights under
> the Convention without being willing to assume the correlative
> duties. (quoted by Zuleta, 1983, p. 478)

This view was shared by the majority of those who made statements at
the signing ceremony (Zuleta, 1983, pp. 478–9, 480–1). Not surprisingly, the US government provoked the anger of the Convention's

supporters when it announced that it intended to take advantage of those provisions which it favoured, while not abiding by those it opposed (*Newsweek*, 20 December 1982).

The problem of the status of non-parties is not without security implications. As will be seen in detail later, the US government was almost completely satisfied by the military dimensions of the Convention, particularly those parts concerned with navigation and overflight: but can non-parties consider such freedom of navigation to be fully secured in future? (Zuleta, 1983, p. 480). Judging from the stand taken by signatories at Montego Bay against a 'pick and choose' attitude on the part of non-parties, one might conclude that future freedom of navigation cannot be assumed to be fully secure. This might therefore become a point at which signatories can apply pressure on the United States, for bargaining purposes, as a means of encouraging US concessions elsewhere. The signatories did not seem unmindful of this option. Tommy Koh, for one, reminded the United States that its security and military interests would be 'better protected by the treaty than without it' (quoted by Rosen, 1981). It remains to be seen whether this veiled threat will be implemented.

Despite the problems facing a less than universally ratified Convention, there is little reason to expect anarchy at sea. And if a 'sea of troubles', of a sort, is the outcome, it is important to remember the untidiness of so much of the recent history of the law of the sea. Of the fifteen treaties dealing with the law of the sea which were ratified and still in force at the start of 1982, only three had been ratified by more than eighty nations and only one had been supported by more than one hundred (Robertson and Vasaturo, 1983, pp. 700–1). Indeed, the history of the law of the sea has been predominantly a story of the evolution of customary rules through state practice (Knight, 1977, p. 34). The factors contributing to order at sea have always been relatively strong. Historically speaking, therefore, some of the confidence of the US delegation in customary law rested on strong foundations.

Even though anarchy will be avoided, the future at sea promises more uncertainties than was the case in the immediate past. What finally emerges will be the result of the interplay between hard bargaining, legal claims and state practice over a long period. The outcome may be messy, but it will not necessarily be untenable. The situation contains many disputes, but extensive conflict is unlikely. Much is bound to emerge, as in the past, by customary development, but we should expect a variety of unacceptable unilateral claims, backed in some cases by force. Together, the speed of change and the uncertainty of evaluations will mean that it will take many years before what appeared to be the developing norms in UNCLOS III will be codified. By the time they are, they may themselves already be threatened by newer developments still.

The future maritime context with which we shall have to deal, assuming no cataclysmic breakdown of international order or mind-boggling spread of international harmony, is the further development of the troubled common. This is an example of the 'constant problem' aspect of the international ordering process in which, as Buzan has explained, 'the achievement of higher levels of regulation and standardisation does not necessarily bring problems to an end, but solves some lower-order problems at the expense of creating higher-order ones' (1978, p. 48). In short, as somebody once said about life in general, the evolution of the law of the sea will continue to be 'one damned thing after another'.

Notes: Chapter 2

1   E. D. Brown has used the phrase 'policy-oriented jurisprudence' to refer to what he regards as the 'very low level of objectivity' which has been exhibited in much of the recent writing on the law of the sea. Much writing 'appears to be designed to support *a priori* conclusions' rather than to analyse the law objectively (1983, p. 524).

2   In the subsequent discussion it should be understood that the 'miles' referred to are nautical miles, that is, 1·151 statue miles, or 1·852 kilometers.

3   By 1972 national claims regarding the territorial sea were getting out of hand. Out of 111 states, only twenty-five accepted the traditional three-mile limit. Fifteen nations claimed between 3 and 12 miles, fifty-six claimed 12 miles and fifteen others claimed more. Of the latter, eight claimed 200 miles (Alexander, 1983, p. 567).

4   Under Article 305 the Convention is open for signature until 9 December 1984, but it subsequently remains open for accession under Article 307.

5   The sources of international law are twofold. First, there are formal agreements, notably treaties, in which the parties undertake to carry out certain obligations. Secondly, there is state practice, that is, custom and usage in relations between states. The former is known as *conventional* international law, the latter *customary* international law. The material sources of customary international law are numerous (diplomatic correspondence, military manuals, and so on) as are the 'elements' of custom (duration, uniformity and consistency of practice, generality of practice, the existing sense of legal obligation, and so on). Treaties and other formal agreements are normally thought to be binding only on the parties, but customary international law is thought to be binding on the whole international community (Brownlie, 1973, ch. 1). Not surprisingly, there is sometimes disagreement about the precise status of a particular practice: is it or is it not a norm of customary international law?

6   UNCLOS III adopted a resolution establishing a Preparatory Commission for the Sea-Bed Authority on 30 April 1982. Its main responsibilities involve drafting the rules and regulations for seabed mining and implementing the system for the protection of the pioneer investors (Robertson and Vasaturo, 1983, pp. 698–9).

3

Into the Future
UNCLOS IV, V, VI, etc.

At the beginning of this century Picasso painted an arresting sculptural portrait of Gertrude Stein. 'But Gertrude doesn't look like that', one of her horrified friends is supposed to have complained. 'She will. She will' was Picasso's reply.

Whether or not Picasso's forecast was correct in this case, great paintings and great pieces of literature certainly can change the way we look at the world. The same is true for some agreements between states. The League of Nations Covenant, for example, made it almost inconceivable that the international community might again try to manage without a global multi-purpose international organization. When the League collapsed, it was therefore a case of: 'The League is dead: long live the UN.' UNCLOS III and its Convention should be seen in a similar light: a significant change has come about in the way nations think about the sea, though it will be many years before the full implications of this fact work themselves out. The lasting effect of UNCLOS III will be to ensure that to a greater extent than ever before, the sea will be conceived as an extension of the land. This will be the result of the attitudes, processes and norms which have been generated and in some cases legitimized in the course of the conference. The growth of national and in some cases international control of the seas will be a future fact of the maritime environment.

In order to speculate profitably about the implications of the changing law of the sea, it is necessary not only to think about the immediate post-Convention situation; it is also necessary to try to envisage the longer-term trends and prospects. This includes the wearying thought that UNCLOS III was not the end of the conference circuit, but merely the end of the first lap.

Creeping Jurisdiction

The last chapter described the recent history of the law of the sea as 'one damned thing after another'. The 'damned thing' which has been most exercising the minds of law-of-the-sea-conscious strategists and national security managers is all tied up, in one way or another, with the phenomenon of 'creeping jurisdiction': that is, the extension of national or international rules and regulations, and rights and duties over and under the sea, in straits and coastal zones, on and under the seabed, and in the vast stretches of the high seas. In recent times the traditional 'free seas' have been falling back before the advancement of national claims which have increasingly become legitimized on the international stage.

We are living in a transitional period of maritime affairs. We are seeing a shift from a regime entirely dominated by the traditional maritime powers to one in which all coastal states (and even non-coastal states) demand a bigger say in ocean affairs and claim greater rights in the exploitation of ocean space. The new sea-conscious group of nations face greater responsibilities than ever before in the management of ocean affairs. Even if the 'best will in the world' were to be present — and how often is that evident in international politics? — nobody expects that this transitional process will be easy or free from conflict.

In recent years there has been what has appeared to be an almost irrestible tendency for national jurisdiction to creep beyond the existing three-mile territorial sea. The pressures have been a mixture of nationalism, economic ambition, environmental concern and a legalistic keeping-up-with-the-Joneses. At present, the limit of jurisdiction is set by the 200-mile EEZ, which places about 32 per cent of the oceans (about 28 million square miles) under some form of national administration. As will be discussed in detail in Part Two, this is a matter of great concern for those governments which want to operate their warships in distant waters. Naval powers have been concerned at both the geographical extent of the creep and the character of the rights being claimed by and given to national governments. One worry, for example, is the possibility that warships might be required to give coastal states prior notification before entering their EEZs — a maritime version of air defence identification zones. A step in this direction was taken by pollution-conscious Canada, as a result of its efforts to control the movement of merchant ships. Under the Eastern Canadian Traffic Regulations System (ECAREG) all ships over 500 g.r.t. entering the ECAREG traffic zone are required to request clearance twenty-four hours in advance. The stated objective of the regulations is to reduce the danger of pollution and to increase traffic safety. This system could well extend national control beyond 200 miles (Gold and Johnston, 1979). It is likely that such regulations will spread, for all governments — to a greater or lesser extent — are interested in ensuring good order in the waters off their coasts. But what seems so reasonable from an environmental and management viewpoint can have major security implications. Are such regulations the harbingers of a trend towards a 200-mile territorial sea? Will the pressure for management also come to encompass warships? Will the desire for traffic control eventually spill over into what is now 'high seas'?

A sophisticated answer to such questions requires a judicious balancing of the forces of continuity and change. But we live at a time when change is having its head, and it is vital to realize that as farmers of the sea we are scarcely beyond the Hottentot stage, and that as engineers we are only at the beginning of the maritime industrial revolution. Presently, we are merely at a take-off stage in which there is growing sense that the sea will be a vital source of food and energy. The oceans can now be seen as a major resource in global terms, and not simply, as in the past, a medium for traffic, a barrier to communication and a marginal economic asset. As a result, the promise represented by the oceans — and hence a sense of the significance of the threat of being deprived of it by pollution or politics — is slowly sinking into the official mind, though it has long excited enthusiasts in the maritime community. In future, technology, interest and the will to govern seem set to fill out large chunks of the map of the sea with appropriate forms of national and international administration as inexorably as railways, the industrial revolution and nationalism spread control throughout the land masses in the last century.

The process of 'creeping jurisdiction', as just described, has attracted other names. It has been called 'the ocean enclosure movement'. Some have described the growth of national jurisdiction over the sea as 'unilateralism'. Neville Brown has given it the label 'parcellation' (1977, p. 145). One suggestive, though inelegant, contribution is Gary Knight's concept of 'propertization', to convey the idea that the oceans are becoming increasingly impregnated with all the characteristics of 'real' (that is, territorial) property. These characteristics include the granting of property rights, the making of claims, the outbreak of boundary disputes, the imposition of regulations, the duty to avoid nuisance, and so on. But whatever the name — and another will be introduced in the next section — it is evident that between them, 'creeping jurisdiction', 'the ocean enclosure movement', 'unilateralism', 'parcellation' and the 'propertization' of the oceans are creating a new maritime environment, and one which could greatly affect the mobility of warships and the utility of naval strategy in the decades ahead.

Territorialization and the Spread of Psycho-Legal Boundaries

Another term which can be used to describe the process of creeping jurisdiction is 'territorialization'. Again this is a somewhat clumsy word, but it is one which should put subsequent discussion about naval developments into better perspective. Although international lawyers might quibble with the word because of its 'dry land' connotations, or its connotation with the specific concept of the 'territorial sea', the use of the word can be justified in political terms. This might not help the cause of legal clarity, but then how much of politics does?

'Territorialization' is the idea that national administration over the land is simply extending seawards in terms of rights and duties concerning good order, the exploitation of resources and the exercise of sovereignty. In this context we should conceive 'territory' in the sense in which it has been employed by ethologists, and in particular by Robert Ardrey in his book *The Territorial Imperative* (1967). According to Ardrey's theory, man's behaviour in relation to his sense of possession over, protection of and possible expansion of particular patches of territory is analogous to the territorial behaviour of animals. Ardrey argued that this 'imperative' was genetically determined in the case of both men and animals. Such arguments about the roots of human behaviour are irrelevant for present purposes: we are only concerned with the manifestations of the undoubted sense of ownership which so greatly affects human actions.

In the study of animals, 'territoriality' refers to an area in which one group is dominant and believes that it has rightful possession. Consequently that group will resist intrusion by others. The 'territorial' sense has existed in relation to patches of land ever since human groups became settled farmers. In modern times it has been expressed politically in the concept of sovereignty, and by the creation of armed forces as badges of that sovereignty, as well as its defenders. There is now a growing trend for nations to project that territorial sense over adjoining patches of water. A mixture of legal, technological, economic and political developments are reshaping the attitudes of nations about the sea: there has been a remarkable change in this respect even compared with the mid-1960s. UNCLOS III was both an effect and a cause of this trend, which Hedley Bull has felicitously called a form of 'maritime territorial imperative' (1976, p. 8).

Recent years have witnessed violent manifestations of this imperative. The war over the Falklands/Malvinas during the final stages of UNCLOS III showed just how strong competing feelings about sovereignty can be, even between two nations which, historically speaking, have not been 'enemies'. Possession of the seas surrounding the islands, as well as the question of whose flag flew at Port Stanley, played some part in the calculations of the two governments; how large a part cannot be determined until official records become available. Similar imperatives were evident, but with less costly results, in the Anglo-Icelandic fisheries confrontations of the mid-

1970s. Although British warships carefully refrained from intruding into Iceland's legally defined territorial waters, the Icelandic government nevertheless accused the British of 'invasion' (*New York Times*, 1973, p. 3). This suggested that the zone claimed by Iceland had taken on a deeper meaning than that normally attached to areas of salt-water.

In addition to acting as or keeping out 'invaders', ships can also be used to try to symbolize a nation's possession over a claimed area of sea. This was the aim of the two Argentinian fishing boats which, in August 1983, entered the Falklands Protection Zone which had been declared by Britain following the ending of the war (O'Shaughnessy, 1983; Fairhall, 1983). The boats were attempting to demonstrate in a practical way — by movement in the manner of territorial animals — the belief of their owners that a particular patch of water belonged to their country: 'We made our little contribution to Argentine sovereignty' said one of the skippers. It had been the latter's intention to reach the islands 'flying the Argentine flag'. As a result of this enterprise, the Argentinian Navy's High Command, which had not performed brilliantly in the war, was yet further embarrassed, for the fishermen had exposed its inability to offer protection to Argentine vessels venturing into waters formally claimed by Argentina. On this occasion the vessels were quickly and peacefully escorted out of the zone by British warships.

The accumulation of such incidents, small in themselves, indicates the growing importance of feelings about sovereignty over the seas. Even in less tense situations nations can become sensitive about the movement of foreign vessels, and especially warships. This was evident at the start of 1983 under a newspaper report headed 'Soviet warships sail within 50 miles of US coastline' (Halloran, 1983). The report told of two Soviet warships which had broken off from a squadron which had been visiting Cuba; they subsequently sailed to a point 50 miles from the Mississippi delta, the closest such sailing since Soviet ships had begun their periodic deployments to the Caribbean in 1969. The two Soviet warships, which were under US Navy surveillance throughout, at no time attempted manoeuvres that could be called 'provocative', and at no time did they approach the three-mile territorial limit of the United States. However, it was reported that they were 'well within the 200-mile economic or fishing zone which the United States claims'. There was nothing illegal about the activities of the Soviet warships, of course, and the United States itself sends warships within similar ranges of the Soviet Union in the Baltic Sea, the Arctic Ocean and the Sea of Japan. Nevertheless, despite this, and the fact that the Soviet warships did not present a military threat, their very presence in waters over which the United States had claims jarred the American political sense of whose warships should be where on the world map. In the subconsious mind, the maritime territorial imperative was exerting its effect.

Although the strength of the sense of possession over offshore waters varies between nations, the trend is unmistakable; and as the examples of tiny Iceland and the superpower United States show, this maritime territoriality is present at both ends of the international political spectrum. Illustrations could also be taken from the middle of the spectrum, with countries such as Canada, with its long military commitment to 'sovereignty protection', or Libya, with its claims to the waters of the Gulf of Sirte. Given this trend it is not too far-fetched to suggest that the time is not distant when national sensitivities will be such that alien incursions into nationally claimed sea space will be felt as keenly as are unauthorized incusions into air space. Feelings about national sovereignty are at least as strong as they ever were, and in some cases they are stronger; and for the first time in the case of some countries, these feelings are being directed seawards. One result of all this is that ships, and especially warships, are an essential aspect of those trappings of sovereignty which are so important to the self-respect and authority of governments. The governments of coastal states need badges of sovereignty over the seas in the same way that they need a seat at the United Nations and a national airline.

In the decades ahead the territorialization of the oceans will focus on the developing concept of the EEZ. Regardless of the fate of the Convention, UNCLOS III will be seen as having helped to precipitate and legitimize this concept in a way which now seems impossible to reverse. Almost overnight − on a historical time-scale − the EEZ concept filled out 32 per cent of ocean space with new national rights and duties. The irreversibility of this development is clear from the way in which the US administration, while rejecting the Convention's seabed mining terms, nevertheless embraced its many other provisions, including the extension of the functional sovereignty of coastal states out to 200 miles. It must be said that some states refuse to accept that the EEZ concept has already become a norm of customary international law, but this is not the verdict of the majority. In the latter's opinion, the EEZ is here to stay (Appendix: Tables 2 and 3).

The EEZ concept has been appropriately described as 'a zone sui generis', since it is neither high sea nor territorial sea as normally understood. However, some writers have been reluctant to concede its uniqueness. Underlying D. P. O'Connell's comments on this matter, for example, is an assumption that EEZs are essentially high seas gone wrong; they have fallen upon bad times as a result of keeping bad company (1978, p. 16). This viewpoint is diametrically opposed to that of those who see the EEZs as simple extensions of national jurisdiction over adjacent sea areas for legitimate economic and political purposes. In contrast, O'Connell insisted that the issue had to be looked at 'historically', though why this is so is not compelling. Politically, it would seem to be more profitable to look at the issue in terms of present realities and future expectations rather than 'historically'. Those who propound the ethnocentric-navalist perspective claim that the EEZ is essentially an area of high seas which has now become subject to certain limited jurisdictional rights 'which are in the nature of police rights rather than sovereignty'. In O'Connell's words the EEZ is 'high seas, and superimposed on that you have certain coastal state rights with respect to [the] enjoyment and protection of marine resources'. Thus, O'Connell concludes that the residual character of the EEZ is high seas. This represents the attitude of the traditional naval powers, including the Soviet Union. Typically, the latter insisted on a non-sovereignty clause regarding the EEZ, and does not concede that it has already become a norm of customary international law.

To those unschooled in the verities of the navalist tradition, O'Connell's thesis will not be self-evident. It will not be obvious why the EEZ should, in essence, have the 'residual' character of high seas rather than the 'emerging' character of territorial sea. The explanation for O'Connell's viewpoint lies in the remarks in Chapter 1 to the effect that international law is an extension of politics by other means. O'Connell was defending the traditional maritime interest, and he gave the game away in this respect when he stated that the 'great fear' (presumably the Anglo-American navalist fear) is that of the self-fulfilling prophecy: if people go around saying that the EEZ is to be understood as an extension of national jurisdiction rather than as an area of 'residual' high seas, then the EEZ may well increasingly grow to resemble the territorial sea. Depending upon one's viewpoint, this could be regarded as an adverse trend in maritime affairs or, alternatively, as a step towards progress in the international legitimation of national aspirations.

Clearly, the practical and legal evolution of the EEZ concept will not be without dispute. Plenty of demarcation problems remain to be settled regarding claims to extended jurisdiction, but the most interesting and potentially troublesome developments will be related to claims for various functional competences in this 'zone sui generis'. It is likely, for example, that some coastal states will undertake actions and enact legislation which will interfere with the rights expected by naval powers in EEZs; they will claim that they are acting in the interests of good order at sea and in accordance with their developing rights in a zone which is unique in the law of the sea. The danger of vessel-source pollution is one possible cause of friction.

Although warships enjoy sovereign immunity from environmental protection regulations within EEZs, coastal states do have rights within their EEZs to adopt non-disciminatory rules and standards against vessel-source pollution and to enforce these when necessary. Future rules and standards are to be established through the Intergovernmental Maritime Organization (IMO) or through a general diplomatic conference. But already, a number of coastal states have adopted domestic legislation with regard to vessel-source pollution which is more severe than that of the International Maritime Organization Convention. As a result, as Lewis Alexander has argued, 'The passage of "potential polluters", such as nuclear-powered vessels, vessels carrying nuclear or other "hazardous" cargoes, and ammunition ships, through the EEZs of some coastal States may in time be jeopardized, treaty or no treaty' (1983, pp. 585–6). The writing is on the wall for ships of war. Warships, in some sense, are the ultimate 'potential polluters'.

Both coastal states and naval powers have to face similar questions regarding the future of the EEZ. What is permissible in a 'zone sui generis'? And are rights there enjoyed by designation or default? There is much scope for disagreement on such questions. An Indian specialist on the law of the sea has offered the opinion that some ostensible military rights in the EEZ cannot be allowed 'owing to the nature and characteristics of the EEZ being implicitly a sui generis zone having a specific legal regime' (Admiral Frank L. Fraser, Chief Hydrographer of the Government of India, in Gamble, 1979, p. 400). Spokesmen of the naval powers will not agree, and are unlikely to for a long time to come. But the pressure is on the naval powers, and they have good cause to be worried. Although during UNCLOS III they insisted so firmly, and generally with success, on maintaining their existing rights, long-term trends in the maritime environment seem to be against them, and the politico-legal battleground will be the EEZ. As one knowledgeable international lawyer has noted: 'Admittedly, the EEZ is a zone *sui generis* but the safeguards for the freedom of the high seas written into the new Convention on the Law of the Sea appear less than impressive when measured against the exclusive rights accorded to the coastal State' (Brown, 1983, p. 522). Obviously not every piece of accumulating jurisdiction will adversely affect military navigation. But the secular trend is adverse to the naval interest — as traditionally and conventionally understood — despite the rights enshrined in the 1982 Convention. There comes a time when a collection of grains of sand becomes a heap.

Regardless of the details of the law of the sea which emerge in the next few years, the paramount political fact will be that one man's distant water is another man's maritime backyard; and that all coastal states want a bigger say in their own backyards. Creeping jurisdiction at sea is here to stay. As Gary Knight has put it, there is 'substantial evidence that this is a permanent and probably irreversible trend' (1977, p. 32). So, even if the Convention laboriously cobbled together by UNCLOS III fails to get the support of the present US administration and the governments of other major industrialized states, the long-term future of naval mobility is under challenge. It may take half a century, but unilateralist drives to parcel up parts of the ocean will continue and will be legitimized by the territorialist mood of the international community. As this development unfolds, and as state control intensifies or expands over larger patches of sea, greater meaning will be invested in the new boundaries which are an inevitable outcome of the process. Nations will feel protective and sensitive – indeed patriotic – about these patches of ocean. Hence it is appropriate to talk about the spread of what might be called 'psycho-legal boundaries' at sea (Booth, 1983, pp. 373–96).

The Challenge to Navies

The territorialization of the seas and the proliferation of psycho-legal boundaries will be a fact of naval life for the indefinite future. The process represents a challenge to that mobility which has always been the essence of naval strategy. The history of naval affairs repeatedly shows that warships of the right type and in the right number can give nations which possess them strategic access to those distant places, resources and political developments which are thought to be important for the national interest. 'The sea is one' as an old British Admiralty maxim had it, and hence a country with a powerful navy has always been said to have the potential to be a 'neighbour' of all countries with coasts.

The objective of naval strategy is the use of the sea (Booth, 1977, ch. 1). States are interested in using it for three general purposes: the passage of goods and people; the deployment of military power for diplomatic purposes or for use against targets on land or at sea; and the exploitation of resources in or under the sea. Navies exist as a means to further such purposes. Their objective is to secure the sea for one's own nation, and to be in a position to attempt to prevent others from using the sea in ways which are to one's disadvantage. In the process of fulfilling their objectives navies have three characteristic modes of action: military, diplomatic and constabulary. Each mode of action requires mobility, to a greater or lesser degree, and each, in its different way, has been or will be affected by creeping jurisdiction. The spread of psycho-legal boundaries in each case presents challenges and opportunities.

The basic problem for naval powers is created by the confrontation between the process of creeping jurisdiction and the need of warships to have mobility. To date, the traditional naval establishments have seen the confrontation solely in terms of challenge, but in Part Two it will be argued that opportunities are also being created. For the moment it is important only to note that naval establishments and their supporters believe that creeping jurisdiction will simply add legal and political inhibitions to the already growing costs involved in the exercise of naval power in a post-imperial money-conscious world. They only see a further increment being added to the debit side in cost-benefit calculations regarding the 'peacetime' utility of warships. In particular they fear that the process of territorialization will give coastal states increasing bargaining power, and some say over the mobility of foreign warships. If coastal state rights grow, and come to include rights over the passage of foreign warships, then the latter's mobility will probably have to be paid for in some way.

The naval powers clearly understand this possibility. Indeed some of the pressures involved have already been felt by US officials. Ambassador Elliot Richardson, then the Special Representative of the President at UNCLOS III, revealed in 1980 that cables had crossed his desk appealing for the 'blurring or delay' of activities such as the sending of ships and aircraft into or over disputed waters.[1] He said that the writers of the cables had justified caution in US warship deployment 'on such grounds as the "adverse effect on other matters on which we are seeking their support", "jeopardy to important American economic interests", "repercussions on sensitive bilateral developments" and the like'. One Ambassador, Richardson reported, 'went so far as to recommend the outright cancellation of routine overflights of the 200-mile zone' (1980, p. 909). This revelation is a most interesting sign of the maritime times. It indicates the pressures which territorialization has already had on former expectations about naval mobility. If a US Ambassador can suggest cancelling routine overflights across another country's EEZ, will it be long before a particularly territorialist group of coastal states strongly demand the prior notification of overflight or warship transits across EEZs? Will it be long before they demand prior notification as a *quid pro quo* for support on political, legal, or economic issues? As will be seen in Chapter 4, the issue of prior notification was quietly raised in the final stages of UNCLOS III. It will certainly be heard again, and louder.

Naval establishments understandably fear that the proliferation of psycho-legal boundaries and the in-filling of the enclosed areas with claims such as the prior notification of warship transit will add yet further obstacles to the fulfilment of their professional tasks. And in the West at least, they are not entirely confident that if an issue such as warship transit becomes serious, their diplomatic representatives will stand up for naval mobility rather than be tempted by the prospects of a quiet diplomatic life. The major naval establishments do not relish the prospect of future legal struggles over naval mobility, since their professional lives have been overloaded with problems since 1945, and they already believe that they have enough on their plates. In the late 1950s, when the strategies of the greatest military powers came increasingly to rest on nuclear weapons, the role of navies was cast in doubt. A decade later, and through the 1970s, 'naval diplomacy' came into vogue as a justification for the peacetime development and rationale of surface warships, and for the Soviet Navy as well as for the navies of the Western maritime powers (Cable, 1971 and 1981; Luttwak, 1974; Booth, 1977; Dismukes and McConnell, 1979). Ironically, a few years later, it is the peacetime exercise of naval diplomacy more than any other role which appears to be threatened by the future development of the law of the sea. During what we call 'peace' international law, including the law of the sea, is more salient than during those periods when military 'necessities' rather than legal norms tend to shape policy. In war, it is always said – and with ample justification – the law is weak.

The in-filling of ocean space with new forms of jurisdiction will not necessarily be a speedy process. We would not be justified in simply extrapolating the accelerated developments of the late 1960s and 1970s. So when we are speculating about major changes in the law of the sea we should be thinking in terms of a decade or more rather than single years. Nevertheless, however long or incremental the drift to *mare clausum*, it is one which the naval powers will watch carefully; and, just as predictably, they will seek to resist it. To make matters worse, although the superpowers share some common interests in maintaining naval mobility, the territorialist members of the international community might well seek to exploit the superpowers' global geopolitical competition – a rivalry which does not seem likely to abate in the 1980s and 1990s. Scott Allen has explained this worrying prospect from the US perspective as follows:

> If less-developed countries of the Southern Hemisphere fall victim to subversive insurgencies dominated by the expansionist policies of the Soviet Union, the Western alliance will find its rights of access to the seas threatened. Legalistic territorialist arguments would be used to justify claims against free use of the sea-lanes, the straits, and access to the far shores through special zones, enclosed seas, and historic bays. Nationalistic propàganda would be backed by well placed Soviet naval and military aid. It would then be for the Western nations to decide, collectively, or individually, whether access to vital straits and the far coasts should be a benefit available only to those flags under the protection of the Soviet Navy. (1983, p. 47)

If such a situation were to come about, it would be fraught with dangerous possibilities. Both superpowers would have reason to fear that their rival might gain an advantage, though the Soviet Union would have more cause to worry, because of the disadvantages the Soviet Navy faces as a result of its maritime geography, because of the country's relatively low influence around the world's rimlands, and because of the continuing vitality of Western political, economic and military power. A rational solution to the mutual fears of superpower strategists on this issue would be for them to enter an agreement about rules of behaviour, in which they would undertake not to seek unilateral advantages in circumstances which would lead to the encouragement of territorialist claims. Such an agreement would be rational, but there is little reason to expect it in the international politics of the late 1980s and 1990s, if the crude superpower diplomacy of the early 1980s is any guide.

Not only might the territorialization of the sea become enmeshed with superpower competition, but problems might also arise in North–South relations (Allen, 1983, p. 48). Allen has drawn attention to the possibility that the coastal states of the Group of 77, in possession of a voting majority in the General Assembly or in any future law of the sea conference, 'can simply redefine the scope of their national jurisdiction'. If, as a result, coastal jurisdiction continues to advance, 'the last vestige of the high seas may vanish'. The technology for occupying and exploiting the seabed is on the way and what Allen called the 'political basis' for such a trend appears to have been established. Of particular concern was what he thought to be the 'expandable' nature of the principle of the 'common heritage of mankind':

> If it can be applied to the seabed, why not to the fish in the high seas, as well as those in the exclusive economic zones? Why not to the vast thermal energy resource in the tropic oceans? Why not to the access to the sea, and its navigational properties? Why should skippers not pay needy, less-developed countries a fee for access to the oceans that wash their shores? Is the sea not a common resource possessed by all mankind, as are the resources of the Antarctic? The moon? (1983, p. 48)

Allen listed even more areas of potential expansion, including, ultimately, land-based mineral resources now under sovereign control: after all, like manganese nodules, they are where they are as an 'accident of fate'. One can easily imagine the disadvantaged of the world readily concurring with such an argument. This would obviously not be the view of the traditional maritime powers.

The territorialist trend, leading to *mare clausum*, is generally seen as offering no advantages to the traditional maritime powers. From the latter's perspective man's effective use of the oceans is hindered by the closed sea principle. Again, Scott Allen has expressed this viewpoint

48

forcefully, based on his fear that the 1982 Convention was a step on the slippery slope.

> The year 1982 saw that discredited doctrine's reemergence *[mare clausum]*. What year will see its downfall is unclear. The change will not likely be accomplished by a few holdout nations, such as the United States, but rather by the emerging smaller sea powers of the Southern Hemisphere ... The nations of the Southern Hemisphere must see their own self-interest in *mare liberum*, freedom of the seas, as they have seen it in *mare clausum*. That can happen only when they themselves have the ability to use the sea. (1983, p. 49)

It must therefore be a primary aim of Western maritime policy, in Allen's eyes, to help the nations of the less developed world to realize the benefits of the freedom of the sea by helping them to use the sea.

In order to bring about such an outcome, the leading Western maritime nations would have to pursue a policy of enlightened self-interest: but their behaviour in the final stages of UNCLOS III does not give one much confidence that they have the vision to see such possibilities. By rejecting the spirit of 'the common heritage of mankind' in favour of the mean spirit of every-man-for-himself the Reagan administration not only threatened the future of the Convention, but it also put at risk some important US national interests: it placed free enterprise dogma before its strategic and other maritime interests, and it showed that it preferred to accommodate the commercial outlooks of a handful of domestic seabed mining companies rather than to identify with the aspirations of the bulk of the international community. With the United States having unravelled the package deal of UNCLOS III, it would not be surprising if, in the future, some states decided to retaliate by acting in an obstructionist manner on questions relating to the movement of foreign warships through EEZs. As was suggested earlier, by slipping out of one bargain, the Reagan administration may have opened up far more problems than it imagined — or failed to imagine.

Third World nations are aware, to a greater or lesser degree, of the strategic dimensions of the law of the sea issue. During the earlier stages of UNCLOS III some Third World spokesmen claimed that the support of the naval powers for a narrow territorial sea represented not so much a defence of the internationality of the oceans as a tactic by which they could legally place their warships as close as possible to the shores of coastal states. During UNCLOS III, however, economic rather than strategic concerns were the major preoccupation for the Group of 77. Once the economic issues become more settled, Mark Janis, among others, speculated that national security issues would come more to the fore in Third World thinking about the law of the sea (1976, pp. 69—70). It can be assumed that such a possibility would be all the more likely in the event of a period of future North—South acrimony, when Third World spokesmen may be searching for bargaining tools. If they are, they may find them off their shores. If coastal states come to regard their EEZs 'as subject to their sovereignty for purposes of regulating navigation and overflight and related activities' — as Elliot Richardson feared (1980, p. 906) — the implications for naval strategy and military overflight would be very far-reaching indeed. As potential political bargaining chips, EEZs may yet prove more valuable than the manganese nodules of the deep seabed.

Ocean Enclosure: How Far Can It Go?

Gary Knight has identified four stages in the history of the law of the sea: 'unrestricted freedom of the seas', 'reasonable use of the seas', 'regulated use' and what he has caalled the fourth and final stage, namely, 'property rights' in the ocean (1977, pp. 33—4). But there is a possible further stage. This would be the full enclosure of the ocean, a 'genuinely global *mare clausum*, a regime providing government, law and order — including a monopoly of limited force — for the whole of the world's last common' (Young, 1974, p. 262). Hollick has described this as the 'logical endpoint' of contemporary maritime trends, that is, a 'total carving up of ocean space into national areas with international cooperative efforts dictated by the circumstances of particular areas and uses' (1981, p. 17). The trend towards a global *mare clausum* is now a thinkable prospect, and as such is a fit subject for strategic speculation (Part Two, below).

After the rapid expansion of national jurisdiction to 200 miles during the 1970s, the years immediately ahead should see a hiatus in the enclosure of the oceans. This is not because of any inherent 'logic' in the figure of 200 miles, but rather because there is a mutual interest in giving the existing changes a chance to settle. But even before UNCLOS III was finished, some voices asserted that the EEZ represented only a minimum acceptable compromise for the African states, and that if they failed to achieve satisfaction, they would follow a new and more radical approach to solving ocean problems (Njenga, 1975, pp. 87—105). Such assertions should not be dismissed as mere rhetoric. If the recent history of the law of the sea suggests anything, it is that the only fault is in being over conservative. Looking back at the development of the law of the sea in the 1970s — and we are perhaps too close to appreciate it fully — its most remarkable feature was the pace of change, even in the face of the vested interests of the traditional maritime powers. It is not surprising, therefore, that so many have concluded that the trend towards creeping jurisdiction seems irreversible. That said, most specialists would also agree with Lewis Alexander that the ocean enclosure movement, which has recently been so dynamic, 'may be approaching a temporary plateau' (1983, p. 561). While we are crossing his 'temporary plateau' in the years immediately ahead, Alexander has identified six possible developments which point towards the further in-filling of ocean space with national jurisdiction (1983, pp. 588−90):

(1) *The continued expansion of maritime claims within the current jurisdictional framework.* Some countries which have not yet asserted a 200-mile zone may do so. Others may expand their claimed competences from exclusive fishery zones (EFZs) to exclusive economic zones.[2]

(2) *Increased expressions of nationalism in offshore jurisdictional zones.* This trend would involve increased toughness in the interpretation of national rights. There would be a greater readiness to arrest foreign fishing vessels, to refuse consent to foreign marine scientific research in one's EEZ, and to seek greater restrictions on the passage of warships and aircraft in and beyond the territorial sea.

(3) *Improved environmental protection measures in the EEZ.* The right of coastal states to protect their marine environment is guaranteed by the Convention. It is therefore likely that there will be greater efforts in this area. By imposing greater controls on navigation, there should be a diminution of the threats to the quality of the marine environment.

(4) *Uncertainties as to the binding force of Convention text articles.* This problem will open up several areas of dispute. Some claims which go beyond the framework of the Convention will be challenged, while some states may fail to live up to the provisions of the text (or, if they are a non-party, they may simply deem them inapplicable).

(5) *The development of a modus vivendi between and among states with adjacent or opposite EEZs.* Rather than face the problems caused by an excess of nationalistic-territorialist claims, coastal states may realize the advantages of at least ad hoc agreements on such common problems as maritime boundary delimitation.

(6) *The gradual re-emergence of marine regional arrangements.* Moves can be expected towards regional arrangements to adopt uniform regulations on matters such as pollution control or marine scientific research.

As a result of such developments, Alexander concluded that jurisdiction will continue to creep, even on what he characterized as the post-Convention 'plateau'. His general argument seems unchallengeable.

In answer to the question 'how far can creeping jurisdiction go?' the ultimate answer is simple: 'much further, and in theory all the way'. Although it is true, as Buzan has suggested, that it would appear that the 200-mile zone 'encloses most resources of interest' (1978, p. 8), one must accept that there will now be more interest than previously in what is left unregulated. In the late 1970s, for example, it was reported that Soviet fisheries research was tending to concentrate in the waters of the mid-oceans, where no controls would operate. It should also be added they were operating as well off the coasts of some African states where EEZs had been declared, but where effective supervisory power was lacking (Young and Sebek, 1978, p. 260). An estimated 20 per cent of the fish being caught at the end of the 1970s was outside 200-mile zones (*The Economist*, 23 July 1977, p. 17). Some governments may seek forms of functional jurisdiction beyond the 200-mile limit, in order to exploit exclusively the fish stocks which lie outside. There are other reasons for trying to extend control. Governments may see extension as the only way of dealing with particular forms of vessel-source pollution. Or they may wish to act in order to pre-empt seabed miners just beyond their EEZs (Hollick, 1981, p. 17; Alexander, 1983, pp. 588–9). There is profit and therefore political interest in what are now the high seas.

One would hesitate to envisage further creep beyond the present EEZ if the rationale behind the 200-mile zone was stronger. But this boundary has an arbitrariness which suggests that change will not be irresistible. The breadth of the EEZ has its origins in the claims of Chile, Ecuador and Peru in the 1951 Declaration of Santiago. In this case a 200-mile zone happened to cover the productive fisheries areas off their coasts (related to the Humboldt current and nutrient-rich areas). Their claim for exclusive jurisdiction for designated purposes came to be known as the 'Patrimonial Sea', a phrase already suggesting a sense of territoriality much stronger than that of the neutral acronym 'EEZ'. In words which have a very contemporary ring to them, the Santiago Declaration recognized their seas as 'irreplaceable sources of essential food and economic materials' necessary to further the goals of economic development and independence. Once established and promoted by the Latin American states, 200 miles then became the magical figure for the 1970s. It was sold to some African and Asian states, who then embraced it with enthusiasm when they discovered that the sea could be more than a medium for the transport of imperialist warships.

The arguments which led to the growth of the 200-mile zone could also be used for more distant horizons. The Humboldt current does not have the universality of the old three-mile cannon shot. In theory, another 25 miles of ocean might be desirable from a particular national viewpoint, but one hardly expects the next jump to be to 225 miles. Round figures or simple divisions have a strong pull. On this basis, the extension of EEZs to mid-ocean would appear to be the next possibility. One of the principles behind the old three-mile limit, measured by the range of cannon shot, was that 'the dominion of the land ends where the power of the arms ends' (Colombos, 1967, pp. 92–3). In practice, this limit persisted long after the range of weapons exceeded 3 miles, while even the 200-mile limit (let alone the twelve-mile territorial sea) falls far short of the military reach of all countries with warplanes. Such talk about a mid-ocean EEZ may seem fanciful. In the short term it is. But it is salutary for sceptics to be reminded of the fact that it is only a relatively short time since Western opinion scoffed at the 'bizarre' Latin American claims for the extension of national jurisdiction out to 200 miles. These days, the maritime environment is not one where it is profitable to be backward-looking.

A further geographical extension of jurisdictional zones may be a long-term prospect. In the meantime, a more likely possibility is the intensification of national regulation within existing EEZs, that is, functional rather than geographical creep. This is a 'natural' tendency for governments, and in many cases for no ulterior motives, simply the desire and pressure to govern efficiently. As a result, governments will be inclined to intensify the regulations within the EEZ; and the Convention will not necessarily constrain the in-filling of ocean space, as some would hope. For in the words of Arvid Pardo, 'since the limits of national jurisdiction are not clearly defined in the Convention, coastal states fronting on the open ocean can continue, within broad limits, to extend their control in the marine environment as their marine capabilities increase and their national interests appear to dictate' (1983, p. 497). The Convention itself will not necessarily constrain creeping jurisdiction, but undoubtedly there will be greater creep of both a geographical and functional kind in the absence of a universal Convention.

The most troubling of the feasible medium-term possibilities for naval powers would be the growth of a strong movement in favour of a 200-mile territorial sea. To speculate about such a possibility is not to indulge in fantasy, since the idea has already been talked about. But it is not a short-term prospect. A 200-mile territorial sea can be ruled out for the time being as a result of the provisions of the 1982 Convention, an absence of sufficient support and the fact that for some time ahead international attention will be focused on the problem of ratifying what has been agreed, rather than pushing out new laws (Alexander, 1983, pp. 561–2). But even before UNCLOS III, as many as eight states were already making what seemed the preposterous claim of a 200-mile territorial sea (Alexander, 1983, p. 567); and by 1983 the number had increased to fourteen, though admittedly they did not constitute a group of powerful 'maritime' states (Appendix: Table 1). It is not inconceivable in future that the territorialist ambitions of more states will be channelled into claims for a 200-mile territorial sea, if only, in the first instance, for bargaining purposes. The hullabaloo from the naval powers will be deafening.

Somewhere short of the idea of a 200-mile territorial sea, but a future problem for the naval powers, is the possible growth of special 'security zones' at sea. The problem will be all the greater if these zones become identified with 200-mile limits. Security zones form one of the areas of 'special competence' which have evolved over the years, though they have not received general acceptance in the practice of states, nor in the Convention text. One of the difficulties with these zones is the 'extreme vagueness' of the term 'security', as a result of which it has been feared that the granting of 'security' rights in offshore zones would open up the way for abuses. Furthermore, anxiety has been expressed that the recognition of such rights would also 'go far toward' equating rights over the contiguous zone and rights in the territorial sea. In any case, international lawyers have claimed that security zones are unnecessary, since questions of self-defence against imminent and direct threats are covered by the general principles of international law and by the Charter of the United Nations (Brownlie, 1973, pp. 213–14).

Despite being unnecessary yet the source of various legal problems, security zones are a political fact of life. In the early 1980s about eighteen states had claimed extraterritorial 'security zones' in which passage by warships and military aircraft required prior notification and approval (Alexander, 1983, p. 587). Of these, the most important have been those claimed by North Korea, Vietnam and Syria (Alexander, 1983, p. 574). In 1977 North Korea declared a military zone extending to 50 miles from its coast, in which navigation by any vessel or overflight by any aircraft was prohibited without prior permission. Vietnam, in the same year, announced a 24-mile security zone in which foreign warships must seek permission before entry. Syria has a similar claim, but for 35 miles. In addition, a number of other coastal states passed laws which require prior notification, and sometimes approval, before warships can enter their territorial sea.

By far the most extensive security zone in recent years, but this time declared in the special circumstances of a limited war, was the 200-mile 'Total Exclusion Zone' announced by the British during the Falklands War of 1982. The reasoning behind the extent of the zone is not entirely clear – 'the wider the better' might be the rule of thumb from a military viewpoint – but it did undoubtedly represent a tactical blunder in relation to British law of the sea policy, since it strengthened the identification of security zones and EEZs. It contributed to strengthening the tendency to regard the behaviour of foreign war-ships within 200 miles of one's coast as legally different from the same behaviour beyond that distance. This is an attitude which the naval powers do not want to encourage, and this may have been one of the reasons why, when the Falklands had been recaptured, the British government replaced the 200-mile 'Total Exclusion Zone' with a 150-mile 'Protection Zone'. Unlike the Total Exclusion Zone, the Protection Zone required the complete exclusion of only military vessels and aircraft (Fairhall, 1983). The Argentinian government protested to the United Nations that the Protection Zone was an attempt to achieve 'British domination' over the area, and was unlawful (*Guardian*, 23 September 1982). Despite the protests, the zone remained in being and was maintained with a tough attitude.

Security zones have not received general acceptance in the practice of states, nor have they been legitimized by the Convention. Never-theless, they remain a fact of life and a potent reminder that one man's blue water is another man's maritime backyard. Because of the sensi-tivity which nationalistic states have regarding the presence of alien warships off their coasts, security zones are a phenomenon which will not disappear: indeed, they may be expected to spread. This is espe-cially likely to be the case in tense situations, such as the Falklands War. On that occasion the Argentinian cruiser *General Belgrano* was thought to be threatening British ships within the zone, even though the *Belgrano* itself remained outside. But because it was seen to be threatening, it was thought to be 'fair game' for attack. Like empires, and for much the same reasons, security zones have a tendency to expand.

Although we seem to have reached a 'temporary plateau' as far as the ocean enclosure movement is concerned, there are powerful pressures for change. As Elisabeth Mann Borgese has explained, industrial nations need to regulate the penetration of the industrial revolution into deeper and wider offshore zones, developing nations have to defend their coastal waters against the pressures of modern distant water fishing fleets and factory ships, while no state can tole-rate spying devices and polluting activities in their coastal waters (1982, p. 712). As a result, we can expect limited jurisdictional creep to take place even while we are on the 'plateau'. The main trend for the moment seems likely to be in the direction of claims for denser func-tional competences rather than for further geographical reach, but the latter can by no means be ruled out, especially in the longer term. In this respect, the most decisive step towards a world of closed seas would be the development of a concerted movement to legitimize the idea of a 200-mile territorial sea.

The growth of coastal state regulations within the 200-mile limit will be one of the preoccupations of the law of the sea community in the years ahead. The problems thrown up may be approached on a bilateral, regional, or global scale, but in the light of the UNCLOS III experience, the majority of the international community will probably prefer to approach the issues comprehensively and globally. Obviously, the law of the sea will continue to evolve; and given the costs of getting things wrong these days, it is not too early to begin speculating about the post-Convention world. This might not be easy to encourage, since some conference-watchers seem inclined merely to say with relief 'UNCLOS I and II are dead: long live UNCLOS III'. But UNCLOS III, in its turn, will have its day, and there might be advantages in already contemplating strategies for UNCLOS IV. Part Two will examine the military dimensions of possible future changes in the law of the sea in a territorialist direction.

Changing ocean usage of one sort or another will create new pressures on the law of the sea. At some point, therefore, some aspects of UNCLOS III will need changing. There will be a requirement for an UNCLOS IV or V, etc.; or perhaps a conference in semi-permanent session; or even the creation of a new permanent agency within the United Nations to oversee the oceans. And as far as the latter suggestion is concerned, could the process of international institution-building have a more promising focus? Without doubt, a permanent or semi-permanent negotiating body would accord well with the needs of the time. In view of the complexities of the issues involved and their global implications, there is a need for UNCLOS to become, like UNCTAD and SALT/START, not so much a set of negotiations, but more of a way of life. Some would argue that there will be no need for an UNCLOS IV, on the grounds that UNCLOS III dealt with all the issues and that new ones can be incorporated into its structures, rules and processes.[3] From this viewpoint the 1982 Convention is seen as a blueprint for future attempts to achieve a comprehensive law of the sea (Robertson and Vasaturo, 1983, p. 711). Whatever perspective is adopted, it should be appreciated that UNCLOS III was only a stage in a never-ending process, albeit a very special stage. UNCLOS III represents the end of the beginning — the 'beginning' being the international community's fuller awakening to the uses (and abuses) of the sea.

Like SALT, UNCLOS III will have a life, of sorts, after its death. The pressure for a new conference is all the more likely in the event of a massive collapse of the hopes of 1974–82. A newly conceived conference would have the effect of clearing some of the stale and unpleasant diplomatic air caused by the late change in US policy: it might well prove easier to create a new conference rather than tinker with the remains of the old. As Elliot Richardson has argued, 'It is difficult . . . to conceive of a process, short of the convening of a whole new conference, that could make substantive changes in a Convention that has already been opened for signature' (1983, p. 512). A new conference would also make it easier for the United States to re-enter the global process. The analogy with US policy towards the creation of the League of Nations and the United Nations is striking. After being instrumental in the League's establishment, the US government rejected the organization at its moment of conception because of domestic pressures. The subsequent non-participation of the world's major power in the life of the League contributed to ensuring that the organization collapsed sooner rather than later, and at some cost to the non-participating world power. The lesson was learned, and a wiser administration later made sure that the United States was a major influence on all stages of the creation and running of the League's successor. If this analogy has any validity, it suggests that things will have to get worse before they get better, but it does give some cause for long-term optimism: it suggests that both US policy and the Convention will be improved.

The UNCLOS III approach, dominant between 1974 and 1982, represents only one way of tackling the problem of the developing law of the sea. In time the UNCLOS process — by whatever name and with whatever set of roman numerals — may not be as important a feature of the developing law of the sea as it has been in recent years. During our time on the plateau, there may be a diffusion of thinking about the subject, and specific law of the sea problems may be dealt with by bilateral or regional agreements (Hollick, 1981, p. 15).

The lasting effect of UNCLOS III will be to ensure that to a greater extent than ever before the sea will be seen as an extension of the land. History will look back on UNCLOS III as having been a vital stage in this process. It catalysed ideas and generated new norms; it was both system confirming and system transforming; it legitimized and it created; and it gave the international community an agenda for the future when it contemplates the seas. And contemplate the seas it must, for economic necessity and temptation, the search for energy, the threat of pollution and the problem of overfishing will remain with us, and hence the requirement for the management of the oceans will grow. Not all the pressures on the law of the sea will have direct or immediate military implications. Indeed, for the moment the direct military implications of the 1982 Convention will be minimal; but in the longer term the effects of the norms generated by UNCLOS III will be far-reaching. The situation might not change dramatically for twenty years or so — commercial seabed mining is unlikely before the end of the century and neither population pressure on world food resources nor pollution are yet as bad as they can or will be — but there is no doubt that the years ahead will see the in-filling of ocean space with new psycho-legal meaning. It is technologically possible, economically unavoidable and politically tempting. The cumulative effect of these changes might be to bring about what later will be called a 'paradigm shift' in the peacetime military uses of the oceans. The conservatively minded might look at the oceans in 1983 and say 'Gertrude doesn't look like that'. But those with both a sense of historical perspective and feel for the flow of events will surely answer, 'She will. She will.'

Notes: Chapter 3

1 At the time Richardson was writing, the problem involved was that of dealing with states claiming territorial seas greater than 3 miles.
2 The EEZ concept was first presented at UNCLOS III in 1974. By 1982 fifty-six countries had established EEZs. Thirty-six additional states had declared EFZs, forgoing for the time being the extra rights available to them in the EEZ (Alexander, 1983, p. 570; Appendix: Tables 2 and 3).
3 Article 312 (*Amendment*) states that after ten years from the date the Convention entered into force, a state may propose specific amendments (but not relating to activities in the Area) and request the convening of a general conference whose decision-making procedure would be the same as UNCLOS III (that is, 'by way of consensus') unless otherwise agreed. Under Article 313, however, a simplified amendment procedure was proposed. This did not necessitate a conference, but merely written communication. The latter does not allow consensus decision-making, but instead gives each state an effective veto on amendments.

PART TWO

The Implications

4

The 1982 UN Convention: The Military Dimension

Although the military dimension of UNCLOS III demanded less space in the public record than the problems relating to seabed mining, military considerations did help to determine the policies of some states, including some of the most important. It is necessary, therefore, to begin this detailed analysis of the Convention with a survey of the interests of those states which wanted to ensure that the outcome did not interfere with their aim of securing maximum naval mobility.

The Interests of the Naval Powers

The military priorities of the major naval powers were never difficult to discern through UNCLOS III. In 1980 they were frankly outlined, from the US viewpoint, by Elliot Richardson, who was then still the Special Representative of the President for the Law of the Sea Conference and head of the US delegation to UNCLOS III (1980, pp. 902–19). As a former Secretary of Defense, Richardson was more sensitive than most delegates to the naval dimension of the problem, and so his words – and worries – deserve special attention.

Although Richardson's arguments were specifically concerned with the needs of the United States, they were also relevant to a greater or lesser extent to all the other countries with an interest in deploying warships at some distance from their own coastlines. For the United States, above all other countries in the modern world, is the maximalist naval power, the one with the greatest perceived interest in the widest possible freedom of navigation. On this matter, the United States can therefore be allowed to speak for the rest – something which, in any case, it is rather difficult to stop its spokesmen from doing on any matter these days. The identity of interests among the naval powers was underlined during UNCLOS III by the similar positions adopted on security questions by the United States and the Soviet Union.[1] In Richardson's laconic words: 'As between the superpowers, consensus on the importance of the law of the sea to global mobility has not thus far been a problem' (1980, p. 910). For the superpowers, as for the lesser naval powers, their interest in continued naval mobility was much more of a core interest in the law of the sea negotiations than was the constraining of that mobility by those states with little or no interest in displaying naval power beyond their own coastal waters.

Throughout UNCLOS III the national security interest played a major role in US policy-making, though certainly not to the exclusion of other interests (Moore, 1980, p. 83). National security interests, particularly relating to navigation, provided an irreducible set of requirements on issues such as the transit of warships through straits. So, for example, the United States would not have conceded a twelve-mile territorial sea without an agreement concerning 'transit passage' through straits. Other delegations were aware of the high priority given by successive US administrations to the national security interest, and this gave them some scope for manipulating a compromise over deep seabed mining, an issue on which the Third World attached a high priority. But in the end some Third World spokesmen exaggerated the priority of the naval factor in US thinking.[2] Despite its hard-line image on military matters, the Reagan administration switched its priorities from defence to free enterprise ideology. In the opinion of one US politician, the Reagan administration reversed the ratio of US interest in the Convention from 80:20 national security: deep seabed mining to the exact opposite (Robertson and Vasaturo, 1983, p. 688).

The decision to shift emphasis by the Reagan administration was matched by two changes in the attitude of the Department of Defense. According to Leigh Ratiner, who served various US administrations as an adviser and negotiator at UNCLOS III on seabed mining, energy and national security issues,

First, there was a much greater emphasis particularly on the civilian side of the Department, on the importance of American access to strategic raw materials as a national security interest and, second, there was a belief that if the treaty finally entered into force without US participation, most of those provisions which were favourable to the security of the United States would be accepted as customary international law, and that therefore the treaty rights would be available to all states whether or not they become parties to the treaty. (1982, p. 1011)

As a result of changes of opinion on these two questions, the Department of Defense came to have 'significantly less enthusiasm for the treaty' than had been the case under earlier Presidents.

According to Richardson, the United States had five main naval interests during the negotiation of the final stages of the text of the Draft Convention (1980, pp. 915–16). These were, and had been, consistent aims over the years:

(1) LIMITING THE EXPANSION OF THE TERRITORIAL SEA

The US aim was to establish a twelve-mile maximum for the territorial sea in order to contain the ambitions of those coastal states which were claiming sovereignty beyond 12 miles. The US concern on this issue began in 1974, when seventy-six countries were claiming territorial seas ranging from 12 to 200 miles. To make matters worse, in the following six years another twenty-five countries expanded their claim. The spread of such claims emphasizes the way in which the very process of law-making in this area not only legitimizes changes but also can generate them. Of the 101 states with claims beyond the traditional three-mile territorial sea, about three-quarters favoured a twelve-mile limit. But it was not just the expanding geographical claims which were worrying the naval powers; there were also some equally troubling functional claims. As Richardson put it, 'In addition to new territorial limits, certain of these claims call for prior notification to or authorization by the coastal states for the passage of warships or nuclear-powered ships, thus significantly restricting the traditional rights of innocent passage' (1980, p. 904). Nor was this all. As will be seen later, the claims regarding the territorial sea also threatened the rights of passage of warships through straits. Maintaining these rights proved to be one of the major interests of the naval powers in UNCLOS III.

Historically, naval mobility had been served by the doctrine of the freedom of the seas; this had given warships (and in time aircraft) complete freedom of movement outside the narrow zones designated as territorial sea. Within territorial seas, the movement of foreign warships and aircraft was governed by the concept of 'innocent passage'. This gave surface warships the right to transit, without prior notification, but 'innocence' required that the transit be not prejudicial to the 'peace, good order, or security' of the coastal state. Submarines and aircraft were not given the same freedom: innocent passage did not embrace the right of aircraft overflight or of submerged submarine transit (Richardson, 1980, p. 905; Smith, 1980, ch. 2). In that it would mean an extension of these limitations, a twelve-mile territorial sea was not ideal from the naval viewpoint, but there was no escaping the fact that by 1980 only twenty-three states still adhered to the old three-mile limit. The Convention therefore offered the naval powers an instrument by which they could try to stop the further qualitative and quantitive creep of the territorial sea.

Perhaps the main threat of a creeping territorial sea was the restriction of warship access through straits where passage had previously been 'free'. As it happens, some 116 of the world's straits, including some of the most important, were threatened with losing their high seas corridor as a result of the states on either side being granted a twelve-mile territorial sea (Neutze, 1983, p. 47). Given the strategic importance of 'free and unimpeded passage' through straits (to be discussed in detail later), it was a major US interest to maintain or even improve upon the existing rules. In the process of trying to achieve this, a new concept of 'transit passage' emerged:

> Transit passage is the freedom of navigation and overflight for the purpose of continuous and expeditious passage of the strait. The right of free passage applies to all ships whether on the surface or submerged and includes the movement of ships and aircraft in military formations as required by the circumstances. (Richardson, 1980, p. 915)

Under the new concept, therefore, coastal states would not be permitted to control the transit of foreign warships in territorial waters which were also straits: coastal states could not 'suspend or hamper any critical element' of transit passage, whether it be submerged, on the surface, or in the air. At the same time, the 'legitimate interests' of the coastal states would nevertheless be protected; these were defined in terms of safety and pollution rather than in terms of protecting the 'tranquility' of the coastal state (Smith, 1980, p. 38).

If foreign warships and aircraft had been made subject to the right of 'innocent' rather than 'transit' passage, as a result of the sixty-three additional straits being overlapped by the territorial seas of their opposing coastal states, the implications for strategic mobility would have been far-reaching. Richardson expressed it from the US perspective as follows:

> On that argument, the legal right to overfly a strait could be gained only with coastal state consent, submarines would be obliged to travel on the surface, and surface assets would be subject to varying assertions of coastal-state regulatory power. All the world's most important straits would be subject to these restrictions . . . The result could seriously impair the flexibility not only of our conventional forces but of our fleet ballistic missile submarines, which depend on complete mobility in the oceans and unimpeded passage through international straits. Only such

freedom makes possible the secrecy on which their survivability is based. (1980, p. 905)

If the issue of transit through straits was a matter of considerable concern to the US Navy, it was a vital issue for the geographically disadvantaged Soviet Navy (Richardson, 1980, pp. 905, 912). In international straits, as in the territorial sea, the naval powers saw the Draft Convention as a legal barrier against the growth of threats to their long-existing navigation rights.

(3) THE MAINTENANCE OF PASSAGE THROUGH ARCHIPELAGIC SEAS

Under the concept of the 'archipelagic sea' certain states sought new regulatory powers over those extensive areas of ocean between and around their island territories. In response to these claims the United States and the other naval powers wanted a guarantee of freedom of navigation and overflight through archipelagos 'on terms equivalent to transit passage through straits'. The difference between passage through archipelagos and straits, in Richardson's words, was that sea lanes through archipelagic seas, 'instead of being determined by the configuration of the land, would be defined by courses and distances, with a right of deviation up to 25 miles on each side of this axis'. This was satisfactory to the naval powers; they were willing to accept some limits on access in order to ensure a satisfactory transit agreement.

(4) THE MAINTENANCE OF TRADITIONAL RIGHTS IN THE AREAS COVERED BY THE NEW EEZS

It is generally agreed that the most material innovation of UNCLOS III was the concept of the EEZ, which gave coastal states sovereign rights over the living and non-living resources up to 200 miles from their shores. Following this extension of coastal state jurisdiction over 32 per cent of the surface of the oceans, the naval powers feared further qualitative as well as geographical creep. They were anxious in case national control over these new zones did not remain limited to economic matters but spread into other fields: 'If this vast area ever comes to be regarded by coastal states as subject to their sovereignty for purposes of regulating activities, the result would be to curtail drastically what Professor Bernard H. Oxman has aptly called "the sovereign right of communication" (Richardson, 1980, p. 906). The naval powers therefore hoped to ensure that the Convention preserved their traditional freedom of navigation and overflight within the areas now covered by the EEZs.

Richardson insisted that the freedom in question, 'both within and beyond 200 miles', must be qualitatively and quantitatively the same as the traditional high seas freedoms: 'they must be qualitatively the same in the sense that the nature and extent of the right is the same as the traditional high-seas freedoms; they must be quantitatively the same in the sense that the included uses of the sea must embrace a range no less complete — and allow for future uses no less inclusive — than traditional high-seas freedoms' (1980, p. 916). In the EEZ, as elsewhere, the naval powers hoped to use the Convention to slow or preferably stop the growth of what were regarded as unacceptable claims.

(5)   THE CREATION OF A CAREFULLY BALANCED AND COMPULSORY SYSTEM OF
DISPUTE SETTLEMENT

In view of the changing maritime environment which spawned UNCLOS III, and the inevitable problems which would result from the process of adjustment, the US government not only wanted its navigation rights secured, but it also wanted 'the right to bring suit against a state that interferes with navigation or overflight'. This matter was of lower priority than the others, but it was hoped that by ensuring that suit could be brought in matters of dispute, the 'advocates of reason and restraint within foreign governments' would be strengthened whenever those governments contemplated eroding established freedoms. The right to bring suit, Richardson argued, 'would help relieve us of having to choose between acquiescence and defiance each time a claim is made . . . [and] . . . would give us an important new option in our efforts to control and discourage such claims'. Again, the United States saw the Convention as a means of creating a legal environment in which US perceptions of its rights would be 'essentially unchallenged' (Richardson, 1980, p. 914).

The five major interests of the United States just outlined were also shared by the Soviet Union. Despite their different geopolitical situation, ideologies and policies, the superpowers had a mutual interest in preserving their freedom of navigation in distant waters and in preventing the law of the sea from falling further down the slippery slope towards territorialization. But there were important differences between the superpowers, as well as similarities, and some worrying problems resulted from aspects of the Soviet stance. (Butler, 1971, and Sebek, 1977, are standard works on Soviet law of the sea policy in general. For introductions to the naval dimension see Janis and Daniel, 1974, pp. 71–87; 1976, pp. 23–38; and Young and Sebek, 1978, pp. 255–62.)

Since the late 1960s the Western world has come to live with the knowledge that the Soviet Union has developed a modern navy with a worldwide capability. Unfortunately, the extent of the alarmism displayed in the early stages of this development has had a 'crying "wolf"' effect on later opinion. The developing Soviet Navy was always a growing problem and serious consideration for Western navies, but as a result of decisions taken in the late 1970s a marked 'step-up' in capability is under way, the effect of which will be to offer a real challenge to the US Navy from the mid-1980s and beyond (MccGwire, 1981, pp. 125–81). One inevitable consequence of having an increasingly powerful and global navy is to strengthen a country's interest in strategic waterways. However, any movement towards a more restrictive law of the sea regime will complicate Soviet strategic access, and already its navy is hindered by geographical disadvantages. In order to reach the open oceans and areas of strategic interest around the world, Soviet warships must pass through choke points which are mostly under the control of Western or Western-leaning states, or through the EEZs of countries which are not particularly pro-Soviet. In addition, the Soviet Navy is split into four widely divided fleets, which increases the requirement for sheer warship numbers, while adding to the difficulty of concentration. Together, the investment of the Soviet state in a global navy and its natural lack of what Robert Herrick once called 'waterfront real estate' ensures that the Soviet Union always takes the law of the sea very seriously.

The importance of law of the sea questions in Soviet thinking has been evident in the writings of the Commander-in-Chief, Admiral S. G. Gorshkov, and in the extent of naval involvement in Soviet policy-making on the law of the sea (Gorshkov, 1979, pp. 46–58; Janiś, 1976, pp. 23–38). But Soviet policy throughout UNCLOS III did not seem to have been as riven by bureaucratic differences as that of the United States, nor did its naval security interest ever seem threatened to the same extent as in Washington by any over-zealous adherence to traditional ideological precepts. In the event, the Soviet approach to the negotiations was pragmatic rather than ideological, and in a conservative rather than revisionist direction.

The Soviet involvement in UNCLOS III, like its involvement in most international organizations, has been for damage limitation purposes and propaganda rather than as a result of a commitment to common principles about the development of international society. To a lesser degree even than most Western states, the Soviet Union has not identified with the evolution of a 'New International Economic Order'. This played no part in its policy at UNCLOS III. Furthermore, the Soviet Union would be well satisfied to live without the Convention if certain of its vital interests in the law of the sea were accepted as norms of customary law, notably the twelve-mile territorial sea and the transit passage regime. As it was, in the process of UNCLOS III both the Soviet Union and the United States had 'a common interest in finding a way of reconciling the freedoms of navigation and overflight

67

important to themselves and other major maritime countries with the national control of coastal resources and international control of sea-bed resources important primarily, though not exclusively, to developing countries' (Richardson, 1980, p. 911). As a result, compromise was inescapable for the Soviet Union.

While the superpowers share a number of broad interests on law of the sea questions, the commitment of the Soviet government to the principle of 'open access' does not stand too much probing, as Young and Sebek have argued so effectively (1978, pp. 225–62). Stressing the extent to which Soviet legal theory has been neglected in Western manuals of public international law, Young and Sebek have given a series of warnings to those who have believed, or who have wanted to believe, the 'myth' of an almost complete identity of interests between the West and the Soviet Union on law of the sea matters (p. 261). It is important to note, for example, that Soviet support of the principle of open access 'did not involve any back-pedalling as far as the already "closed seas" around the Soviet Union were concerned', since the Soviet Union does not accept for its own coastal waters the obligations suggested by international law (Young and Sebek, 1978, p. 255). Soviet domestic law bars foreign warships from entering the Soviet territorial sea without prior permission and allows for the permanent closure of parts of it to all foreign shipping. These laws, in the words of Young and Sebek, 'have remained unchallenged in Soviet territorial seas, while the Soviet Navy and merchant fleets have continued to enjoy rights of innocent passage elsewhere'. A similar situation has existed in seas claimed as 'internal waters', which in practice includes all the Arctic seas (p. 256). Soviet policy-makers have been less successful with their doctrine of 'regional seas', in part because of their concern that by claiming a special regime for the Baltic, the Black Sea and perhaps the Sea of Okhotsk and the Sea of Japan – with limited rights of access for non-coastal states – they might establish a fashion which would work to the Soviet Union's disadvantages in the Mediterranean, Caribbean and elsewhere (Young and Sebek, 1978, p. 257).

Because the Western law of the sea community – like Western military strategists – spends much more time contemplating its own navel than examining the minds of its adversaries, insufficient attention during UNCLOS III was given to Soviet thinking. This problem was compounded by the low profile sensibly adopted by the Soviet Union. Consequently, some of the inconsistencies and hypocricies mentioned by Young and Sebek went largely unnoticed. Not for the first (or last) time on maritime matters, the Soviet Union got away with it. This has notably been the case with the Soviet violation of the Montreux Convention, when it sent its small carrier, the *Kiev*, through the Turkish Straits in July 1976 (Froman, 1977, pp. 681–717). The Western powers acquiesced in this bending of the law but they can less well afford to acquiesce in any Soviet attempts to lean on its neighbours and extend its maritime frontiers in the strategically sensitive and resources-rich regions of Spitzbergen and the Barents Sea (Young and Sebek, 1978, pp. 259−60; Booth, 1981, pp. 3−21). A diplomatic quiet life can always be secured by turning a blind eye to one's problems: but only in the short run. In the long run anyone who relies on meeting trouble with a blind eye is bound to be tripped up.

In a variety of important ways, therefore, Soviet law of the sea policy represents a challenge to the West; it should not simply be assumed that because it has shared some interests with the United States on some issues, it has a uniformity of outlook all down the line. Consequently one might question the extent to which some American spokesmen have identified United States and Soviet interests (Richardson, 1980, pp. 910−14), have seen Western interests to lie exclusively in a regime offering the maximum freedom of navigation (Clingan, 1980, pp. 82−93) and have seen the West's 'natural' adversaries in UNCLOS III as those Third World states favouring the enclosure of the oceans (Allen, 1983, pp. 46−9). As Young and Sebek concluded, these and several other major assumptions in Western thinking about the law of the sea may now be outdated (1978, pp. 261−2).

Whatever the differences between the superpowers, the reasons for their conservative posture on matters affecting warship navigation are quite obvious. As was discussed in Chapter 3, the basic problem is that creeping jurisdiction is seen as a threat to naval mobility, and hence to the traditional assets of warships as instruments of foreign policy in peacetime. If surface warships had been about to go out of business in the 1970s then the issues raised by the territorialization of extensive areas of ocean would not have been important. This was not the case. Despite the escalating costs and growing vulnerabilities of surface warships, future fleets were on the drawing board, and by the turn of the 1970s/1980s it was apparent that there would be a greatly expanded US naval programme under the Reagan administration, while the signs were becoming clearer of a powerful Soviet naval challenge being built for the 1990s (George, 1978; MccGwire, 1981, pp. 125−81).

Nor were warships, including surface ships, going out of business elsewhere. In 1982 the recovery of the Falkland Islands by British forces following their occupation by Argentina underlined for at least this 'medium maritime power' that surface warships were indispensable for some tasks: without surface ships and organic air power, the islands could not have been retaken. One round earlier, Argentina could not have hoped to have occupied and then successfully secured the Falkland Islands without its own surface ships − short of an abject British surrrender. In other parts of South America, and in Asia, warship construction as well as procurement is taking place in non-traditional naval powers, such as India and Brazil (Larus, 1981, pp. 77–83); Ferreira, 1983). Indeed, there is a general trend towards naval modernization in most parts of the world, and certainly in those of any strategic significance (Blechman and Berman, 1979; Booth and Dowdy, forthcoming). Obviously states which have an interest in using the sea — and it has been argued that UNCLOS III has raised general awareness in this respect — also have an interest in having some capacity to prevent that usage being challenged. Hence the continuing relevance of conventional naval power.

From the maximalist perspective of the United States, the need to guard against its use of the sea being opposed requires 'the capacity to project force to any part of the globe where significant US interests or responsibilities are challenged' (Richardson, 1980, p. 906; Allen, 1983, pp. 46–9). The development of a more restrictive maritime regime, it has been generally assumed, would make it increasingly difficult to bring national power to bear at sea and from the sea. The maximalist US position in this regard has been summed up as follows:

> Our economic well-being . . . is continually more dependent on overseas trade and more vulnerable to distant political developments. The combined result is to compel increased reliance on the strength, mobility and versatility of our armed forces. To fulfill their deterrent and protective missions these forces must have the manifest capacity either to maintain a continuing presence in far-flung areas of the globe or to bring such a presence to bear rapidly. An essential component of this capacity is true global mobility — mobility that is genuinely credible and impossible to contain. (Richardson, 1980, p. 907).

In practice, a naval power requires that its sea and air units have access to maritime areas of national interest 'without at any time being obliged either to defy some challenge to their right to do so or to make a vast detour in order to avoid such a challenge' (Richardson, 1980, p. 908).

One fear of US planners, along the lines earlier indicated by Scott Allen, has been that if challenges to access did arise, then superpower competition over rights would follow in train. Richardson warned that it 'must be assumed' that the Soviet Union would be prepared to go to 'great lengths' to ensure the mobility of its air and naval forces. As a result,

> In the contest for control of strategic waterways thus made inevitable, the least the United States would seek to accomplish would be to neutralize whatever combination of carrots and sticks was

employed by the Soviet Union, lest we find ourselves acquiescing in Soviet control . . . For if the USSR has no assurance that such an interest will be respected under binding legal arrangements, it will feel compelled to bring to bear whatever resources may be necessary to win control over the chokepoint. (Richardson, 1980, pp. 913–14)

Undoubtedly, Soviet planners would have the same fears about the United States, with the additional worry that the United States possesses more economic, political and military leverage in most parts of the world. As a result of conflicting interests and shared suspicions, superpower competition in the Third World would be further intensified.

From the viewpoint of the superpowers, therefore, the peacetime utility of warships requires 'rules of law compatible with the routine deployment of ships and planes' (Richardson, 1980, p. 908). Freedom to use the sea is seen to be essential for the continued use and effectiveness of 'naval diplomacy' (Booth, 1977, pp. 33–6). Any restriction to freedom of mobility would increase the costs of using the naval instrument. In Richardson's view these costs would probably involve 'some form of political, military, or economic concession' to coastal states, in addition to the competition between the naval powers for influence over strategically located states.

Those states wanting maximum freedom of navigation for warships saw themselves to be at the top of a slippery slope during UNCLOS III. If their naval interests were to be upheld, they had to use the law in order to block, as they saw it, the excessive proliferation of maritime claims. As Richardson succinctly put it, 'the superpowers have trouble enough in an increasingly pluralistic world without being forced into marginal conflicts over the peacetime movement of their military forces' (1980, p. 911). As a result, it was natural that the US Department of the Navy and the Department of Defense were 'strongly' in favour of a comprehensive treaty (Admiral S. D. Cramer, USN, in Gamble, 1979, p. 406). This, it seems, was also the opinion of the British Foreign Office and Ministry of Defence (Watt, 1982).

The naval powers therefore attempted to use UNCLOS III as a means of maintaining those well-established rights which were coming under challenge through the 1970s as a result of the 'maritime territorial imperative'. If the naval powers could not secure their interests through legal means, they would be confronted by the need to secure them by power, and in the face of the claims of most of the world community. 'The result', as Richardson explained for the United States, 'will be expensive not only to our bilateral relationships but to our reputation as a well-intentioned and law-abiding member of the world community' (1980, p. 909). Having the reputation for acting legally is important, for both foreign and domestic opinion. The effects of having a different reputation could not be precisely forecast, but they would obviously be negative.

For a bundle of reasons, therefore, the naval interest was firmly on the side of the Draft Convention through the final stages of UNCLOS III. If there were to be no universally agreed rules, the naval powers believed they would have to pay diplomatic and other costs to deploy their warships in peacetime. The cumulative effect of such costs might become greater than their naval strategy could stand.

The Satisfaction of the Naval Interest

It should be stressed at the outset that from the standpoint of the major naval powers there is no doubt that the naval interest was well served by the 1982 Convention. This is evident from the following endorsement by Commander Dennis R. Neutze (who at the time was Legal Adviser to the Deputy Chief of Naval Operations in the US Navy):

> The treaty process has resulted in a rather clear victory for the proponents of naval mobility. Not only do the navigational articles define a regime that is generally satisfactory from a naval perspective, but the action taken on amendments to the text clearly defines the outer limit of coastal state authority (1983, p. 48).

The US Navy — and therefore all the other navies favouring mobility, but not requiring it in practice to the same extent — had every reason to feel satisfied at the Convention. It had withstood efforts to amend it, and had secured the strategic aims which Richardson had outlined so frankly in 1980.

The major achievements of the Convention were listed and discussed in Chapter 2. Those with particular relevance to the military dimension were: the twelve-mile territorial sea with a right of innocent passage; transit passage in straits; coastal state rights over living and non-living resources in the EEZ, but freedom of navigation and overflight for other states; coastal state rights over the living and non-living resources of the continental shelf; the validation of the concept of archipelagic seas, but including the right of 'archipelagic sea-lanes passage' for others; the confirmation of traditional freedoms on the high seas; and the creation of a comprehensive dispute settlement mechanism. As a result of these agreements, the Convention was a legal endorsement of traditional expectations and practice regarding naval mobility. The major objectives of the major navies had been well secured.

From the standpoint of the US Navy — but he could have been speaking for other naval powers — Commander Neutze concluded that the outcome should

- Slow the proliferation of excessive maritime claims.
- Provide a legal yardstick against which the validity of maritime claims can be judged.
- Provide a more stable environment in which to plan and conduct future naval questions.
- Permit the conduct of naval operations in most cases without the political costs we now pay in exercising our navigational freedoms. (1983, p. 46).

In general the Convention had validated the freedoms traditionally enjoyed by the naval powers. One noteworthy change to the traditional regime was the extension of the territorial sea. But as long as this did not entail the 'closing' of hitherto international straits, this was a relatively insignificant change. A twelve-mile territorial sea was already rapidly becoming the norm of customary international law; and, as will be made evident later, a twelve-mile innocent passage regime is not one which will seriously interfere with modern naval operations. Furthermore, this change was more than compensated for in the eyes of naval establishments by the extension of the 'transit passage' provision to straits. Transit passage represents a major gain on what had existed previously, since it permits both submerged transit and overflight, and permits transit not merely in the high seas corridor but anywhere within the strait.

Overall, what the Convention achieved was a nice compromise between traditional naval interests and contemporary political and economic aspirations regarding the sea. The naval powers had wanted to maintain the maximum possible freedom of navigation; this included innocent passage through territorial waters, unimpeded transit through straits and archipelagos, and high seas freedoms elsewhere. Threatening these needs was the coastal state pressure for greater control over adjacent waters — the territorialist trend discussed in the last chapter. The Convention thereby represented a satisfactory resolution of the tension, actual and potential, between requirements for naval mobility and pressures towards creeping jurisdiction. Its framers had managed to legitimize creeping jurisdiction over about 32 per cent of the oceans while maintaining the essential features of global naval mobility.

As a result of the UNCLOS III compromise, naval mobility seems assured for the life or half-life of the 1982 Convention. That said, it must be noted that the satisfaction of at least some of the naval powers, notably the United States, needs always to be read with a footnote to the effect that the provisions of the Convention, such as the dispute settlement machinery, may not be available for non-parties. So, naval mobility *seems assured* as a result of the work of UNCLOS III, but international politics are not always what they seem, and UN Conventions are no exception. It will therefore be necessary for the naval powers to be wary about their navigation rights in the years ahead. Their satisfaction will ultimately rest on the practice which will follow the coming into force of the Convention: the latter's words are not enough. The need for caution in this regard was underlined by a US Navy spokesman soon after the Convention was opened for signing. While expressing himself well content with its provisions regarding naval matters he was professionally circumspect:

> The navigation articles do not impose unreasonable burdens on the naval powers, nor adversely affect legitimate interests of the coastal states. In the final analysis, the degree to which each of the conflicting interest groups has been successful will depend as much on how the treaty's ambiguities are resolved as on its literal language. (Neutze, 1983, p. 46)

Ambiguities and Problems

It was only to be expected that the 1982 Convention on the Law of the Sea would contain 'ambiguities'. Ambiguities could not be avoided in such a complex document, cobbled together over such a long period by so many different nations. Indeed, agreements are often the starting point rather than the end of arguments between nations. In the event, the surprise is that there are so few 'ambiguities' in the text, that is, provisions with more than one possible interpretation, or which are vague or uncertain of meaning. This is the case in its military aspects, as elsewhere. But there are some ambiguities and problems with military significance, and these will be indicated below. As in Chapter 2, the discussion of the relevant provisions is not given in order of importance, but in order of appearance in the Convention.

PREAMBLE

The Preamble represents the 'spirit of the Convention', and in this sense takes its ideological flavour from its origins in the outlook of the developing states which gave UNCLOS III its momentum, from the pro-New International Economic Order thinking which was prominent in the 1970s, and from the ritualistic peaceful incantations of any United National forum. Consequently, the Preamble stresses that the Convention should contribute to 'the maintenance of peace . . . for all peoples of the world', promote the 'peaceful uses of the seas and oceans' and assist the strengthening of peace, security, co-operation and friendly relations among all nations'.[3]

If such words are supposed to mean anything, and represent more than diplomatic window-dressing, it is possible that those in future who would use warships for coercive purposes may have to face the prospect of being criticized for not acting in accord with the spirit of the Convention, as identified in the Preamble. In practice, however, states bent on the pursuit of vital national interests will determine their policy on the basis of stronger considerations than diplomatic piety. States will remain the arbiters of their own interests and be-haviour, and since all governments — even the most bloodthirsty — regard their own policy as synonymous with a policy of peace, they will not be deterred by the spirit of a Convention, or even the UN Charter. Furthermore, throwing the Preamble — diplomatically speaking — at the naval powers in particular instances could well help to discredit the Convention in the eyes of the naval powers, just as the United Nations itself has been discredited in the eyes of some of its more important members as a result of the hostile rhetoric of a section of Third World members.

One prospect facing the naval powers, over the long term, is that the Preamble will be one of the elements contributing to a shift in the way the international community regards the military uses of the oceans. The Preamble might be part of the cumulating legal trends which, together with economic and political pressures, might tip the scales against peacetime naval missions; it would thus constitute, as Elizabeth Young brilliantly foresaw in the mid-1970s, 'a kind of de facto arms control' (1974, p. 262). Even so, when it comes to vital issues for the naval powers, the Preamble, and other legal inhibitions, will merely be — to update a pertinent comment of Sir Charles Webster — a scrap of paper across the opening of a missile tube.

PART II   TERRITORIAL SEA AND CONTIGUOUS ZONE

Section 3   Innocent Passage in the Territorial Sea
Article 18 *(Meaning of passage)* stipulates that passage shall be 'contin-uous and expeditous', and it explains what this entails. Clearly there is some scope for dispute about the meaning of 'expeditious' in parti-cular cases, but more serious is the scope for disagreement in Article 19 *(Meaning of innocent passage)*; this states that passage is innocent 'so long as it is not prejudicial to the peace, good order or security of the coastal state'.

The meaning of 'innocent passage' has long been open to the possi-bility of different interpretations, honest and otherwise. With this in mind, Article 19 attempts to clarify the concept, and lists twelve criteria for assessing the meaning of 'innocent'. These include: first, matters concerning the character of the mission of the warships concerned (are they threatening or using force against the coastal state? or are they violating the principles of the UN Charter?); secondly, matters relating to the actual activities of the ships during passage (are they practising with weapons? or are they gathering information?); thirdly, matters relating to environmental, fishing and research activities by the ships (is there any 'wilful and serious' pollution?); and, finally, the rather open-ended provision against 'any other activity not having a direct bearing on passage'. These criteria offer plenty of scope for any state which may wish to challenge the passage of the warships of another state, for warships are always gathering information of one sort or another, if only of an environmental kind. In practice, if a problem of interpretation is foreseen, naval powers could bypass it by having their warships avoid the territorial sea of the country or countries concerned; they may well be reluctant to do this, however, for fear of setting a precedent. Rights which are not exercised are liable to lapse.

The coastal state under Article 25 *(Rights of protection of the coastal State)* 'may take the necessary steps' in its territorial sea to prevent passage 'which is not innocent'. However, under Article 24 *(Duties of the coastal State)* it 'shall not hamper the innocent passage of foreign ships' except in accordance with the Convention. Although the Convention satisfied the governments of the naval powers, some knowledgeable observers were sceptical; they were concerned rather than satisfied by the fuller elaboration of the innocent passage provision, since decision as to whether the provisions were fulfilled was still left in the hands of the coastal state. Consequently, Michael Reisman concluded, 'the emerging trend in this area of law must be viewed, from a national security perspective, as increasingly melancholy' (1980, p. 65). When Arvid Pardo criticized the concept of 'innocent passage' in the Convention as 'unacceptably vague' he was doing so from a different perspective (1983, p. 494). From a legalistic viewpoint Pardo is correct, but in political terms it is difficult to imagine how a more precise instrument could have been fashioned. However, Pardo continued to make the important point that Article 19 'does *not* state that a ship complying in every way' with the provisions of the article enjoys the right of innocent passage, since 'a coastal State still enjoys the discretionary power to decide whether passage of a foreign vessel in a particular case is or is not prejudicial to its peace, good order, or security'. (On innocent passage in general, see Colombos, 1967, pp. 132–5; Butler, 1971, pp. 51–70; Reisman, 1980, pp. 60–5.)

Despite the uncertainties surrounding the concept, and the fact that its scope has been increased to 12 miles, there is no reason why the naval powers need feel threatened by the new innocent passage regime. As in the past, it should work reasonably well (on the past see O'Connell, 1975, pp. 139–45). What may be more troublesome is the further spread of special 'security zones'. The more there are, the more this restrictive concept will be legitimized. Its expansion threatens innocent passage, and in so doing strengthens coastal state expectations regarding the prior notification of warship passage. Already, states' acquiescence in practice to the rules of security zones or the Soviet territorial sea (Young and Sebek, 1978, pp. 255–6) will weaken the general principle of innocent passage.

Inspection is a difficulty faced by coastal states when monitoring innocent passage. In many instances it will not be easy to determine whether a violation has taken place: whether, for example, a foreign warship has undertaken any 'research . . . activities' in territorial waters. This difficulty will be even greater in the case of Article 20 *(Submarines and other underwater vehicles)* since detecting illegal submerged passage is a problem for even the most technologically advanced states, as recent episodes in Scandinavian waters have shown, when what have been believed to be Soviet submarines have evaded Swedish and Norwegian trackers in relatively narrow sea areas. It will obviously be easier for coastal states to identify foreign nuclear-powered surface ships and perhaps even ships carrying nuclear substances (Article 23); their passage might become threatened in time if the relevant 'international agreements' came to include the spread of 'Zones of Peace'. The legitimization of this latter idea would strengthen the hands of those states wishing to hinder the transport of nuclear materials in whatever form.

PART III   STRAITS USED FOR INTERNATIONAL NAVIGATION

Section 2   Transit Passage
Article 38 *(Right of transit passage)* grants 'all ships and aircraft' the right of transit passage as defined in the Article. As with innocent passage there is room for disagreement in particular cases as to whether the passage of a warship, or warships, is 'solely for the purpose of continuous and expeditious transit', and it is for the straits state to determine whether any particular passage violates the provisions of the Article. A more serious source of dispute is whether ships and aircraft operating under this right fulfil the duties specified in Article 39, notably the duty to refrain from 'any threat or use of force against the sovereignty, territorial integrity or political independence of States bordering the strait, or in any manner in violation of the principles of international law embodied in the Charter of the United Nations'.

Transit passage does not allow 'research or survey activities' without prior authorization, but here again there is some scope for disagreement, since, as was mentioned earlier, warships are invariably involved in 'research or survey activities' of one kind or another, and this is particularly the case with submarines, with their constant need for up-to-date environmental information. One problem for straits states, as for coastal states and the territorial sea, comes in determining whether a violation has actually taken place. However, it is important to note that the right of transit passage is strongly protected in Article 44 *(Duties of States bordering straits)* by the provision: 'There shall be no suspension of transit passage.'

There are two other potential problems surrounding the transit passage concept. The first is that the Convention provides no 'useful definition' of 'straits used for international navigation' (Pardo, 1983, p. 494). It is difficult, therefore, to know whether 'transit passage' is applicable to straits which are rarely used by foreign warships. In view of this Pardo has argued that it would have been useful to have included an annex in the Convention listing those states 'recognized as used for international navigation', and also it would have been useful to have prescribed 'compulsory and binding settlement' of any dispute regarding the proper status of a particular strait. The point is taken. As it stands, this is a matter which will be worked out in practice, and in all likelihood on the basis of might is right. This will serve the military interests of the naval powers. A second problem relating to transit passage is the absence in the text of an express right of submerged passage. The US Navy and government took it as understood that submerged passage was included in this right (Moore, 1980, pp. 77, 95−103), but others have questioned whether the text gives adequate navigational safeguards (Reisman, 1980, p. 48). Again, state practice will almost certainly settle this question in favour of the naval powers.

Section 3   Innocent Passage

Under Article 45 *(Innocent Passage)* certain straits are excluded from the transit passage provisions. These are strategically unimportant exceptions. A professional sceptic might ask: 'But will they always be?' The answer is: 'Almost certainly yes, though one can never be sure.' In addition, the same problems apply to the meaning of 'innocent passage' here as were discussed in relation to innocent passage through territorial waters.

In one respect, however, there may be greater pressure on the innocent passage concept in straits than in territorial waters. This results from the heavy traffic which occurs in some of the most busily used straits, notably the Straits of Hormuz and Malacca, and the English Channel. In such locations the growth of maritime traffic, together with the natural desire of the straits states to minimize accidents and pollution, is likely to lead to the growth of more restrictive traffic control.[4] As a result, the control of shipping will take on more aspects of the control of aircraft at busy international airports. Fears have been expressed, and not always for sensational purposes, of the terrible consequences which might result from collisions between supertankers and nuclear-powered ships in busy sea lanes near well-populated and well-developed coastlines. The explosion, following a collision, of an ammunition ship in Halifax harbour, Nova Scotia, in 1917 — the worst explosion in the world at that point — is a terrible reminder of the possibilities.

With growing dangers from accidents, pressure will be placed on the concept of innocent passage; the cause of traffic and pollution control could be used to restrict the access of some types of ship through particular waterways. There could well be an attempt to endorse such regulations with special vigour in cases when relations between the straits states and particular users are strained. In such circumstances, the straits state will rarely be in a position to prevent a naval power from moving its ships, though it is possible, but the naval power will have to face increased risks and possibly costs in exercising passage, and in some cases this might call a particular mission into question.

PART IV   ARCHIPELAGIC STATES

Article 58 *(Right of innocent passage)* gives archipelagic states the right to 'suspend temporarily in specified areas of its archipelagic waters the innocent passage of foreign ships if such suspension is essential for the protection of its security'. This provision could be used to limit navigation in specific instances, and each state is the final arbiter of what is 'essential' for its security. This does something to limit the force of Article 53 *(Right of archipelagic sea lanes passage)*, which gives archipelagic states the right to designate sea lanes and air routes, for the passage of 'All ships and aircraft'. Submarines are not mentioned in Article 53, and for this reason the opinion has been expressed that 'the language of the treaty is not entirely clear' in this respect (Neutze, 1983, p. 45). However, Neutze claims that it was 'generally understood by Conference participants that the right of archipelagic sea-lanes passage includes submerged transit as well as the right of overflight'. (On the 'preposterous' nature of undocumented understandings, see Reisman, 1980, p. 75). What is 'generally understood' in international forums is, of course, always open to subjective interpretation, and reinterpretation. There is therefore some scope for dispute, but precedent, difficulty of detection and interception, and naval power interest are likely to ensure in practice that what is not prohibited is permitted on the matter of submerged transit and overflight.

Article 56 *(Rights, jurisdiction, and duties of the coastal state in the exclusive economic zone)* gives the coastal state the right to fix 'installations and structures' in its EEZ. These, including artificial islands, could be designed and placed in such a way as to interfere with foreign warship navigation in general and submarine navigation in particular. Article 60 (7) represents a partial check on this possibility, but it refers only to 'recognized sea lanes essential to international navigation'. Against possible threats to navigation should be set the principle that all ships and aircraft should enjoy the freedoms of navigation and overflight referred to in Article 87 *(Freedom of the high seas)*. This implies that what is not prohibited is permitted: and what is not prohibited is extensive. As Elizabeth Young pointed out in relation to one of the earlier drafts of the Convention, the silence of the document on military matters hides a number of rights for navies, such as the right to deploy weapons, to conduct naval exercises and to hold weapons tests within the EEZs of other states (1978, p. 200).

There is obviously some room for disagreement as to the precise status of the 'military exclusions'. This was made clear in Admiral Fraser's earlier argument to the effect that the EEZ regime does not allow states to hold weapons tests within the EEZ of other states (Gamble, 1979, p. 400). However, the prevailing view to date – though it could change – is that states have all the traditional high seas uses except where those uses are not explicitly prohibited by international law (Brown, 1983, p. 560). All this makes Article 88 *(Reservation of the high seas for peaceful purposes)* sound like a pious piece of rhetoric. The EEZ, of course, is not the same as 'high seas', and this leads to a quirk in the Convention, for there is a sense in which the Convention could be said to have strengthened the duty to maintain the peaceful uses of the oceans in those areas designated 'high sea' over those designated 'Exclusive Economic Zone'. There is no specific commitment to 'peaceful purposes' in the latter. This distinction was presumably not intentional on the part of the framers of the Convention.

Some qualification of the earlier discussion about 'military exclusions' is suggested by Article 59 *(Basis for the resolution of conflicts regarding the attribution of rights and jurisdiction in the exclusive economic zone)*. This provision leaves open the question of 'what is not prohibited' in the EEZ. Article 59 states that in cases where the Convention 'does not attribute rights or jurisdiction' to the coastal or other states within the EEZ, 'and a conflict arises between the interests of the coastal state and any other State or States', the conflict should be resolved 'on the basis of equity and in the light of all the relevant circumstances, taking into account the respective importance of the interests involved to the parties as well as to the international community as a whole'. This could mean everything or nothing. But it does give some scope for states to question warship activity within their own EEZs; and there may well come a time when a particular state feels strongly about it. In response, for example, to naval manouevres in its EEZ, a state might claim that the Convention did not 'attribute rights' on the matter. Article 87 *(Freedom of the high seas)* might be the naval power's defence, but in reply it might be argued that this does not apply, since the EEZ is not the same as high seas (Article 86). In this case a 'creative ambiguity' would have arisen as a result of this sui generis character of the EEZ.

A more direct problem than the one just considered is the possibility of disputes over the rights of 'geographically disadvantaged states' (Article 70) and over matters of EEZ demarcation (Article 74). However, the likelihood of violence over such disputes in most parts of the world seems low (Buzan, 1978, pp. 8–15). Another potential cause of dispute arises from the right of coastal states to adopt non-discriminatory rules and standards against vessel-source pollution, and to enforce these when necessary. This could have potential military implications, especially where states adopt, as some have already, domestic legislation which is stronger than the Convention of the International Maritime Organization. In Lewis Alexander's words: 'The passage of "potential polluters", such as nuclear-powered vessels, vessels carrying nuclear or other "hazardous" cargoes, and ammunition ships, through the EEZs of some coastal states may in time be jeopardized, treaty or no treaty' (1983, p. 586).

Whether or not matters such as those just discussed lead to disputes, one interesting question is whether states have the right to exclude themselves from having disputes concerning their military activities, in the EEZ and elsewhere, submitted to the dispute settlement machinery which constitutes Part XV of the Convention. According to Article 298 *(Optional exceptions to applicability of Section 2)* a state may, when signing, ratifying, or acceding to the Convention, or at any time afterwards, 'declare in writing that it does not accept any one or more of the procedures provided for in Section 2' (compulsory procedures entailing binding decisions) with respect to several 'categories of disputes'. Prominent among these exceptions in paragraph (b) of Article 298 is 'disputes concerning military activities . . . and disputes concerning law enforcement activities in regard to the exercise of sovereign rights' or, finally, jurisdiction excluded from that of a court or tribunal with respect to some aspects of marine scientific research and fisheries. Despite the pious utterance of the Convention about the 'peaceful' uses of the seas, whenever it comes to the crunch, it is reticent about actually prohibiting military activities directly.

PART VI CONTINENTAL SHELF

Article 77 *(Rights of the coastal states over the continental shelf)* gives the coastal state sovereign rights 'for the purpose of exploring' the continental shelf, as well as exploiting its natural resources; but in exercising its sovereign rights over the continental shelf the coastal state must not undertake activities which 'infringe or result in any unjustifiable interference with navigation or other rights and freedoms of other States' (Article 78). What constitutes 'unjustifiable interference' could be a matter for interpretation, especially where less-than-friendly political relations exist. Furthermore, since the coastal state is granted the exclusive right to construct and to authorize and regulate the construction, operation and use of artificial islands, installations and structures on the continental shelf (Article 80) it is in effect given a licence to develop the continental shelf in ways which could have military significance. In some areas the islands, installations and structures could be strategically placed in such a way as to monitor submarine transits, not to mention surface traffic. Whether this would constitute 'unjustifiable interference' is an open question, but even the possibility that islands, installations and structures could be so used might prove a serious deterrent to a state interested in transiting submarines with no desire to reveal their presence — the normal practice. In this respect Soviet concern about the possible military significance of the structures required by Norway to exploit the energy resources of the Barents Sea reveals the sorts of problems which may arise, albeit in a particularly sensitive area.

PART VII HIGH SEAS

Section 1 General Provisions

Article 87 (*Freedom of the high seas*) states that the high seas are 'open to all states'. Five freedoms are specified, namely, navigation, overflight, the laying of submarine cables and pipelines, the construction of artificial islands and other installations, fishing and scientific research. This list is not all-encompassing, however, since it is preceded by the following: 'It [freedom of the high seas] comprises, *inter alia*, both for coastal and land-based states . . .' The phrase *inter alia* obviously leaves open the possible use of the high seas for additional and unspecified purposes, including presumably the traditional businesses of warships.[5] Typically, UNCLOS III drew a discreet veil across this rather crude but essential form of international intercourse. Nevertheless, it could be argued that the scope for military activity on, under and above the high seas was limited by the immediately following provision, Article 88 (*Reservation of the high seas for peaceful purposes*). This is the shortest Article in the Convention, but in spirit it is the most far-reaching: ostensibly it challenges the historic role of oceans as battlegrounds, roads to war and areas for the peacetime demonstration of military power. It boldly states that the 'The high seas shall be reserved for peaceful purposes'. What could be simpler, or finer? But for a long time to come such a declaration can only be regarded as a resounding platitude, of no practical relevance. Terrible wars have been fought in the name of 'peace'. Civilization-threatening deterrents have been deployed at sea in order to maintain 'peace'. 'Peace' can be a mere armistice in which communists seek to further the struggle by other means. Governments can undertake almost any action, and justify it as 'peaceful'.

It is not inconceivable that a state might decide for political reasons to invoke Article 88 against a naval power deploying warships on the high seas for purposes it regards as hostile. Such a possibility might not seem likely — everyone understands the penchant of UN bodies to scatter platitudes on the pages of its Conventions — but there might be barrack-room governments which will try to use Article 88 to embarrass the naval powers. Such governments could invoke Article 88 and the 'spirit' of the Convention as expressed in the Preamble against an unfriendly country deploying warships. However, the text of the Convention does not itself equate warships and 'non-peaceful' purposes; Article 95, for example, recognizes that warships will use the high seas by granting them 'complete immunity' from the jurisdiction of any state other than the flag state. As with states which deploy warships for deterrent purposes, the Convention accepts that warships are not exclusively engaged in activities which are synonymous with 'the threat and use of force'.

The naval powers themselves see their warships, above all, as instruments of peace — whether it be the status quo of the Western powers or the revisionist 'peace' of the Soviet bloc. In the particular case of the superpowers, their ballistic missile firing submarines (SSBNs) are seen as the pillars upon which strategic deterrence rests. Each of the naval powers honestly argues, from its national point of view, that the forward deployment of its own warships serves the cause of peace; and each nuclear power would argue that the world is significantly safer because of the silent presence of its SSBNs in the oceans. Such 'military' activities are strongly defended by their supporters as being 'peaceful'. This is also the case with naval diplomacy, when states use their warships in order to try to prevent adverse and violent changes in the political environment. In a world of sovereign states, 'peaceful' and 'military' are not necessarily antithetical.

The phrase 'for peaceful purposes', like the Convention as a whole, is a compromise. The phrase is not defined and indeed is not capable of a universal operational definition. The framers of the Convention therefore wisely chose not to sacrifice the opportunity for political compromise on the altar of legal clarity. Consequently, as Pardo has argued, a 'useful' compromise was struck, since the phrase 'for peaceful purposes' accommodates those states which wish to limit the military uses of ocean space, while 'it does not seriously inconvenience' those who believe the extensive military use of the oceans 'is a regrettable necessity' (1983, p. 493).

PART XI   THE AREA

Section 2   Principles Governing the Area

Articles 138 and 141 (*General conduct of States in relation to the Area* and *Use of the Area exclusively for peaceful purposes*) both stress the use of the Area 'in the interests of maintaining peace and security' and 'for peaceful purposes'. This theme is repeated in Article 147 which reserves 'exclusively for peaceful purposes' the use of installations in the Area, and Article 143 which states that marine scientific research in the Area 'shall be carried out exclusively for peaceful purposes and for the benefit of mankind as a whole'. This could be argued as ruling out all military-related research in the Area, unless one argues that one's own national military research is necessarily for the benefit of mankind as a whole — a dubious proposition. But such discussion is academic or at least premature, since it is presently difficult to conceive the requirement for direct military activity in the Area.

Article 145 (*Protection of marine environment*) could be used, like a number of earlier provisions, as an excuse for trying to control the passage of ships carrying nuclear materials. But first a more environmentally sensitive international community would have to emerge.

PART XIII   MARINE SCIENTIFIC RESEARCH

Article 238 gives all states the right to conduct marine scientific research, but Article 240 (*General principles for the conduct of marine scientific research*) declares that such research shall be conducted 'exclusively for peaceful purposes'. Again, 'peaceful' is left conveniently undefined. It can be assumed, however, that it was not the intention of the framers to interpret 'peaceful purposes' as simply being the opposite of 'military purposes', since a ban on research for military purposes would seriously interfere with a wide range of essential military tasks, notably the research necessary for submarine and anti-submarine warfare. The question of military-related research is of particular sensitivity in the territorial sea, where Article 245 reserves for the coastal state the right to regulate, authorize and conduct marine scientific research there. This provision should be of no small interest to that state, which everyone assumes to be the Soviet Union, which has been conducting clandestine and provocative submarine operations — possibly for 'research' purposes — in the territorial waters of Norway and Sweden in recent years.

84

Coastal states have the same authority over marine scientific research in their EEZs and on their continental shelves (Article 246), except that in the latter case it is stated that coastal states shall, 'in normal circumstances, grant their consent' to such projects on the understanding that they be carried out 'exclusively for peaceful purposes and in order to increase scientific knowledge of the marine environment for the benefit of all mankind'. Again, it can be expected that some states will wish to conduct clandestine 'research' in such areas in disregard of the Convention. Some navies, particularly those which operate submarines, require extensive environmental intelligence, and occasionally some countries need to conduct electronic surveillance from the sea. In such cases, the governments concerned will not be inclined to pay attention to Article 248, by which states are obliged to give a full description of 'the nature and objectives' of their project (see also Article 268). Because of the absence of a clear dividing line between 'peaceful' and other types of 'marine scientific research', this is a subject about which not too many questions will be asked. Those who do ask them will be looking for political trouble rather than precise answers.

Only a few nations have the capability of carrying out major marine scientific research at considerable distances from their own coastlines, and 'most of the distant-water research carried out by these few nations occur within 200 miles of the shorelines of other countries' (Alexander, 1983, p. 587). This fact alone underlines the scope for trouble in this area. Before UNCLOS III it had been accepted that a state was free to carry out marine scientific research except in another's territorial sea or continental shelf, where permission was needed. During UNCLOS III the Third World succeeded, against the efforts of the industrialized world, in securing the jurisdiction of coastal states over marine scientific research in their own EEZs (Article 57). As a result, in Alexander's words, 'ultimately about one-third of the world's ocean space (and in many respects the most scientifically interesting portion) will be closed to foreign research vessels except through the acquisition of prior consent'. And although normally such consent is expected to be granted, 'it seems likely — for political, economic, or other reasons — that consent for foreign scientific research projects may at times be withheld or seriously delayed' (Alexander, 1983, p. 588). Much will depend upon the relationships which exist between particular pairs of states, and the outcome is more likely to be determined by power and interest than by law of the sea considerations.

In this matter, as in others, it is incumbent on smaller powers to stand up for their rights, if they are not to be lost by default. An unfortunate precedent in this regard was established at the end of the 1960s as a result of British behaviour towards the Soviet Union. In

1969 the Soviet government refused permission for a British fishery research vessel to work in the Barents Sea. The British government acquiesced, and subsequently did not seek to conduct research in the area. However, when the Soviet Union soon afterwards announced its intention to conduct research in the North Sea into oil-pollution from seabed installations, the Russians made no request and the British made no inquiry (Young and Sebek, 1978, p. 259). Although this episode occurred over a decade before the UNCLOS III Convention, it is an indication of the way in which equity can defer to power in international politics, if the relatively weak are too meek. The development of a stable and moderate international system requires the small occasionally to be defiant, as well as the strong occasionally to be restrained.

PART XV   SETTLEMENT OF DISPUTES

The issue of 'military exclusions' was discussed earlier. In addition to the problems identified, the issue also exposes the provisions of Part XV and gives a hollow ring to Article 279 *(Obligation to settle disputes by peaceful means)*. The latter requires that the parties to the Convention 'settle any dispute between them concerning the interpretation or application of this Convention by peaceful means', preferably by 'peaceful means of their own choice' (Article 280) or, failing this, by the procedure laid down in Part XV. The latter gives states the right to bring suit against 'unreasonable' claims. But this right is potentially a two-edged sword. For it also gives 'unreasonable' states the opportunity to bring suit against conservative states on law of the sea matters, and to argue, perhaps, that rights (including military rights) are present only by designation, and not by default.

PART XVI   GENERAL PROVISIONS

Article 301 *(Peaceful uses of the seas)* stipulates that parties to the Convention, in 'exercising their rights and performing their duties' under it, 'shall refrain from any threat or use of force against the territorial integrity or political independence of any state'. This Article, at last, fleshes out the meaning of 'peaceful' in a way which is not done elsewhere: it equates 'peaceful' with refraining from the 'threat and use of force'. But this does not represent a serious restraint on military activity, since a right to the 'threat and use of force' in self-defence is enshrined in the UN Charter, and all states see and certainly tend to justify their own military activity in terms of national self-defence.

From this examination of the Convention's potential military ambiguities and problems, four main conclusions emerge. First, the analysis of the detail of the text reveals nothing which need change the general conclusion reached earlier to the effect that the Convention satisfies the military requirements of the naval powers. Although the text does reveal that there is some room for interpretation and dispute on some of the Convention's provisions, these do not amount to anything significant. Indeed, since the subject matter is complex, since words are not perfect tools and since the Convention was the product of negotiations between the whole of the international community, the document is remarkable for its relative precision. It has become apparent in the course of discussion that the most slippery concept in the text is that of 'peaceful purposes'. But if the delegates at UNCLOS III could have worked out a universally operational definition of what constituted 'peace', 'peaceful', or 'peaceful purposes', then there would hardly be a need for the Convention, or even the United Nations itself. This is one of those problems which, if we could resolve it, we would not need to.

Secondly, it is justifiable to conclude that the text in detail proves to have been a masterly compromise between the interests of the naval powers and the other members of the international community. Both groups should be able to live with the outcome. Despite earlier fears among the naval establishments about some of the possible results of the UNCLOS III process, the long labour has, militarily speaking, merely produced a mouse.

Thirdly, despite what has just been said, the Convention is not entirely free from ambiguities and sources of dispute in the military domain. It remains to be seen whether they will amount to anything serious in practice; and the reasonable expectation is that they will not. What is likely to be of more interest is the possible challenge to the legality of various military uses of the ocean raised by those who believe that important aspects of this matter remain 'undetermined' (Pardo, 1983, pp. 494–5). Pardo lists the following:

(A)   transit of foreign warships in the territorial sea without prior notification to, or consent of, the coastal State;
(B)   reservation of vast areas of high seas for significant periods of time for missile testing or other security purposes; and
(C)   emplacement of anti-submarine warfare devices on the continental shelf of another State, without the latter's consent.

In one sense Pardo is incorrect in arguing that such issues are 'undetermined', for they were covered in UNCLOS III to the satisfaction of the naval powers, by designation or default. But the more significant point is his demonstration that there is a body of opinion which is not satisfied with the position achieved by the naval powers on these matters, and that there are issues which will be on the agenda in the future.

Pardo believes that it would have been 'useful' had the Convention had something to say on the military uses of the seas. But any radical pressure in this direction might well have finished off the Draft Convention before even President Reagan's attempt on its life in 1981–2. In future law of the sea discussions, however, participants may well be more willing to face military issues directly, having gone as far as presently seems possible on economic and demarcation issues. This being so, Pardo is corrrect in arguing that although most countries will usually go to considerable lengths to avoid confrontations in the maritime environment, military uses of the sea remain controversial, and so 'confrontations will be increasingly difficult to avoid'. The process is likely to be characterized more by erosion than by pitched battle, but Pardo's fears accord well with the trends discussed in the preceding chapter.

Finally, whatever the words of the Convention, those safeguarding the naval interest will judge success by what happens in practice. And what happens in practice will depend on the way coastal states choose to interpret the Convention and on the way the naval powers respond in their operational practices. The 'constructive ambiguities' in the text allow states to try to get what they want, and there is just enough uncertainty in parts of the Convention to allow coastal states to press for more control in their EEZs and elsewhere when they have the time and energy. The major naval powers are well aware of this possibility. Early in 1983 Commander Neutze of the US Navy warned:

the clearest interpretation of the ambiguous language of the treaty will be the actual operational practices of those who base their navigational rights on its provisions . . . It is important that all naval powers, including the United States, demonstrate clearly – through their operational practices over the next few years – their understanding that the language of the treaty has no significance on naval mobility . . . in order to take advantage of the many positive benefits that the treaty's language portends for the future of naval mobility, the United States must continue to operate its forces in a manner that ensures the treaty's language is properly interpreted and demonstrates to the world community that the United States is firmly resolved to maintain its navigational freedoms. (1983, p.48)

Under the assertive title 'Whose Law of Whose Sea?' Commander Neutze was indicating that although the US government had not signed the Convention, it did intend that its view of the 'Law' should operate, and that when it came to naval mobility, the sea still belonged to the naval powers. The more the law of the sea changes, it seems, the more the interests of the naval powers remain the same.

Historic Compromise or Paradigm Shift?

The outcome of UNCLOS III therefore seems reasonably satisfactory from the viewpoint of the future of naval mobility. Naval strategists will find it easy to adapt to the Convention because it basically promises 'business as usual'. But they will have to be watchful of the possibility that its 'ambiguities' might be exploited to their disadvantage, or, worse still, that particular states may take the law into their own hands. The determination of the United States to stop unacceptable developments is beyond doubt. In the years ahead its navy will show operational vigilance, and, if necessary, its actions will be confrontational. One sign of the times, before the Convention was signed, was the incident in August 1981 between United States and Libyan aircraft in the Gulf of Sirte, when the United States contested Libya's claim to sovereignty over the Gulf. If the freedom of the seas as it is understood by the naval powers has to be bought by vigilance and violence, then it will be, and the US Navy will bear the brunt (Richardson, 1980, p. 902; Neutze, 1983, p. 48).

As was concluded earlier, the Convention represents a nice compromise between traditional naval interests and the developing political aspirations of the international community regarding the sea. Whether this will develop into a *historic* compromise remains to be seen, but there are pressures working against this possibility. During UNCLOS III the aim of continued naval mobility was much more of a core interest for the naval powers than was the constraining of that mobility for states with little or no interest in deploying warships at a distance from their own coastal waters. A radical growth of interest in constraining naval mobility on the part of the majority of the international community is one of the factors which could change, and so precipitate a new and more acrimonious period in negotiations about the law of the sea.

If in the near future the outcome of UNCLOS III seems reasonably satisfactory for the naval powers, this might not be the case in a vague 'longer term'. The problems which might arise in this regard will be the result of the territorialist norms and attitudes which have been generated and to a degree legitimized by the UNCLOS III process and the Convention which finally emerged. As was suggested in Chapter 3, some agreements between states can change the way we think about the world, and the law of the sea will never be the same again after UNCLOS III. This means that UNCLOS III might represent the beginning of what might be called a 'paradigm shift' regarding the military uses of the oceans.

The phrase 'paradigm shift' is an inelegant piece of jargon, but it has a certain assertiveness which is lacking in a phrase such as 'change of image' when it comes to describing the potential transformation foreseen — a politico-strategic equivalent of Picasso's portrait of Gertrude Stein. The change in the dominant global viewpoint regarding maritime affairs will come about both as a result of the general territorialist pressures discussed earlier and the growth of a series of claims with particular military implications. What is foreseen, as a result, is the prospect of a far-reaching evolution in the way nations look at the military uses of the sea in peacetime. In modern war, restraints, including those of a legal nature, tend to slip out of sight: but in peacetime legal considerations are important in state policy (Henkin, 1968, pp. 31–87). International law does affect the way states behave. Assuming that a government has the will and the power, international law cannot stop it from doing what it wants: but international law can shape what it wants, and in this way it can exert an influence. What is foreseen in the 'paradigm shift' regarding the sea is a change in the international community's attitudes towards peacetime naval deployments off foreign shores: these will be seen as illegitimate as a result of a combination of political, economic and legal considerations. There will be pressure for limitation and hence there will no longer be relatively cost-free forward deployments. *Mare clausum* will thus have triumphed in about one-third of ocean space. Freedom of naval navigation will have ceased, and the outcome will be what Elizabeth Young, in the words quoted earler, so presciently described at the very outset of UNCLOS III as 'a kind of de facto arms control, not specifically intended or designed as such' (1974, p. 262).

Without doubt, coastal states will want a bigger say in the course of time about what happens in their maritime backyards. It would be surprising indeed, therefore, if the thinking of at least some of them did not turn, in a more determined way than hitherto, towards the goal of achieving greater control over foreign warships and aircraft in, over, or under adjacent waters. Most states are the objects rather than the subjects of international politics: they are the *whom* rather than the *who* in the Leninist formulation; and they naturally want, because of their weaknesses, the maximum restraint on the freedom of action of the more powerful. This being so, it is not difficult to guess one direction in which their efforts might be applied. In the mid-1970s some Third World spokesmen claimed that the support of the naval powers for a narrow territorial sea represented not so much a defence of the internationality of the oceans, but more a tactic by which they could legally place their warships as close as possible to the shores of coastal states (Janis, 1976, pp. 69–70). In short, some Third World spokesmen fully recognized that the law of the sea was a continuation of naval strategy by other means. In the future, more than in the past, they may come to believe that this is a game which should be played by the weak as well as the strong.

As ever, while the mighty are concerned with the freedom *to* do things, the relatively weak are anxious about freedom *from* particular possibilities. And the latter's vulnerability to military pressure could lead them to try to place limitations on naval mobility by practice or by negotiation. In the course of their efforts to bring about favourable changes in this regard, some coastal states might make naval access dependent upon naval powers agreeing to a common stance on a particular foreign policy issue or issues (Richardson, 1980, pp. 907–10). Further efforts at limitation might involve attempts to change, or threaten to change, the Convention. Such a prospect would be all the more likely if, as was suggested earlier, the naval powers were not seen to be playing ball in the economic or other dimensions of the law of the sea. Were there to be pressure to change the Convention, the likely directions can be guessed from some of the proposals discussed towards the end of UNCLOS III. These proposals, according to Commander Neutze, would have been 'disastrous to naval mobility' had they been passed (1983, pp. 45–6). The 'eleventh hour' amendments referred to included an attempt, supported by Romania and others, to alter Article 21 regarding innocent passage in such a way that it would have created a 'warship notification regime';[6] a proposal by Spain that military aircraft transiting over straits must comply with International Civil Aviation Organization procedures (involving checking-in with coastal states' flight-following regulations); and a Turkish proposal to rescind the prohibition against reservations to the Convention unless expressly pemitted by other Articles, which would allow coastal states to select only those parts of the Convention it chose to accept. With varying strength, these amendments were defeated, but each received a not insignificant amount of support. They might have been defeated in UNCLOS III, but they or their like will be seen again.

If some of the proposals in the final stages of UNCLOS III suggest the direction in which the first military claims of the next stage of the law of the sea might develop, what would a completed 'paradigm shift' look like? It will be easier to describe than to bring into operation. Its basic feature will be a 200-mile territorial sea, governed by an 'innocent passage' regime for warships and aircraft. However, this regime would be tighter than the present innocent passage provisions, in order to satisfy national requirements relating to more effective traffic control and pollution safeguards, not to mention continuing interests in controlling the movement of foreign warships. This would mean that prior notification schemes would operate for warships and aircraft, and perhaps passage would be dependent upon consent

(Richardson, 1980, p. 904). In 1983 twenty-three states already had some form of prior notification requirement in their domestic legislation (Alexander, 1983, p. 586). Pollution controls might prevent the passage of nuclear-powered vessels or ammunition ships off particular coasts. Alongside the tightening of innocent passage, transit passage provisions might also be strengthened, again by claims for prior notification schemes for warships and aircraft. At the same time, if there were to be the grim and unstable world in the years ahead which many have foretold, one might expect the spread of special security zones and other unilateral claims which would further threaten military mobility. Finally, there might be a concerted effort to operationalize the meaning of the phrase 'exclusively for peaceful purposes' in such a way as to delegitimize the movement of foreign warships beyond their own coastal seas. This would mean defining 'peaceful' in terms of 'non-military' or 'non-armed' rather than 'non-aggressive'.

Whatever reasons groups of nations may have for pressing for tighter controls over military mobility at sea, such efforts are both encouraged and legitimized by the stress on 'peaceful purposes' in the Convention. As was mentioned earlier, the phrase 'exclusively for peaceful purposes' occurs regularly in the Convention, and sounds platitudinous. However, Pardo has made the pertinent comment that the phrase conveys 'the vague, misleading, but useful impression that the Convention will somehow reverse the ongoing process of intensive militarization of ocean space' (1983, p. 493). There is a strong body of opinion which does not want to reverse the process of militarization, and it is this force which will fuel efforts to constrain naval mobility, and so bring about the 'form of de facto arms control' envisaged by Elizabeth Young.

If all or most of these developments just described were to take place — and none is beyond the bounds of possibility — the result would be more than merely a change in the law of the sea. The outcome would also represent a decisive shift in the attitudes of the international community towards the peacetime use of the sea for military purposes. In many situations permanent forward naval deployments would be a thing of the past, and naval mobility would be restricted. But even if events did move in this direction, later chapters will show that the utility of navies will not thereby come to an end.

Naturally, the naval powers will seek to resist such a far-reaching territorialist trend, just as they tried to use UNCLOS III to restrain creeping jurisdiction. But the pressures will be cumulative, and it may happen that the erosion of 'freedoms' of the sea in one area will spill over into others, with the result that one day the naval Gulliver may find himself tied down. The naval powers will try to defend their interests, by force if necessary, but over a long period they may be less willing to act in such a fashion if the weight of the international community is against them, if they risk poisoning particular relationships, or if territorialist states develop enough punch to back their claims with credible force. In such circumstances the political costs of standing outside the consensus may outweigh the naval advantages of maximum freedom. As a result of cost—benefit calculations, or the temptations of a quiet diplomatic life, even naval powers might, at some time in the future, connive in restrictions on naval mobility.

The progressive limitation of forward peacetime naval deployments on the lines envisaged above may presently seem far-fetched. But a century ago almost everybody in Western Europe would have dismissed anybody who had suggested that colonies were illegitimate and should and would be brought to an end. Most people would have insisted that colonies were part of the natural order of things, that they helped human progress and that in any case they would continue to exist because the great powers would defend their interests by force if necessary. Less than a century ago, a paradigm shift regarding attitudes to colonies would have seemed wildly visionary. Yet colonies are now (almost) a thing of the past. The ending of colonialism, as with other paradigm shifts in international politics, was not the result of a single cause. The diffusion of military power which helped the colonial peoples to fight for and then protect their independence increased the costs of colonies. At the same time, the benefits of the physical control over distant lands and alien people was in decline. Added to these factors was the war-weariness of the colonial powers and the growth of international organizations which helped to delegitimize the idea. There was a loss of interest in empire. The most important factor in this paradigm shift was the fact that colonialism was an idea whose time had passed.

We are a long way in practice from such a dramatic change in the military uses of the oceans, but the idea of an informal arms control regime based on a *mare clausum* is not now unthinkable. *Mare clausum* can and is being talked about. If the voices are relatively few, so they were at the start of the anti-colonial movement. Before the event, paradigm shifts always appear far-fetched. And, let us not forget, international politics is frequently a far-fetched activity. Who would have thought, when Reagan and Andropov were born, that the United States and the Soviet Union would not only become the two 'superpowers' in the international system but would at the same time be members of a global multi-purpose international organization (none had then existed), yet only have the same voting power as Zimbabwe (where?)? Who, in 1939, could have imagined that Italy, then standing alongside Nazi Germany, would by 1949 be a founder member of the North Atlantic Alliance, standing alongside its recent wartime enemies? Ten years can be a long time in international politics.

In the late 1960s one would have been laughed out of the room if one had talked to a naval audience about a *mare clausum*. But now the idea has to be taken seriously. And so it is being, by some within the naval establishments of the developed world. It is seen as a dark cloud on the navalist horizon. This has been illustrated by the publication of a series of articles on the legal threats to navigation in the important *Proceedings* of the US Naval Institute, culminating, in mid-1983, in the publication of Scott Allen's plea for a recognition of what he argued is the universal self-interest in *mare liberum*. We are back in an old and familiar debate. Which way will the pendulum swing this time? Within living memory, after a long period during which colonies were regarded as part of the natural order of things, many nations freed their soil of foreign soldiers. Is it inconceivable that the international community, within the lifetime of the younger generation, will seek to remove foreign warships from seas over which they feel a growing sense of possession?

The answer remains to be seen. Our discussion of the question at this moment could have either a self-fulfilling or a self-denying effect. It was Scott Allen's purpose, for example, to highlight the possibility of a *mare clausum* as a warning to his country and the developed world in general, so that they might prepare defences against a further drift in that direction (1983, pp. 46–9). The stance of this book is more sanguine about the prospect of *mare clausum*, believing it to be both more likely and less inherently undesirable than envisaged by Allen. But neither viewpoint is determinist. The game is there to be won, though at present it does appear that the trends in the maritime environment are pro-territorialist rather than pro-navalist. Economic, political and strategic developments, over a long term, do appear to be working against large peacetime deployments of surface warships at great distances from their own shores. Britain and France, to a large extent, have withdrawn their naval forces from the global scene – an unthinkable thought when their present leaders were born. Within the lifetime of babies born today, the governments of the United States and Soviet Union may come to similar decisions.

The time-scale envisaged is a long one: we are thinking fifty years ahead, not five. It is therefore well beyond the horizons of politicians; they, in all countries, increasingly seem to be seeking to live up to their reputation for thinking ahead only as far as the next election, or coup. But such a time-scale is not entirely beyond the range of naval planners – the 'future fantasy staffs' of the strategic world. If warships are well cared for, particularly if they are kept out of wars, they can last for a very long time indeed. At least forty years can be expected to elapse from the day the pencil is first put to the blueprint to the day when the final warship of a particular series is scrapped. As a result, those who direct modern warships can expect to have to face several technical and perhaps even political revolutions in the course of their profes-

94

sional careers. The history of the *General Belgrano* is fascinating in this respect. This ship, which started out as the USS *Phoenix*, survived the Japanese attack on Pearl Harbor in 1941, only to be sunk by the British nuclear submarine *Conqueror* in 1982. Forty-four years old at its death, the *Phoenix/General Belgrano* had survived the era of total war only to be sunk in an unnecessary struggle for sovereignty between two countries which hitherto had not regarded themselves as enemies. With this history, the *General Belgrano* may be the symbolic warship of our time.

While the idea of a paradigm shift might presently appear fanciful to some observers, particularly the keepers of the old ideas, there are enough straws in the wind to encourage our imaginations. Obviously the process has a long way to go, and its evolution might be fitful, but on top of the rising costs and growing vulnerability of surface warships, the stress on the 'peaceful' uses of the ocean in UNCLOS III, allied to the legitimization of territorialist impulses, might in the course of time prove to be as significant a milestone in the history of naval power as were the lone voices who first called for an end to colonial power.

For the moment, UNCLOS III generated and legitimized various forms of creeping jursidiction, and the 1982 Convention placed some restrictions on the way territorialist ambitions might inhibit traditional naval mobility. A nice compromise was thereby reached between the naval powers and the rest of the international community; and both can live with this compromise if they so wish. Since what was agreed was basically 'business as usual' from the naval point of view, naval strategy in the years ahead will develop, as it always has, more in response to changes in technology, international affairs and domestic politics than as a result of developments in the law of the sea. But if, as was suggested, the long-term effect of UNCLOS III will be to change the way nations regard the sea as a resource and object of politics, then navies will one day have to face the prospect of major adjustments. As the phenomenon of the 'maritime territorial imperative' spreads, navies will have to adjust to a new map of the world's oceans, one characterized by a patchwork of diplomatically significant psycho-legal boundaries. If international law-making and nationalistic-territorial attitudes towards the sea proceed hand in hand, as they did in the 1970s, the consequences for routine naval mobility will be profound.

As this process develops, warships need not be ruled out as instruments of foreign policy; as will be argued in later chapters, this very process could in fact make their use more salient. But this will depend on how far creeping jurisdiction develops, and its precise character; and, even more importantly, it will also depend on whatever technological and political factors are then shaping naval strategy. The details cannot now be predicted; they are a matter for the distant future. All that can be said now is that it is still open whether the agreement embodied in the 1982 Convention between creeping jurisdiction and naval mobility will evolve into a historic compromise, with a life of indefinite duration, or whether it will come to be seen as a milestone in the move towards a paradigm shift regarding the military uses of the oceans, leading to a progressive erosion of former freedoms of naval navigation. If the Chinese historian was justified, over a century later, in declaring that it was 'too early' to pronounce on the consequences of the French Revolution, we are certainly justified in being guarded about the consequences of UNCLOS III which, in the maritime context, attempted to encourage a spirit of equality, fraternity and nationalism − if not *liberté*. In short, the long-term naval significance of UNCLOS III is not yet evident, and cannot be confidently predicted, for the evolution of the law of the sea will be the plaything of too many imponderables. It will only become clear in the light of the terms of the Conventions produced by UNCLOS IV, V, VI, etc., in the decades and half-centuries ahead.

Notes: Chapter 4

1 The mutual interest of the naval powers is brought out, for example, in Janis, 1976, and O'Connell, 1978, pp. 11−18.

2 Early in 1981 Tommy Koh had said that he believed that the United States would eventually decide that its national security and military interests were 'better protected by the treaty than without it' (Rosen, 1981).

3 The problem of interpreting the term 'peaceful purposes or uses' has also been present, but more seriously, in negotiations about space law (Poulantzas, 1970, pp. 266−9). One suggestion was to substitute the term 'non-armed'. Such a provision has relative legal clarity, but is hardly likely to be endorsed by naval powers with respect to the sea.

4 Elizabeth Young has written: 'No underinsured, ill-navigated, chartless, flag-of-convenience-registered 250,000 ton tanker can ever be "innocent" in the English Channel or the Malacca Strait, or, should it find itself there, in the Canadian Arctic' (1974, pp. 262, 265; see also Moore, 1980, p. 79).

5 It is interesting to note that within the compass of 'inter alia' the United States has formally taken the position that deep seabed mining is a freedom of the high seas (Alexander, 1983, p. 702; see also Brown, 1983, pp. 533−7).

6 In 1976 Yemen had introduced an amendment to the effect that 'The coastal State may require prior notification for the passage through its strait in its territorial sea of foreign warships or nuclear-powered ships or ships carrying dangerous substances'. The amendment, which would have reversed the decision of the International Court of Justice in the *Corfu Channel* case, and 'rolled back' more than twenty years of state practice to the contrary, was not adopted (Moore, 1980, p. 110). However, it was not long before it raised its head again.

5

Rights of Passage through Choke Points

As was suggested in previous chapters, the basic problem in the interplay between naval strategy and the present and future evolution of the law of the sea arises from the fact that the 'blue water' of the naval powers is invariably somebody else's maritime backyard. And it is likely to be a backyard over which the coastal state has a stronger sense of ownership and a greater desire to exploit its resources unilaterally. As a result, it is the confrontation between the interests of naval powers in navigational freedom for their warships, and the interests of coastal states in restricting that freedom, which provides the problems which are the focus for the remaining chapters of this book.

The present chapter will examine the possible military implications of creeping jurisdiction in straits and archipelagos. Subsequent chapters will examine the implications on the seabed, in the territorial sea and in EEZs. In each case, the challenges to naval strategy will be examined, both in the light of the 1982 Convention and in the event of movement towards a more restrictive regime.

Security and Straits

In 1960 the Chairman of the US Delegation to UNCLOS II told Congress:

> The primary danger to the continuance of the ability of our warships and supporting aircraft to move, unhampered, to wherever they may be needed to support American foreign policy presents itself in the great international straits of the world — the narrows which lie athwart the sea routes which connect us and our widely scattered friends and allies, and admit us to the strategic materials we do not ourselves possess. (Arthur H. Dean, quoted by Truver, 1980, p. 85)

The 'narrows' of 1960 are now fashionably called 'choke points', but

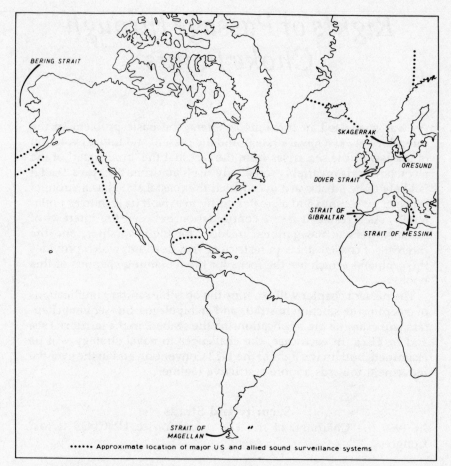

Map 1a Choke points: major straits and ASW barriers.

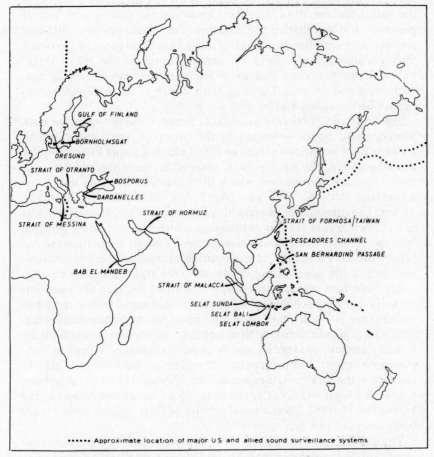

Map 1b Choke points: major straits and ASW barriers.

Arthur Dean's basic argument has lost none of its force in the intervening years. As a result, during UNCLOS III the issue of transit
through international straits attracted more attention than any other
from those interested in the security aspects of the changing law of the
sea.[1] It was also a subject over which there was some argument
between the naval powers and some of the relevant coastal states. In
the end, however, the Convention endorsed the principle of 'transit
passage', and so satisfied the interests of the naval powers. This was
also the case with the different but related problem of warship transit
through archipelegos. Even so, detailed study of the major international straits reveals that there are many outstanding problems,
both local and general. The long-term future of international straits
cannot be considered to be a closed book.[2]

The Strait of Gibraltar is a crucial example of the problem, for both
Morocco and Spain belonged to the group of strait states which
lobbied hard at various stages of UNCLOS III against the concept of
transit passage. The naval powers insisted on the latter, but the strait
states favoured provisions which they believed to be to their own
advantage (Moore, 1980, pp. 100–2, 108–9). Spain, for example,
viewed the question of passage through straits within territorial seas
as a particular case of innocent passage which may not be suspended;
but, conversely, the Spanish government viewed transit passage as
inherently non-innocent. In the opinion of the Spanish government,
and that of the government of Morocco, the right of transit passage
would interfere with the interests of the strait states in the maintenance of an orderly scheme for maritime traffic control within the Strait
of Gibraltar, it would jeopardise their plans for environmental protection and it would threaten their security by allowing overflight by
military aircraft, passage by warships and submerged transit by submarines without their prior permission (Truver, 1980, pp. 184–220). In
the case of the Strait of Gibraltar, as with a handful of other such choke
points, the legal and security issues involved have been compounded
by the fact that the international politics of their adjacent regions are
both complex and explosive.

The naval powers have been firmly united in their assessment of the
implications for warship mobility and aircraft overflight of any extension of national jurisdiction across international straits, such as would
have occurred if the new twelve-mile territorial sea had simply been
allowed to wipe out what had previously been high seas corridors.
Different naval powers would have been affected in different ways
and to a different extent, but each perceived some security risk
resulting from the nationalization of important strategic waterways.
As a result, the naval powers stood firm, and the Convention was a
mark of their success in preserving acceptable navigation rights
through straits.

The position of the naval powers remains that the straits issue is 'non-negotiable'. This is not only for its own sake, but also because of the interrelationship between the straits issue and other aspects of the law of the sea. The naval powers fear that any weakness on their part on the straits issue will be exploited in other areas of the law of the sea. John Norton Moore has called it the 'spillover threat':

> To permit strait states control of warships or commercial navigation could spill over into other areas of coastal state functional jurisdiction, such as any potential economic zone, and occasion increased restrictions in those areas. This spillover threat and the long-run relation between transit rights and other oceanic freedoms are usually ignored by those focussing narrowly on military straits transit rights. There is also a similar spillover effect at work between ship transit rights and overflight rights and between military and commercial rights (1980, p.82).

In the years ahead transit rights in international straits will continue to be the first line of defence of navigational rights in general for the naval powers.

Without the right of transit passage enshrined in the 1982 Convention, 116 hitherto international straits would have become overlapped by territorial seas, with military transit henceforth governed by innocent passage provisions.[3] As was discussed earlier, this would have given the strait states important discretion over the passage of foreign warships. It would be their right to determine the 'innocence' or otherwise of passage. Submarines demonstrate theirs by transiting on the surface, while overflight is not innocent without consent. Had such a regime been allowed to come into operation, the possibility for disputes and conflict between the strait states and the naval powers would have grown because of the ambiguities and uncertainties in the definition of 'innocent passage', the discretion accorded to the strait states, and the need of the naval powers in crises to transit or overfly particular straits regardless of the disposition of one or other of the strait states.

Of particular significance to the superpowers was the risk posed by an innocent passage regime to the invulnerability of their submarines; this was obviously of primary importance with respect to those units (SSBNs) involved in strategic nuclear deterrence (Moore, 1980, pp. 80–1; Reisman, 1980, pp. 49–55). SSBNs, since the early 1960s, have played a determining role in modern strategy, and anything which has been seen as detracting from their ability to move through and hide in the oceans has been seen as a threat not only to the submarines themselves, but to strategic stability in general. Clearly, if SSBNs were required to transit straits on the surface, they would give the game away. Since strategic nuclear deterrence has been seen as providing the basic structure for the whole of East-West relations, and more besides, the future straits regime has been seen to be of considerable strategic significance. And even those states outside the East-West confrontation share an interest in superpower nuclear stability.

Despite the evident logic of the preceding argument, it is easy to exaggerate the importance of straits transit for SSBN missions. It is important to note that Osgood's study of SSBN vulnerability in relation to straits passage in the mid-1970s identified only sixteen straits of significance for SSBN passage among those potentially affected by the extension of the territorial sea to 12 miles. Of these sixteen, only the Indonesian straits of Ombai-Wetar and Lombok and the Strait of Gibraltar were thought to be of critical value, since they connect SSBN operating areas (Osgood, 1974, pp. 1–36). In the intervening years, however, the strategic significance of straits for SSBN transit has diminished even further, as a result of the increased range of submarine-launched ballistic missiles. Both the United States and the Soviet Union now have missiles which can reach their targets without their submarine platforms having to leave waters adjacent to their own coastlines. SSBN passage through straits is now something which is 'nice to have' rather than vital.

Navigational restrictions on submarines and surface ships, whether it be prior notification schemes or movement in designated traffic lanes, would increase their vulnerability. Hostile surveillance and hence interdiction in some circumstances would be made easier. But the issue of straits passage has by no means been confined to warships, for air power has become increasingly important for those wanting to exercise military power in distant areas. Several states have a critical strategic interest in the overflight of straits, for both direct military purposes and resupply. And as the importance of air power grows, the ramifications of this problem will become steadily more serious.

Scott Truver and others have pointed out that if overflight privileges above expanded territorial seas could be denied, a state's ability to resupply overseas forces or allies by air in limited wars or crises short of war could be seriously affected (1980, p. 91). The problem this might entail was amply demonstrated to US planners during the Middle East War of October 1973, when a number of US allies in Europe, threatened by an Arab oil embargo, denied overflying and landing right to US aircraft on their way to Israel. As a result, US planners had to devise an elaborate flight pattern between the United States and Israel based upon the judicious use of aircraft carriers and tanker aircraft in order to transfer replacement aircraft and supplies. This airlift involved 569 flights. The C-5A and C-141 transport aircraft flew from the United States to the Azores, and then into the Mediterranean through a point in the centre of the Strait of Gibraltar. Without the free use of this strait, the United States would either have had to scrap the idea of resupply or, more likely, would have had to pay heavier costs and take greater risks. From the Strait of Gibraltar the American aircraft flew to the vicinity of Crete before turning south-east to Tel Aviv. Throughout their journey the aircraft had obviously to avoid overflying airspace controlled by Arab countries. As Truver noted,

> The possibility that an Arab state, antagonized by the American efforts to aid Israel might take it upon itself to intercept one of the American cargo aircraft could not be dismissed. Perhaps a greater possibility in the future is that radical Arab countries armed with simple surface-to-air missiles (SAM) might take a pot shot at a passing American aircraft. (1980, pp. 90−1, 228)

Such a threat also existed to the replacement aircraft which were also being flown from the United States to Israel. From the Azores, US Navy A-4s were refuelled by tanker aircraft from the carrier *John F. Kennedy*, stationed in the Atlantic near Gibraltar. Later, in the Mediterranean, the aircraft were refuelled on the carrier *Franklin D. Roosevelt* before flying off and finally being refuelled on the last leg by tankers from the carrier *Independence*. Air Force F-4s were refuelled by tanker aircraft based in Greece. This episode shows, with dramatic clarity, the never certain reliability of even old allies, the importance of aircraft carriers, the value of planners able to improvise and the strategic significance of the right of transit through straits.

The 1973 Middle Eastern War presented the issue of straits transit in its most serious light for the United States, but Michael Reisman has argued that problems might well occur in less dramatic circumstances (1980, p. 64). He has speculated, for example, about the possibility of a coastal state seeking to prohibit the passage of US vessels which were providing an ally with food, oil, or other material, 'all of which, under doctrines of modern warfare, can be considered vital to the prosecution of the belligerency'. Even 'symbolic participation' in a regional problem may be circumscribed. In support of his argument Reisman cited the episode in January 1979, when the United States decided to send a force of jet fighters to Saudi Arabia; these had been sent in order to affirm support for the Saudi government, underline US concern in the eyes of Soviet leaders and warn Iranians of the seriousness of US intentions. However, Spain refused to allow the jets to refuel in US bases on Spanish territory, apparently in accordance with the 1970 Agreement of Friendship and Co-operation. The issue here was not directly a matter of the law of the sea: but the episode does illustrate that when states are given discretionary rights, they might well exercise them in unhelpful ways, even with states with whom they have

Agreements of Friendship and Co-operation. Nothing is guaranteed in foreign policy, even between allies.

The American airlift to Israel in 1973 was a costly improvisation, but to their credit US planners and airmen did adhere to the rules of international law. Some states are not always as punctilious. This was the case with the Soviet Union in 1977–8, during its support of Cuban military activities on the Horn of Africa. In the first sixty days of its airlift to Ethiopia, which began in November 1977, the Soviet Union conducted fifty flights. Later, the number dropped to about two a week as the bulk of supplies began to be moved by sea, and as troops began to be moved by passenger plane. Soon afterwards, the International Institute for Strategic Studies in London offered the opinion that the Soviet airlift to Ethiopia had been noteworthy for 'the scope and variety of its flight paths'. The airlift was said to have shown that intervention in Africa was possible with even limited overflying rights, since 'as many as ten [states] were overflown without permission' (IISS, 1979, p. 13). Clearly the Soviet Union was taking risks, to both its aircraft and reputation, but it lacked the options given to the Americans by the Strait of Gibraltar, the possession of a string of large aircraft carriers and the availability of refuelling from land-based tankers. The two episodes do not necessarily 'prove' that the United States is more law-abiding than the Soviet Union: rather they show yet again that superpowers will always exert their power when they believe their vital interests are engaged.

As the importance and flexibility of air power continues to develop, the problem of overflight is one which will grow rather than diminish. This will especially be the case if the years ahead are characterized by instability in many parts of the world, and hence the even further growth of opportunities for superpower involvement. If, in a crisis, overflying rights are withdrawn by one or more states, then rerouting will be necessary if the risks of unauthorized flight are not to be taken. As a result, flight time might be greatly increased both by the need to fly a longer route and by the need to negotiate it. In the course of negotiation, it could be that unwelcome political costs might have to be paid. At the least, one of the key assets of air power — speed — would risk being lost. In marginal situations it is conceivable that political obstacles placed in the way of overflying particular areas might tip the balance against undertaking a resupply or reinforcement mission. Ironically, a decision to abort a mission in the build-up to a crisis, as a result of the pressures of international law, could allow the crisis to get out of hand, with the result that very much more than international law might be at stake. Getting there 'firstest with the mostest' might be more conducive to security in some circumstances than showing complete obedience to international law.

If a more restrictive regime for straits were to come about, the strategic significance of those countries in a position to control the major choke points would be greatly enhanced. Accordingly, a small group of states — whose friendliness could not be assured by either of the superpowers, or any other state wanting to deploy naval power — would have a new opportunity to exercise greater political leverage. In the event of a strait being in the hands of a state or states hostile to a particular naval power, the consequences in a crisis could be far-reaching; this is evident from the obstructionist role which even allies might play, along the lines of US allies during the 1973 Middle Eastern War. A more restrictive regime would legitimize any pressures which a hostile straits state might wish to exercise against a naval power, though it is unlikely that any of the conceivable governments of strait states would forcibly attempt to prevent a major naval power from transiting a strait if the naval power was determined. However, the diplomatic costs of carrying out a politically opposed transit might be high, and the possibility would have to be faced that there might be an increase in military risks. The legal and political problems created by an increase in the rights of strait states would be compounded by the diffusion of modern weaponry, which raises the level and variety of physical threat which could be posed to the naval powers. Modern mines offer a relatively cheap and effective way of closing off straits, or certainly making passage hazardous. This is an option which could be grasped by either a strait state or a state hostile to a naval power. Straits are not particularly difficult to obstruct. In some circumstances a particular strait state might lack both the military and political flexibility to back down. It might decide that it had no alternative but to try to prevent the passage of particular warships.

A more restrictive straits regime would therefore threaten to increase the political and other costs of passage. The threat of costlier or impeded access in the event of a crisis would reduce the significance of a naval power's commitment to its allies. Such uncertainty might affect the calculations of both the naval power's potential friends and its enemies, not to mention third parties. Strait states would therefore have the opportunity to exercise pressure short of actually impeding access; they could exert leverage by attempting to manipulate the vulnerabilities and needs of naval powers. In exchange for unimpeded access, a strait state (even if it is an ally of the naval power concerned) might demand a political, economic, or military price, when, for example, the US Navy — or its Soviet counterpart — wished to move carriers between oceans. Key straits in this regard will be those giving access into the Mediterranean from the Atlantic and into the Indian Ocean from the Pacific.

The problems envisaged above will obviously be most acute during a crisis. Any restrictions placed on the passage of warships could affect reaction time. The granting of the right of prior notification and consent to strait states could postpone a naval power's build-up in the crisis zone, and so weaken the force which could be deployed. More serious obstacles, ultimately physical resistance in the event of passage being denied as 'non-innocent', would raise the international temperature considerably. Any threat to safe passage would distract some ships from their urgent mission, and divert others from priority tasks. If all the costs and inconveniences could not be met, the naval power would be forced to look for an alternative and inevitably longer route; its government might even call off the contemplated action.

Without doubt, a more restrictive straits regime would strengthen the hands of straits states and lead to a significant increase in the strategic and foreign policy problems of naval powers. They, naturally, want predictability in their planning and security in their navigation. A more restrictive straits regime would put these at risk. In the event of obstructionist straits states in such circumstances, the consequences for naval powers might be a diversion of diplomatic effort, possibly a slower reaction time in a crisis, the need to buy off the particular straits states politically, the adoption of a less satisfactory deployment route, or even the cancellation of missions. The nationalizing of straits would therefore seem to threaten the very basis of naval strategy: hence the stout resistance by the naval powers to any such development during UNCLOS III was completely predictable. Stout resistance will also be their posture in future, in the event of any threat to the unravelling of the relevant provisions of the Convention. The conservative and prudent position on straits has been expressed by Michael Reisman as follows: 'The relative importance of different avenues of the oceans in the future will depend on technics, contexts, and needs which cannot be envisaged now. It should be clear that the prudent course is not to surrender any of these maritime highways if it can be avoided' (1980, p. 60). In other words: since nobody can foretell which will be tomorrow's life-lines it is wise to maintain freedoms and keep options open.

Island States

Many of the points made above regarding the relationship between strategy and straits are equally relevant to another type of choke point, namely, 'archipelagic waters'. These are the areas which surround multi-island states, of which about twenty have become independent since the Second World War (Alexander, 1983, p. 572). Before UNCLOS III the waters around the islands of an archipelago had no special status.

By far the most strategically significant island state has been and remains Indonesia, whose scattered islands shape the waterways between the Indian and Pacific Oceans. Indonesia has been the most politically active and physically assertive in its claims regarding ocean jurisdiction. In 1960 the Indonesian government attempted to close off its entire archipelago as a separate unit. This act provoked a strong response from the maritime powers, which feared for the navigational freedoms of their vessels passing through Indonesian waters. The problem became more serious still during 'Confrontation' between Indonesia and Malaysia in 1963–4, but it was successfully met by a combination of diplomatic protest and the exercise of rights of passage (O'Connell, 1975, pp. 134–7). But the episode was not without a few jittery moments.

As a result of the efforts of Indonesia and others, UNCLOS III recognized the concept of the 'archipelagic State', and thus of 'archipelagic waters'; the latter allows ships of all states to enjoy the right of innocent passage. In this sense, archipelagic waters are 'virtually the same as territorial waters' (Alexander, 1983, p. 573). Perhaps more accurately, the Convention text reflects the understanding, according to Moore, 'that in all major respects' the concepts underlying the transit passage of straits and those underlying archipelagic sea lanes passage are identical, including rights of overflight and submerged passage (1980, p. 111). Indeed, Moore insists, without such an understanding the conference would not have accepted the archipelagic concept. Consequently, wide expanses of ocean, formerly high seas, are now virtually territorial waters. This is particularly the case in the Pacific, where, in addition to Indonesia, the other major states with archipelagic claims are situated, namely, Fiji, Papua New Guinea, the Philippines, São Tomé and Príncipe, and the Solomon Islands (Appendix: Table 4). But although wide expanses of ocean are involved, with the exception of Indonesia and possibly the Philippines, the power political weakness of the island states is such that the strategic implications of the new archipelagic waters concept would appear to be insignificant, even if the right of transit passage were to be whittled away. Nevertheless the location and significance of Indonesia alone is enough to ensure the opposition of the naval powers to any further functional creep of island state jurisdiction. In any case, strategy is such a plaything of technology and geopolitical shifts that one can never say with complete confidence that any particular area will always be of low strategic salience. The news headlines of the years since 1945 have been peppered with the names of unfamiliar places, about which most people knew little, but which were suddenly and often tragically thrust into importance.

As in most other respects, the 1982 Convention satisfied the naval powers on the question of the rights of passage through archipelagic waters, though some worries have been expressed regarding the status of submerged transit for submarines (Moore, 1980, pp. 110–11;

Reisman, 1980, pp. 67—71). This apart, the military interest was satisfactorily met as a result of the provision of a fifty-mile sea lane for
archipelagic transit. This is ample space to accommodate most task
forces; merchant ships certainly do not need such a generous sea lane
(Gamble, 1979, p. 402).

Archipelagic waters can therefore be conceived as a special version
of the straits issue. They present naval powers with a variety of
possible problems in relation to regular peacetime deployments, crisis
reactions, the movement of general purpose naval vessels, overflight
and submarine transits. However, the prospect of such problems
becoming serious in archipelagic waters is not, in general, as great as
in straits.

Strategy and Access

It is evident from the earlier discussion that the naval powers are
satisfied by the arrangements embodied in the Convention in relation
to warship transit through straits and archipelagic waters. Any future
drift towards national control over such waters will be resisted for the
same reason that led to the naval powers' opposition to the strait
states in UNCLOS III, namely, that any restrictions would threaten
naval mobility. But greater national control would not necessarily be
an insuperable obstacle to the activities of the naval powers: nor
would it necessarily be an obvious good for the strait and island
states. The implications of international developments are rarely as
simple as they first seem.

One inevitable impact of any change towards a more restrictive
regime would be to place a higher premium on the co-ordination of
foreign policy and strategy, for diplomacy would immediately become
a more important factor in securing military access. This in turn would
increase the need for effective communication betwen the political
and naval arms of government, something which has often been
notable by its absence. Naval establishments already have the responsibility — perhaps not always exercised — of educating their political
masters on the limitations as well as the requirements of naval forces
as instruments of policy. This responsibility would become heavier,
because of the additional costs involved in securing naval mobility
under a more restrictive regime.

The foreign policy implications of a more restrictive regime point
naval powers in the direction of improving relations with those states
which bestride such key straits as Bab el Mandeb, Gibraltar, Hormuz
and Malacca. Thus, the naval tail might come to wag the foreign policy
dog: but there is more to it than that. One only has to identify the key
strait states to appreciate that it should be an aim of any sensible

foreign policy on the part of the Western powers to attempt to be on good terms with these key states in any event, because of their inherent regional significance. If naval considerations were to encourage governments to do what they should in any case be doing, so much the better. But the question of the consent (or otherwise) of the strait states will sometimes be of minor account. On marginal issues the attitude of the strait states will be an important factor to weigh in the balance, but some issues are so vital (the support of Israel in the case of Gibraltar, the securing of oil supplies in the case of Hormuz) that the hostile attitude of any strait state will not be the decisive factor in US (or Soviet) policy-making. It would be a black day for Israel, for example, if Morocco's disapproval of the support it receives from the United States were to be decisive in determining whether or not the US administration dispatched warships through the Strait of Gibraltar.

Over the years some of the key strait and archipelagic states have had difficult relationships with one or both superpowers. These states, as a group, reflect a variety of viewpoints on international matters, and it may be perfectly sensible to harmonize with at least some of their preferences. There was, for example, an evident sense of irritation in O'Connell's account of the potential illegal threat represented by the Philippines to Australian warships transiting to Vietnam in the late 1960s (1975, p. 110). However, had restrictive archipelagic claims been legitimized by international law, and had uncertainty of transit through Indonesian waters been allowed to tip the balance in the Australian debate on the issue, would Australia have suffered? Was its experience in Vietnam a success in Australian foreign policy? Nations sometimes need rescuing from themselves. International law can sometimes help.

Diplomacy should be able to deal with any problems in the definition of 'transit' or 'archipelagic waters' passage to the satisfaction of any determined naval power. In most circumstances almost all strait states will be content to back away in the face of superior power. Indeed, they may well accrue prestige from so doing; being threatened by the mighty is a source of prestige for some countries. Naval powers, for their part, might not lose international support when opposing any strait state as long as they can appeal to a higher court than that of the law of the sea. There is plenty of scope for diplomacy in such circumstances, and a mixture of resolution and bargaining should win the day. The effectiveness of US arrangements regarding warship transit with Indonesia is instructive in this case (Osgood, *et al.* 1975, p. 69). Furthermore, while naval powers tend to dwell only on the possibility of choke point obstruction, there may be occasions when strait states, by their acquiescence, would support and legitimize a naval action. This would presumably be the case if warships were engaged in a UN blockade against the regime of the Republic of South Africa.

The possibility must obviously be faced that things would go wrong from the viewpoint of a naval power in a more restrictive regime. In this case resolution will be at a premium. The Indonesian episode in 1964 is pertinent in this regard. Following threatening Indonesian words, the warships of a British task force made self-defensive precautions while passing through the waters claimed by Indonesia. The latter saw the advantage of giving way. The demonstration of military power does not always backfire. Vietnam encouraged glib as well as profound lessons for liberal democracies. Prestige and respect can sometimes accrue if the international community sees a state acting decisively in defence of its interests. This was further illustrated by the blockade of Cuba in 1962, and the sharp US response to the capture of the *Mayaguez* in 1975. In any event, in most circumstances the taking of self-defensive precautions in the face of a threat to the right of transit passage would be trifling as far as diplomatic incidents are concerned.

A more restrictive regime would undoubtedly give the strait states a stronger sense of legitimacy in venting their hostility against a naval power, especially in time of crisis. This underscores the need for the naval power to have forces in sufficient quantity and with sufficient firepower to get its way without a fight — the true meaning of military *power*. This, for the foreseeable future, suggests that a naval power will need aircraft carriers, for their offensive and defensive potential. One of the lessons of the British campaign to recapture the Falkland Islands in 1982 was the critical importance of having air power at sea.

In concentrating on their own problems, the naval powers have tended to underestimate the degree to which the strait states themselves would face new costs in the event of a more restrictive straits regime. They have ignored, for example, the costs which strait states might have to face if they impede a superpower on a matter the latter thinks is vital. The negative implications of a regime change for strait and archipelagic states are more serious than might at first appear. Perceptibly, these states would take on the role of potential targets, for they would be confronted by the problems of power politics to a new degree. They would have new authority, including duties and commitments which they could formerly avoid. They would be put on the spot. If they found that they lacked commensurate power to discharge their new responsibilities, they might be encouraged to develop their own naval power (thereby perhaps provoking a local arms race or encouraging external meddling for arms sales and influence), or they might be encouraged to seek the support of naval allies. However they reacted (and some no doubt would be inclined to do the minimum), the new situation facing strait states could breed either responsibility (and a propensity to compromise) or the opposite. But without doubt, a more restrictive regime would seriously increase the military and foreign policy problems of those states bordering major straits. As Thomas Clingan has argued, when transit is 'free' strait states do not have to make difficult political choices, and that is often a definite advantage to the foreign relations of the states concerned (Gamble, 1979, p. 417). If there were to be a more restrictive regime, strait states would have more duties, as well as rights, and these would result in greater burdens for them. They might find that they would have either to take tougher stands − putting their ships where previously they put only their rhetoric − or they would have to compromise, or they would have to be satisfied merely with the appearance of authority. In this latter case it is interesting to note that Morocco has claimed straits rights which it has not exercised.

The naval powers could live with a more restrictive straits regime − though it would not be their choice − but it can be questioned whether such a regime would be in the security interest of the Third World in general, let alone the strait states. Anything which is calculated to inconvenience the superpowers might be seen as being to the advantage of the Third World, but such an attitude smacks of theology (or rather demonology) rather than a careful calculation of interests. Third World countries can find good use for superpower military support, for example, and they also need economic assistance. The superpowers are producers of order, for the most part, and states generally have little interest in regional disorder. Occasionally some do.

When naval powers act, it is usually important that they act with legitimacy. Indeed, legitimacy is increasingly important in a world where interdependence is growing and the costs of using force are rising. If a particular foreign policy is seen to be legitimate, then actions which are associated with it will also be seen to be legitimate by the international community. This would presumably be the case even if it meant forcing straits against hostile coastal states. Achieving legitimacy for one's actions is a matter of ensuring that foreign policy is made to work for naval strategy. The problem is to get the foreign policy right, and then acquiring the power to act. Strategists should not underestimate the value of making legitimacy work in support of their military efforts (Fisher, 1971, pp. 185−6). And legitimacy in this respect does not derive solely from the law of the sea. There are higher causes to which a state can appeal, such as the right of self-defence or collective self-defence. In addition, we can easily exaggerate the significance and sensitivity which states might feel about law of the sea questions in the total sum of things in an international crisis. On such occasions states are more likely to be guided by St Augustine's injunction: 'Necessity knows no law.'

In a situation where it is not possible for a naval power to secure

111

international support for its actions, but where it decides to proceed none the less, the very fact that it demonstrates the will to override legal inhibitions while appealing to some higher source of justice promises to make its sense of purpose, and hence its credibility, all the more evident. Furthermore, if a superpower has to act and cannot gain the support of a large sector of the international community, would the hostility of an additional (albeit strait) state matter? If, for example, the United States undertook some naval action in support of Israel against the wishes of the whole Arab world, what would be the special significance of Moroccan disapproval? The outcome in such cases will depend upon the capability and will of the superpower concerned. As it happens, these are qualities whose future is open to discussion for reasons unrelated to any prospective changes in the law of the sea. The threat of land-based aircraft to surface ships is particularly significant. The failure of the maritime nations to keep open the Strait of Tiran in 1967 was a pointer in this respect. In a world of diffused military power, there are likely to be more places where superpower muscle cannot safely reach. There will be spheres of impotence for super-powers, as well as influence.

As far as local wars and crises are concerned, strait states might object to the passage of foreign warships, but they will only attempt to obstruct passage (assuming they have the capability) on the rare occasions when they are in fundamental opposition to the country concerned (Osgood, 1976, p. 15). In the main their interest will be to allow the vessels to go ahead (Buzan, 1978, p. 46). We need not therefore be alarmist about the risks of straits being closed merely because of restrictive changes in the law of the sea. The Montreux Convention is instructive. Despite the limits on passage through the Turkish straits which it imposes, in terms of prior notification, ship type and restriction on numbers, the Western perception over the past ten years has not been that the Soviet squadron in the Mediterranean has lacked credibility in crises. Nor did it stop the Soviet Union from deploying the *Kiev* in 1976, although it is an aircraft carrier and therefore its passage is illegal under the terms of the Convention (Froman, 1977, pp. 681–717).

Whereas one's first impression is that the threat of a more restrictive passage through straits and archipelagic waters would seriously affect the mobility of warships, and therefore their essential instrumentality, when the problem is examined in detail it is possible to be more sanguine about the prospects. This is further confirmed by those commentators who have examined the issue of straits access on a mission-by-mission basis.

There has been much discussion of the impact of a restrictive straits regime on SSBN operations, and the arguments need not be rehearsed here. Although a more restrictive regime would require some readjustments (and inconvenience) in SSBN operations, the essential significance and utility of neither US nor Soviet SSBNs would be affected. This is because of the increased range of their missiles, which enable them to reach their targets even when fired from their own contiguous waters. Furthermore, speed of retaliation is not an essential factor with SSBNs: it is certainty of reprisal that matters. Some of the problems of a more restrictive regime can be overcome through bilateral diplomacy. The United States, for example, managed to effect working arrangements for satisfactory SSBN transit through Indonesian-claimed waters (Osgood, 1976, p. 14). In war, of course, legal restrictions would be almost irrelevant. Military necessity would be the determining consideration.

As far as SSBNs are concerned, the first implication of creeping jurisdiction appears to be a threat to their essential mobility. However, when this question is examined further, one can see that a more restrictive regime would merely be an inconvenience, but even this inconvenience should be sufficient to raise the whole question of the future of SSBNs. Michael MccGwire (1975, pp. 1074−5) has questioned whether they are needed in their present form. Might there not be cheaper and better submarine alternatives for strategic strike than those of the *Trident* class? This matter will be taken up again in Chapter 8.

The problem of resticted straits access would be more serious for surface naval operations than for submarines. The general view is that the threat of impeded access could seriously reduce the effectiveness of forces engaged in the naval presence mission. Particular attention has been drawn to US naval forces in the Mediterranean and in the Indian Ocean (Janis, 1976, pp. 6−7). This matter will be discussed at more length in Chapter 7, but several immediate comments are justified. First, the obstacles likely to be raised by a more restrictive legal regime will be relatively small in comparison with the political, economic and technical factors which will affect calculations about the utility of forward deployment in the years to come. Secondly, although a new law of the sea regime could reduce the effectiveness of presence forces, it need not. We need only examine the build-up and impact of Soviet naval forces in the Mediterranean since the mid-1960s. In order to operate there they have had to transit one set of straits governed by the Montreux Convention, and controlled by a country, Turkey, which has been both a historical enemy and is a member of hostile alliance; and they have had to transit another set of straits dominated by Britain and Spain. Even under these conditions, an impressive military and diplomatic instrument has been developed by the Soviet Union. Thirdly, if a threat to naval access if foreseen, the implication to be drawn might not be withdrawal but *augmentation*, to keep larger numbers of ships permanently on the far side of the straits concerned.

This would obviously have foreign policy implications, such as the need for bases, as well as more obvious economic ones. Finally, if it is argued that reaction-time is such a decisive factor in modern strategy that any possibility of delay might tip the scales between the success and failure of a mission, and if it is feared that there might be delays as a result of interference with straits transit, then it must be concluded that there is no alternative but to maintain one's strength, permanently, in the likely trouble spots. If a hair-trigger response is so desirable, the necessary planning and deployment should take place independently of any law of the sea developments.

Hair-trigger responses are not necessarily desirable in international politics, since it is always much easier to get oneself involved in a crisis or 'shooting war' than it is to extricate oneself satisfactorily. In this respect a more restrictive maritime regime could greatly help decision-making. The possibility that access might be impeded and made more costly should objectively have the effect of creating a politico-strategic 'fail-safe' mechanism. Such a 'fail-safe' mechanism should encourage rationality and discourage knee-jerk responses. This should be of general benefit to the international community in an era in which great power force is both less usable and more costly. Anything which helps to clarify the definition of superpower 'vital interests' is to be welcomed.

The two most significant strategic cockpits which would be affected by a changed straits regime would be the Mediterranean and the Indian Ocean. For reasons which will be discussed later, the logic of these situations point in the direction of a further exploration of naval arms limitation agreements. Although difficult to negotiate, such agreements could give the superpowers the least worse of various more complex worlds.

In addition to surface ships and submarines, the question of the transit of straits also involves the important matter of overflight, discussed earlier. At first sight a more restrictive regime would be unlikely to have a decisive impact. Generally, strait states would not contemplate obstructing the passage of aircraft, as a result of a mixture of diplomatic calculation and lack of capability (Osgood, 1976, p. 15). Not least of the safeguards of the country wanting to overfly nationalized straits would be the fact that aircraft cannot be impeded as conveniently as ships. Any attempt to 'terminate' a flight by a strait state would be a matter of the gravest concern. The resolution shown by major powers in face of hostility, notably the US resupply of Israel in 1973, is a lesson which is not likely to have been lost on observers. Again, this problem seems to imply a need for a prudent naval power to have as many aircraft at sea as possible. Even so, the argument above might be thought too complacent. Any possibility that aircraft might be attacked while transiting a strait might be sufficient to deter action in marginal situations. Perhaps this is to the good. In a dangerous world, in which it is easier to get into wars than out of them, there might be something to be said for the maxim, 'when in doubt, don't'.

Most of the problems surrounding straits transit suggest that the Soviet Navy would be more inconvenienced by a more restrictive regime than would the navy of the United States. It so happens that many activities of the Soviet Navy depend upon access through straits controlled by unfriendly, if not always unco-operative, states (Janis, 1976, pp. 31–32: Richardson, 1980, pp. 905, 912). This suggests that the United States should pay more attention to the possibility of trying to use the law of the sea more explicitly as an instrument of naval policy vis-à-vis the Soviet Union. There may be more to gain from harmonizing with the majority and placing the Soviet Union in a minority position rather than harmonizing with the Soviet Union to defend some existing but expendable naval advantages. The merits and demerits of whether to exploit relative advantages over the Soviet Union in this matter have been the subject of serious discussion among a small group of experts in the United States. The balance of the argument rests with those who have argued the case against exploiting the relative Western advantages over the Soviet Union in this respect: a more restrictive regime would leave Soviet fleets 'hemmed in' by alien waters, without corresponding disadvantages affecting the warships of the Western allies. Rather than exploit such an advantage, Elliot Richardson has argued – and this has been the view of successive US policy-makers – that the United States has its own reasons for wanting unchallenged rights of navigation through straits and that these are more important than the temptation of trying to secure an advantage over the Soviet Union (1980, pp. 912–14; Darman, 1978, pp. 376–8 offers the counter-argument).

The Challenge of Nationalized Choke Points

Over the years the problems facing forward naval deployment have been growing as a result of a mixture of economic burdens, new political complexities and the more powerful weaponry which potential targets can now deploy. A more restrictive straits and archipelagic regime would add a legal impetus to this process. Accordingly, the straits transit issue is likely to remain – at least rhetorically – 'non-negotiable' on the part of the naval powers. Regardless of their preference, however, they may well be forced to negotiate the matter in future because of pressure coming from the strait states themselves. If there is no universal agreement on the 1982 Convention, and the situation develops in such a way that what seemed to have been agreed at UNCLOS III was unravelling, then the issue of straits transit will be high on the international agenda in the minds of some disgruntled countries. And the very importance of this issue to the naval powers makes it an attractive political lever in the eyes of others. Furthermore, there is considerable scope for the spill-over of acrimony and interests between this issue and others. One potential problem of linkage between straits and other issues has been identified by Scott Allen:

> if the words of the spokesmen from the Group of 77 are to be credited, the free passage of ships and aircraft of non-signatories through straits and the right claimed by the United States to extract strategic minerals from the seabed might be threatened. These threats have alluded both to legal challenge and to the necessity for continuous naval protection of US-flag vessels engaged in seabed mining. (1983, p. 46)

In the absence of a widely ratified Convention, a possible threat to the navigation rights of non-parties will exist. And as Leigh Ratiner has put it from the US position, 'This is not the time or place to attempt to prejudge the outcome of such an argument. What is dangerous for the United States is the existence of the argument and the potential uncertainty of its military rights in narrow seas during times of crisis' (1982, p. 1019). Without acceptable agreements or *modi vivendi* regarding transit through choke points, the naval powers have cause to contemplate the worst when reveiwing their contingency planning for crises. In the mid-1970s Elizabeth Young wrote that 'probably no naval vessel can now count on being freely allowed passage through straits in time of trouble, whatever the small print of the relevant convention might say' (1974, p. 266). This was an exaggeration, but her words show that the writing is on the wall. With a more restrictive regime straits could become flashpoints: and the international community could well do without what one writer has called 'ten, fifteen, twenty Berlin corridors' (J. Carter — not the ex-President — quoted by Reisman, 1980, p. 71).

The problem is clearly a worrying one for the naval powers, and hence their resistance to regime change. While the present chapter has questioned some of the extreme navalist fears, Darman's thesis that straits transit and other navigational freedoms are unimportant to the United States — and therefore its allies — cannot be upheld (1978, pp. 378–9). These freedoms are important to naval strategy, though it has been shown that the impact of legal restrictions would not be uniform, and that most of the changes could probably be dealt with satisfactorily. Mission by mission, the implications were seen to be more serious for US general purpose forces and aircraft than for SSBNs, and more serious for the Soviet Navy than its US counterpart. But if new problems would be created for the naval powers, it is not apparent that increased national control of straits or archipelagic waters would inevitably be in the interests of strait and island states. Such a change would confront these states with new dilemmas and responsibilities, and for no more tangible benefit than the satisfaction of being given authority.

Nor is it obvious that nationalizing straits is necessarily to the advantage of the international community at large. Is international order and justice necessarily assisted by the development of rules which complicate the problems of superpower military mobility and at the same time increase the ability of a handful of states to interfere with that mobility? The answer is not self-evident to any but the ideologically committed, but surely the weight of argument favours the supporters of freedom of transit through straits (Moore, 1980, p. 79, 120). All states, whether or not they are maritime, benefit from the unimpeded movement of merchant vessels and goods throughout the world: the free transit of straits is in the interest of international trade, as well as the national strategy of some countries. According to John R. Stevenson, a State Department Legal Adviser, 'If coastal states were given a legal basis for impairing transit virtually every country in the world would find its very economy dependent upon the political good will of some other state by virtue of geography' (Department of *State Bulletin*, vol. 65, 6 September 1971, p. 262). At worst, such a situation could lead to a reversion in the direction of an economic system similar to that of the Middle Ages, with some states exerting *pro rata* tolls at choke points for the passage of tons of steel, barrels of oil, or bushels of wheat. In this as in other respects, the Middle Ages have nothing to commend them.

The resistance of the naval powers will inhibit any radical regime change regarding strait and archipelagic waters for some time to come. And on this issue the interests of the naval powers and most coastal states coincide. As Moore has stressed,

The real stake is not the strategic interests and national needs of any one nation, however, important. Rather, it is no less than the maintenance, indeed strengthening of the common interest in navigational freedom in an age of increasingly complex oceans use and oceans politics. The regime of straits transit is the most essential element in that freedom. And in the real world of oceans politics, it is nonsense to believe that either the United States or the Soviet Union would accept a law of the sea treaty that did not fully protect freedom of navigation through straits. (1980, p. 120).

The superpowers were not willing to contemplate any new restriction on straits transit at UNCLOS III, and this will be their position for years to come. But they will find themselves under increasing pressure from an assertive 'South', if they themselves are never willing to compromise. However, given the stength of superpower feeling on this issue, it will no more be in the interests of the strait states to resist them than it was for the maritime states to resist the trend to a 200-mile zone in the 1970s. Laws without norms are just words, and troublesome words at that. Be that as it may, the tendency for authority over strait and archipelagic waters to be claimed, and to creep, may well revive and grow in the years ahead. If it does, disputes and conflicts are bound to arise. These will serve to highlight the importance of maritime access and the continuing military significance of warships.

While a more restrictive regime would increase the problems of naval mobility, changes in the rules regarding strait and archipelagic waters need not be an insurmountable obstacle for a government whose diplomacy is subtle, whose policy attempts to secure legitimacy in the eyes of the international community, whose force is impressive and whose will is strong. But does such a government exist in the modern world?

Notes: Chapter 5

1 The legal, military and political complexities of the issues involved in the question of straits transit were comprehensively discussed in the debate between Moore, 1980, pp. 77–121, and Reisman, 1980, pp. 48–76.
2 This is evident from the very useful series of books *International Straits of the World* edited by Gerard J. Mangone, published by Martinus Nijhoff. The series provides a comprehensive examination of the political, legal, military and economic issues posed by the extension of coastal state jurisdiction over straits used for international navigation. On the strategically most significant straits see Alexandersson, 1982; Lapidoth-Eschelbacher, 1982; Leifer, 1978; Ramazini, 1979; and Truver, 1980).
3 The width of the major straits is approximately as follows:

Passage	Straits state(s)	Minimum width (n.m.)
Bab el Mandeb	Djibouti/North Yemen	14
Bering Strait	USA/USSR	19
Bornholmsgat	Denmark/Sweden	19
Bosporus	Turkey	Less than 1
Dardanelles	Turkey	Less than 1
Dover Strait	France/UK	18
Finland, Gulf of	Finland/USSR	17
Formosa/Taiwan, Strait of	CPR/Taiwan	74
Gibraltar, Strait of	Morocco/Spain	8
Hormuz, Strait of	Iran/Oman	21
Malacca, Strait of	Indonesia/Malaysia	8
Magellan, Strait of	Argentine/Chile	2
Messina, Strait of	Italy	2
Oresund	Denmark/Sweden	2
Otranto, Strait of	Albania/Italy	41

Pescadores Channel	CPR/Taiwan	17
San Bernardino Passage	Philippines	8
Selat Bali	Indonesia	2
Selat Lombok	Indonesia	11
Selat Sunda	Indonesia	12
Skagerrak	Denmark/Norway	61

The distance in some cases are approximate, because of problems regarding the base lines from which calculations are made. About sixty 'important' straits were threatened with being closed off by the extension of the territorial sea from 3 to 12 miles. About thirty 'important' straits have breadths greater than 24 miles, and therefore contain a belt of high seas even with a twelve-mile territorial sea (Alexander, 1983, p. 585). Map 1, p. 98–9, shows the main straits used for international navigation.

6
The Seabed and Territorial Sea

Whereas the three-mile territorial sea no longer has the military significance it once had — because of the increased range of both seaborne
and land-based weaponry — there has been a widely held opinion that
the strategic significance of the seabed has been growing. However, in
the early 1980s this opinion is not what it was a decade or so earlier.
Then it was given its ultimate expression by a Soviet scientist, who
declared, 'the nation which first learns to live under seas will control
the world' (quoted by Luard, 1974, p. 56). With new technology becoming available, and ideas about using conventional weaponry not
always in conventional ways, there were good reasons in the late 1960s
and early 1970s for believing that a new arms race would take place on
the seabed (Luard, 1974, pp. 49−60). Arms controllers and law of the
sea specialists subsequently focused some attention on limiting military activity on the seabed, but here as elsewhere, the 'naval interest'
favours maximum flexibility, and resists the hardening of rules
(O'Connell, 1975, p. 151).

The Seabed: Militarization and Control

As was mentioned earlier, UNCLOS III grew out of the preparatory
work done by the Seabed Committee of the United Nations. This
committee (1963−73) proceeded relatively satisfactorily with its own
efforts in putting the seabed on the international agenda and in
bringing about some controls on the threat of seabed militarization.
The agreements it reached were strictly confined to the seabed, and
naturally the matter of defining the scope of the agreements was a
lively issue. After much discussion it was decided that the area to be
excluded from the prohibitions of the treaty would be that within the
twelve-mile outer limit of the contiguous zone as measured in accordance with the rules of the 1958 Geneva Convention (O'Connell, 1975,
pp. 154−6). Naval activities in superjacent water were strictly excluded, as was 'legal' military activity in the air space above (Barry,
1972, pp. 87−101). Consequently, as Finn Laursen has argued, the

essential significance of the seabed arms control treaty was its limited scope: it outlaws weapons of mass destruction on the seabed, but detection devices remain legal, as do naval operations in, on and above the water. In this way, according to Laursen, the superpowers 'stopped "creeping jurisdiction" in the arms control area' (1982, pp. 204–5).

During the life of the Seabed Committee the UN General Assembly in 1970 resolved that the deep seabed should be 'the common heritage of mankind' — that stirring declaration of non-ownership which was made at a time when most other trends in the law of the sea were in the opposite direction. The common heritage principle was endorsed by UNCLOS III, as was discussed earlier, though the attempt to put it into operation proved to be the Conference's ultimate stumbling block. The future of the principle remains to be seen, but it is definitely not what it was. There is even a risk of it merely becoming cant, particularly in the mouths of those governments which have done so little to make the most of their own national heritages.

Much of the trouble at UNCLOS III on the subject of the seabed regime did not appear to have an immediate military dimension. The earlier work of the Seabed Committee had helped in this respect. In the event, the strategic implications of the seabed issue at UNCLOS III proved to be indirect rather than direct: they resulted from the fact that disagreement on this issue threatened the whole future of a universally ratified law of the sea.

During UNCLOS III the United States consistently showed that it was ready to act toughly in the absence of an agreement on the seabed. Secretary of State Henry Kissinger in 1976 declared that deep seabed mining was 'the most complex and vital issue to be decided' and that 'If the seabeds are not the subject of international agreement the United States can, and will, proceed to explore and mine on its own'. He admitted that this might eventually lead to 'a race to carve out deep-sea domains of exploitation which will escalate into economic warfare, endanger the freedom of navigation, and lead to trials of strength and military confrontations' (Calder, 1976, p. 640). But this prospect did not deter him: and nothing which happened subsequently leads one to doubt that US determination on this matter has declined.

For one reason or another, therefore, directly or indirectly, the military aspects of seabed development have demanded the serious attention of both those states able to think about deploying advanced technology and those with an ideological commitment against the progressive militarization of the seabed. In the case of some governments, including the Soviet Union, the prospects led them to support the complete demilitarization of the seabed (Young, 1978, p. 240). In practice, however, it has not proved possible for the international community to go beyond the Seabed Treaty, which entered into force in 1972, and which prohibits the emplacement of nuclear weapons and other weapons of mass destruction.

Within its own terms, the Seabed Treaty has worked satisfactorily over the years (Vayrynen, 1978), though it has been criticized by some arms controllers on the ground that it does not go far enough. The latter viewpoint has been expressed with particular force by Alva Myrdal:

> It is seldom explicitly admitted that the Seabed Treaty does not inhibit military activities of real interest, that it does not limit installations on the ocean floor for military purposes other than the embedding of weapons of mass destruction. It does not prohibit the installation of facilities which service crawling or free-swimming military systems, even those with nuclear weapons, nor the temporary stationing of nuclear missile submarines on the ocean floor. Thus, the treaty does not stop the nuclear arms race under international waters. Still less does it place any obstacle in the way of that arms race of wider import based on mobile carriers: submarines with ballistic missiles; vast and sophisticated anti-submarine warfare systems; manned and unmanned underwater stations; moored platforms for bunkering, refuelling, repairing, signalling etc. It does not limit the deployment of hordes of detection devices on the seabed (1976, pp. 100–1)

In short, the treaty did little to inhibit the military uses of what Myrdal called the 'underwater environment', as opposed to the seabed proper.

So for naval uses other than the emplacement of weapons of mass destruction, the whole area of inland and territorial waters remains available to the relevant coastal state. And as O'Connell has argued, 'There is also no doubt that the seabed of the continental shelf is also available to the coastal State, but the question is whether this availability is exclusive' (1975, p. 157). Again, the doctrine of the freedom of the seas confronts the principle of the common heritage, and this leaves some scope for argument: 'this very ambiguity can become the occasion of dispute leading to resort to naval force to expel the intruder upon the continental shelf or to sustain the intrusion' (O'Connell, 1975, p. 158).

With creeping arms control inhibited, Myrdal foresaw the prospect of a 'nonstop arms race' under the sea, particularly in view of some of the 'stupendous' technology which was believed to be just around the corner. Other arms controllers have shared these fears, worrying not only about the deployment of unconventional technology, but also about conventional technology used in unconventional ways (Luard, 1974, pp. 49–60). Other observers have been less concerned, and have argued that there has been altogether too much exaggeration about the military uses of the seabed. O'Connell, for example, has claimed that seabed submersibles are 'so speculative' that 'precise evaluation of the issues' is precluded (1975, p. 151). In addition, he has suggested that no serious consideration has actually been given to the possibility of locating nuclear delivery systems on the seabed; this, he says, is

> because of the great cost involved and the fact that construction work on several fixed installations could not altogether escape notice and hence detection. This would defeat the purpose of seabed location, which is concealment only. If mobile systems, called 'creepy-crawlies', were used they would be so huge and cumbersome, and would involve such design problems to enable them to be locomotive on a rugged seabed, that they were seen as only a dubious alternative to SSBNs (O'Connell, 1975, p. 153: compare Luard, 1974, pp. 49–52)

So far, the evidence seems to have justified O'Connell's caution rather than the fears of Myrdal and Luard regarding a seabed arms race.

Despite the attention given to the military aspects of the seabed at the turn of the 1960s and 1970s, the issue has largely dropped out of sight. International attention on the seabed was subsequently focused on the economic dimension; and there is little reason to suppose that this will change in the immediate future. Furthermore, there would seem to be no hope at all for Myrdal's plea for an extension of arms control activities to waters superjacent to the seabed. Underwater arms control looks no more likely to be in season in the 1980s than other aspects of arms control. And while arms controllers wring their hands, the development and deployment of communication and detection devices in the seas proceeds apace. The outcome, in Myrdal's words, is that 'the oceans are becoming more and more thoroughly bugged. Some forms of acoustic surveillance are mobile, but some are fixed. There may be hundreds or thousands of fixed sonar systems in the oceans, bottom-mounted, upward-listening, interconnected with each other and transmitting information to airborne or satellite-borne receivers' (1976, p. 101). Or, she might have added, connected directly to shore stations.

A variety of acoustic arrays have been and are employed, with names like CAESAR, BRONCO, SOSUS, PROJECT ARTEMIS and SPIDER (see Map 1). Some have been deployed on the continental shelf, some on the deeper seabed (Luard, 1974, pp. 54–6; O'Connell, 1975, pp. 148–51; Friedman, 1980, pp. 120–3; Bracken, 1983, pp. 14–15, 18, 61, 184, 190). As a result of the proliferation of such military-related equipment, some arms controllers see only hypocrisy in Article V of the Seabed Treaty, in which the parties agreed to 'undertake negotiations in good faith' concerning further measures in the field of disarmament for the prevention of an arms race on the seabed. There is obviously some imprecision here in the criticisms of arms controllers like Mydral, since the seabed and the use of the superjacent water are obviously not the same thing. More important than the fear of a seabed 'arms race' in the minds of strategists and others is the fear that the bugging of the oceans may one day progress far enough to threaten the very invulnerability of SSBNs, and hence all the more serious because the improving accuracy of land-based missiles already threatens the survivability of fixed land-based systems. Furthermore the employment of any fixed installations on the deep seabed for surveillance purposes will be in violation of the international agreement to keep the ocean floor as the common heritage of mankind, and available for 'peaceful purposes' only (Mydral, 1976, p. 102).

In the Seabed Committee, some countries had taken the commitment to 'peaceful purposes' to mean the complete demilitarization of the seabed. This was not the US position. The latter made clear that it did not consider that 'peaceful purposes' precluded naval activities on the seabed which were not prohibited by a specific treaty negotiated within the framework of a disarmament agreement (O'Connell, 1975, p. 159). This attitude was unsatisfactory from the point of view of some arms controllers: they could envisage the prospect and danger of nations demanding the right to establish 'security zones' around those parts of the ocean floor which were being exploited for oil or mineral extraction. And what weaponry might they deploy for these purposes? At this point, the worries of the disarmer Myrdal and the strategist Kissinger converged. The problem, as Mydral expressed it, is that 'There is an inherent contradiction and incompatibility in legislating internationally to use the seabed and ocean floor for exclusively peaceful purposes and at the same time allowing nations to pursue clandestine military activities of any kind in that area' (1976, p. 102). One of the problems, as indicated earlier, revolves around the never-to-be-settled meaning of 'peaceful purposes'. In 1967 the Assistant Secretary to the US Navy declared that the US Navy had used the sea bottom 'for many purposes for many years', and he warned that any agreement formally ensuring the peaceful use of the sea bottom could interfere with some national security enterprises (quoted by Luard, 1974, p. 59; see also O'Connell, 1975, p. 159). Military activity and peaceful purposes are not necessarily incompatible when seen through the national security lens, and so the concerns and disappointments of disarmers such as Myrdal will continue.

Out of Sight: Out of Mind

Despite the anxieties in some quarters about the prospective militarization of the seabed, the 1977 conference to review the Seabed Treaty was conducted in a relatively relaxed mood. This was because of the limited significance then attached to the seabed by the superpowers, in comparison with their relationship in the long-running and centrally important Strategic Arms Limitation Talks. The political and military issues involved in the seabed were not thought to be so conspicuous as to warrant major negotiations (Young, 1978, p. 243). For similar reasons, the military aspects of the seabed caused no ripples in the final stages of UNCLOS III. But the future remains uncertain, partly because underwater military activity is both a highly technical and secretive subject. This makes it difficult for those without access to frontier scientific-military information to assess the possible implications for the law of the sea. For most observers, the subject tends to be a matter of 'out of sight: out of mind'. This is to the satisfaction of the superpowers, since concealment is the essential strategic feature of the military use of the seabed.

In the immediate aftermath of the 1982 Convention, all seems quiet on the seabed. 'Peaceful purposes', of course, will continue to be defined subjectively, in order to include any placement of listening devices. This freedom, as was mentioned earlier, was predictably and not unreasonably supported by the US Navy. In this respect it is the seabed on the continental shelf rather than the deep seabed proper which is more likely to be a focus for dispute, because of the national rights accorded over the continental shelf. Some states can be expected to be assertive about the latter. In its adherence to the Seabed Treaty in 1973 India announced that there could be no restriction of its sovereign right to verify, inspect, remove, or destroy any weapon, device, structure, installation, or facility which might be emplaced on or beneath its continental shelf by any other country. The position of the United States was that the rights of coastal states were restricted to purposes of exploration and the exploitation of natural resources; coastal state rights therefore did not concern military equipment. The 1982 Convention left this uncertainty unresolved.

Article 77 of the Convention grants states sovereign rights over the continental shelf only for 'the purpose of exploring it and exploiting its natural resources'. Under Article 80, coastal states' rights regarding artificial islands, installations and structures on the continental shelf would seem to be restricted to economic purposes. Seabed law is open to interpretation in this regard. The possibility of similar disputes also arises over the meaning of 'scientific' research, particularly when located in strategically sensitive areas. As was made clear in Chapter 4, there is no clear dividing line between what is obviously 'military' on the one hand, and what is 'non-military' on the other when it comes to scientific research. The dividing line is particularly difficult to draw in the case of the mass of environmental information which it is necessary to collect for effective submarine and ASW activities.

In the latter stages of UNCLOS III one hitherto largely neglected aspect of the exploitation of the seabed was accorded increased strategic significance, particularly by the Reagan administration. This was the question of access to 'strategic minerals' on the seabed. Interestingly, Elliot Richardson had not mentioned this factor in his 1980 listing of major US strategic interests in the law of the sea. In terms of the history of UNCLOS III, therefore, this was very much an eleventh-hour issue. Whether its rise to last-minute prominence means that it had been an oversight earlier, or was now suddenly useful as a 'joker' in the pack, or a bargaining tactic, remains to be settled by historians, when the records of US policy-making become available.

The security implications of seabed minerals had not been a central issue in early law of the sea discussions. After President Reagan had come to power, however, it was said to be one of the factors which helped to change the attitude of the US Department of Defense in favour of the administration's reversal of policy on the Draft Convention. Reagan's Foreign Policy Advisory Council and Stategic Minerals Task Force were worried about the concentration of enormous economic and political power in the Seabed Authority, which they feared would be dominated by Third World nations. This prospect was unwelcome because the United States lacked assured, continuing and non-discriminatory access to critical minerals needed for its industry and defence (Robertson and Vasaturo, 1983, p. 688). Until Reagan took office, the Department of Defense had supported the Draft Convention on security grounds, since it promised to preserve military mobility; defence planners did not believe, for example, that internationalizing the ocean floor would interfere with naval activities. However, they were persuaded, in time, by those who argued that internationalizing the seabed would seriously limit American access to scarce minerals. The risk they foresaw was obvious: what was and is less apparent is the degree of danger involved and the likelihood of its occurence. For the Department of Defense it is not inconceivable that cognitive dissonance was at work: it was psychologically necessary that the organization inflate the importance of the negative security implications of the proposed deep seabed regime in order to strengthen the administration's economic objections, and to justify putting to risk what had been agreed regarding the navigational aspects of the Convention.

It is now widely agreed that the prospects for deep seabed mining are not what they once were (*The Economist*, 31 May 1980, p. 86). Even so, a prudent defence planner in a country which is not well endowed with strategic minerals is bound to give worried attention to the matter. This will particularly be the case if that country happens to be the United States. In this respect, for once, geography has been kinder to the Soviet Union, by endowing it with a greater range of strategic minerals. The problem faced by the United States with respect to seabed minerals is whether its interests are better served by the seabed provisions under the existing Convention, or by a continued refusal to sign. To date, the Reagan administration has remained committed to the latter, though voices like that of Elliot Richardson are convinced that this policy represents a serious error. In Richardson's view, the Convention would benefit his country's 'strategic interest in an alternative source of nickel, copper, cobalt, and manganese. It would be ironic if, in the name of that same interest, we handed over the exploitation of seabed minerals to our industrial competitors' (1983, p. 513).

Seabed mining, by current projections, will not develop in such a fashion that it will decisively affect man's use of minerals, or the international economy. But it could seriously change the economy and security arrangements of some countries. Zaïre, for example, whose export earnings are largely dependent upon cobalt, could become badly hit by successful seabed mining. On the other hand, the economic prospects of some countries could be improved. In particular, successful seabed mining by the industrial nations could free them at least to some degree of their dependence on a variety of unstable countries for the supply of critical minerals. Germany and Japan are two countries which are well developed in seabed mining. Like the United States, some sectors of their governments see more advantages in the national rather than the international exploitation of the minerals of the seabed.

The absence of an agreed seabed regime will foster the every-man-for-himself attitude which is present in those countries most able to exploit underwater technology. Mining companies, supported by their governments, will be tempted to grab what they can on the seabed, much to the distaste of the proponents of the common heritage of mankind doctrine. But seabed unilateralism could provoke a range of responses from some members of the disgruntled majority, including sabotage, covert attacks and commodity or diplomatic boycotts (Buzan, 1978, p.14). Some of these actions would require naval protection for the mining companies. It would presumably be given, out of principle as well as commercial interest. At an early stage of UNCLOS III Henry Kissinger warned everybody that if there was no international regime, the US Navy would be well able to protect US companies.

Of more immediate military importance than the problem of protecting or disrupting seabed mining is the question of the control of underwater detection systems. However, it is difficult to foresee any alternative at present to the continuance of the familiar free-for-all, especially given the importance of tracking submarines in the naval thinking of both superpowers and their major allies. The seabed will remain the main medium for submarine detection, short of some radical breakthrough in tracking devices operating from space. While underwater listening devices retain their importance, navies will resist legal obstacles to the choice of their location, which in turn will affect plans for tracking and deployment (O'Connell 1975, p. 146). On the other hand, most governments would welcome the chance of keeping foreign sensors and listening devices out of their own maritime backyards as a result of international agreement. That said, those states interested in deploying such devices in the maritime backyards of their adversaries will on balance accept the risks of a free-for-all situation. Such states regard it as important that they are able to deploy sonabuoys, hydrophones and other detection devices on the seabed of the continental shelves of other states, especially where straits or other narrow waters restrict the transit routes of the adversary's submarines on deployment to their operational stations. 'Diplomatic difficulties have occurred in just this connection', O'Connell commented coyly in the mid-1970s (1975, p. 149). While there are doubts about the legality of the seabed emplacement of detection equipment, the prevailing view is that such installations are not illegal provided they do not interfere with the rights of the coastal state in the exploration and exploitation of its continental shelf.

The arcane strategic rivalry in the ocean depths is dominated by US-Soviet competition (Burns, 1978), although the desirability in strategic theory of the two superpowers tracking each other's SSBNs is questionable. If theories about maintaining invulnerable second-strike capabilities are valid, it is imperative that states be solicitous about the survivability of their adversary's retaliatory forces. Attempting to track his SSBNs (which increases one's chances of destroying them in war) is a destabilizing heresy in Western deterrence theory (though in practice operations are carried out to this end). This is an issue which has important arms control implications, and will be discussed further in Chapter 8. As matters stand, with the emplacement of sensors for the tracking of all types of submarines, there would not appear to be many places in the US–Soviet confrontation which are not either within the jurisdiction of the superpowers themselves, their allies, or their adversary. Emplacement is therefore either acceptable or 'fair game' for interference. The one potentially dangerous area of dispute over this problem is the Norwegian-Soviet boundary in the Barents Sea, and in the north-east Atlantic in general. This is the great underwater cockpit of modern strategy.

If there is to be a third great battle of the Atlantic, it remains to be seen to what extent its outcome will depend upon information gathered in peacetime from seabed listening devices. But it is safe to assume that they will play some part, and so for the foreseeable future both superpowers will oppose restrictions on seabed surveillance. The United States will be to the fore in this, because of its reputed lead in the state of the art, and its geographical advantages (the fact that its allies control strategically located seabed real estate). As long as the northern members of NATO remain bound together, seabed military use by the United States in critical areas of confrontation will continue: even sensitive allies can permit such out-of-sight-out-of-mind activities. But if a more restrictive law of the sea regime were ever to develop, the bargaining power would grow of those countries with the relevant waterfront, namely, Norway, Denmark (Greenland), Iceland and the United Kingdom. It would also further increase the military significance of these countries in the eyes of the Soviet Union (Booth, 1981, pp. 7–12). Nevertheless, the implication for defence planning of a more restrictive seabed regime is not, in O'Connell's opinion, as 'sinister' as some have supposed. This is 'because the problem of legal obstacles to the location of acoustic facilities is in fact one that naval staffs believe they can live with' (1975, p. 150).

The possibility exists that the seabed may come to be seriously used in future for naval purposes other than the emplacement of detection devices. Interest may be revived in the seabed deployment of nuclear weapons, in either a fixed or mobile mode; this possibility will surely be re-examined if other strategic systems become decisively threatened, though at present the prospect of such an eventuality would seem to be low. The disadvantages of seabed nuclear systems appear likely to continue to outweigh their possible advantages, as was the case in the late 1960s when the Seabed Treaty was originally negotiated.

From this examination of seabed military activity it seems unwise to become excited either about the prospect of an 'arms race' on the seabed, or the problems which would occur were there to be tighter control of military activities on the seabed (in addition to the already controlled weapons of mass destruction). Actual technology has not raced science fiction as quickly as some in the late 1960s forecast, while apart from the Spitzbergen area neither the issues nor the capabilities yet exist for far-reaching conflict as a result of seabed disputes. ASW will obviously remain a critical aspect of the naval confrontation, but in carrying it out the geographical situation of one's allies will be more important than the law of the sea. In this respect, US advantages could in fact be strengthened by a more restrictive law of the sea regime.

Although the alarms of the late 1960s and early 1970s regarding the militarization of the seabed have become muted, the possibility does remain over the longer term that the superpowers will become engaged in a serious competition to acquire strategic locations on the seabed (Luard, 1974, p. 55). Its military use and occupation cannot be entirely dismissed, since it is conceivable that exotic technology will one day be developed. If such an occupation of the seabed does take place, Laurence Martin foresaw in the late 1960s that it might lead to an effort to establish exclusive jurisdiction over parts of the seabed, or at least identification zones analogous to those in the air (1967, pp. 34, 67, 138; see also Craven, 1966, pp. 36–52; Delaney and Townsend, 1979, pp. 37–41). Such an outcome would not only puncture the 'common heritage' concept, but also end the concealment of at least some underwater military activity. It is a possibility, though presently a distant one. And it is likely that if one state began the process, it would produce a spiralling effect, thereby increasing the possibility of conflict and further justifying increases in military potential at sea (Luard, 1974, p. 59).

The major naval powers, as O'Connell has argued, have 'divided interests' on important naval issues, since at one and the same time they are concerned with the defence of their own coast and with the carrying out of naval activities on a global scale. On balance, O'Connell concluded that navies would prefer there to be no restrictions on the use of the deep seabed, but that if there were to be restrictions, they should be minimal (1975, p. 148). For the moment, the naval powers are satisfied with the combination of the Seabed Treaty and the 1982 Convention, since together they limit the restrictions which arms control might bring about. These agreements allow considerable latitude for military activity, and many changes would have to come about before the naval powers felt that important military interests were becoming threatened. While this is so, any disputes over the seabed will be the consequence of clashing economic ideologies rather than clashing military interests.

But who knows in the long term? This area of strategy, like every other, is dragged or pushed along by the tyrant of technological 'progress'. The momentum of innovation constantly complicates the present and undermines any confidence about the future. It subverts the already limited reassurance which the superpowers are able to give to each other, and so constitutes an independent threat to stability in addition to that of competing national interests.

Troubles in the Territorial Sea

Historically speaking it has been the limit of the territorial sea and the perennial question of innocent passage[1] which as much as anything has demanded attention in law of the sea negotiations (O'Connell, 1975, pp. 138–45). In naval operational planning since 1945, however, discussion of the territorial sea has largely been restricted to the problem of limited wars, notably the US involvement in Vietnam, or the confrontation between Malaysia and Indonesia (O'Connell, 1975, pp. 132–8). By the early 1980s, after the legitimization of the twelve-mile limit by UNCLOS III, interest in the territorial sea came to be focused on the mysterious activities of submarines off the coasts of Scandinavia.

Since the late 1960s there have been frequent sightings of submarines — presumed to be Soviet[2] — off the coasts of all the Scandinavian countries, but especially Norway and Sweden (Map 2).

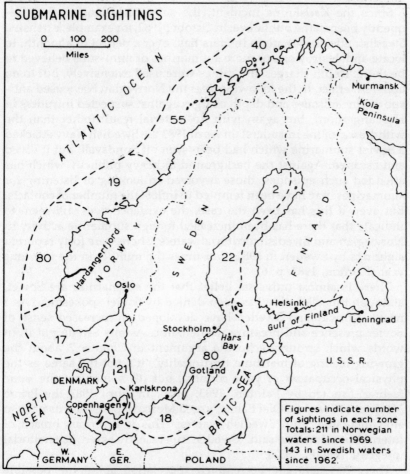

SUBMARINE SIGHTINGS

Figures indicate number of sightings in each zone Totals: 211 in Norwegian waters since 1969. 143 in Swedish waters since 1962.

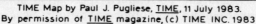

TIME Map by Paul J. Pugliese, TIME, 11 July 1983.
By permission of TIME magazine, (c) TIME INC. 1983

MAP 2 Submarine sightings in Scandinavia.

Norway reported 211 sightings in its waters since 1969 and Sweden 143 sightings since 1962 (Painton, 1983, p. 7; Bildt, 1983, p. 168). Despite their number, the incursions did not attract widespread public interest until October 1981, with the famous or infamous 'Whiskey on the rocks' incident, when a Soviet Whiskey-class submarine ran aground near the Swedish naval base of Karlskrona. The submarine was believed to be carrying nuclear weapons, and it took ten embarrassing days — for all concerned — before it was finally hauled out to sea again. The presence of nuclear weapons inevitably added considerably to the diplomatic strain and political significance of the affair.

Since the Karlskrona incident, the submarine problem has frequently been in the public eye. In October 1982, for example, extensive Swedish efforts took place in Hårs Bay, over a period of a month, to locate and destroy one or more submarines or mini-subs believed to be there. Depth charges and mines were used extensively, but to no apparent effect. In the following year the Norwegian Navy used anti-submarine missiles and depth charges against suspected intruders in Hardangerfjord, but again with no material result (other than the withdrawal of the intruders). In April 1983 the Swedish Navy attacked a Soviet submarine which had been seen off Sundsvall, but it dived and escaped. Against the background of heavy publicity which has attended such episodes, those involved in looking or listening for submarines may have been tempted to inflate the number of contacts. But even if this has been the case, the evidence does still seem to indicate that there has been increased foreign submarine activity in Norwegian and Swedish territorial waters. There were forty reported sightings by Sweden in 1982, four times the number in the previous year (Painton, 1983, p. 6).

There is almost universal belief that the submarines are Soviet, although this allegation has been denied by Soviet spokesmen. As a result, Norway and Sweden have developed an increased sense of Soviet presence and pressure in the Baltic. As one Swede put it, in words which strongly echo the argument in Chapter 3 about the growing feeling of maritime territoriality, 'It's not the same as the physical occupation of your country, but it's somewhat the same feeling' (quoted by Painton, 1983, p. 6). In April 1983 the Prime Minister of Sweden, Olaf Palme, urged Moscow to instruct its navy to stop incursions into Swedish waters: 'This is a serious breach of international law', he said. 'Sweden must clearly assert its territorial integrity' (Fields, 1983).

There has naturally been much speculation about the possible Soviet motives behind this submarine activity. Several theories have been suggested (*The Economist*, 16 October, 1982, 14 May 1983; Bildt, 1983; Painton, 1983):

Intelligence-gathering
Soviet naval planners, like others, have an insatiable appetite for up-to-date information about foreign harbours and other aspects of the coastal environment, especially near bases or possible landing grounds in war.

Updating war plans
There is a widespread opinion that in the event of war the Soviet Union would try to invade Norway through Sweden, as part of its effort to gain control of the waters of the north Atlantic. An opinion has also been gaining ground, strengthened by the shooting down of the Korean airliner by Soviet forces in September 1983, that Soviet defence planners have become edgier since 1979–80 as a result of various pressures from the United States and elsewhere. Since they apparently believe that the threat of war has perceptibly increased, they have decided that they must modernize their war plans for the Baltic (and elsewhere), even at the risk of increasing regional tension and incurring some political embarrassment. Updating war plans involves surveying the locations and practising operations for such contingencies as mining, sabotage raids, the blockading of ports and bases, diversionary activities and major landings. This military explanation for Soviet behaviour has been steadily gaining ground in Western defence circles, including within Scandinavia itself.

Acclimatization
This is an operational aspect of the preceding theory, and involves submariners getting used in peacetime to the depths, temperatures, currents and coastal configurations of areas in which they would operate in war. Acclimatization was also the explanation put forward for some unusual – again presumed Soviet – submarine activity in the Gulf of Taranto in the Mediterranean in 1982 (*Time* magazine, 15 March 1982, p. 19).

Electronic surveillance
Submarines are sometimes used to collect electronic information when it is not possible or appropriate to do so from land or on board a surface ship. Radars, radios and microwave telephone links can be monitored by submarines.

Training
Rather than scrapping some of its older diesel submarines, it has been suggested that the Soviet Navy might use them to train junior submarine captains by sending them on reconaissance missions off Sweden and Norway. In these waters, it has been argued, there is enough opposition from local forces to sharpen inexperienced

officers, but without excessive danger to the boats themselves. Certainly, the ASW capabilties of the Scandinavian countries is not as great a deterrent as that posed by the Royal Navy, which so far has discouraged (as far as is known) the entry of Soviet submarines into British territorial waters. But if training is the primary Soviet objective, it suggests a very compelling need, given the possible price.

Political pressure

This theory proposes that the Soviet objective has been to press the Swedes and Norwegians into accepting a permanent Soviet military presence in their waters, and so establish a tacit recognition on their part that the waters of the Baltic are a Soviet lake. This is also presumably one of the objectives behind Soviet support for the idea of the Baltic as a 'sea of peace'. It has also been suggested that the submarine pressure may be employed as a warning to the Scandinavian countries against closer co-operation with NATO.

Whatever the actual motive, or motives, behind Soviet submarine activity in Scandinavian waters, Western defence observers remain baffled, for none of the explanations offered is completely convincing. However, some mixture of motives, including contingency planning, intelligence-gathering and acclimatization, seem more plausible than the theory of 'political pressure'. Soviet planners must know how easily the latter could misfire, and in any case political signalling by means of submarines is extremely difficult. In order to exert pressure the submarines must be detected but not destroyed, and perceived as Soviet but able to be denied. The dividing line between failure and success in such an activity would appear to be too narrow to be acceptable to the Soviet political leadership — assuming they are involved. Acute embarrassment and a serious deterioration in relations with the Scandinavian countries would result from a destroyed and hence definitely identified Soviet submarine. Furthermore, there is some evidence that Soviet sources are aware of the adverse political effects for the Soviet Union of the stories of repeated submarine incursions into the territorial waters of Scandinavian countries (Bildt, 1983, p. 169). For one thing, such activities would appear inconsistent with a policy aiming to achieve recognition of the Baltic as a 'sea of peace' — unless it is calculated that the Scandinavian countries can be persuaded to accept the idea of a sea of peace as part of the price of securing the withdrawal of the submarine pressure. If political pressure can be ruled out as a motive, it seems, as Carl Bildt, a member of Sweden's Submarine Defence Committee, has argued, that the Soviet naval authorities must now be able to point to 'rather urgent military requirements' if they are to demonstrate to their political masters that the net effect of their incursions 'will be positive from the overall

Soviet perspective'. If this is the case, Bildt ominously concluded, 'the implications for Sweden and other affected countries are very grave indeed' (1983, p. 169).

One effect of these episodes in Scandinavian waters has been to draw attention to the already 'malleable' state of the law as it relates to submarine contacts in the territorial sea (O'Connell, 1975, pp. 142–5). For their part, faced with increased intrusions, Scandinavian coastal defence forces have taken a stronger line. Sweden, for example, now allows its on-the-scene commanders to determine how to attack the intruding submarines, without having to wait for clearance from headquarters, as was the procedure in the past; and they are now authorized to attack intruders without warning, to try to force them to the surface. This new attitude is significant. As one Western diplomat in the region noted: 'For the Swedes, at one time the only thing worse than having Soviet subs in their back yard was the prospect of actually sinking one and leaving a lot of dead Russians below. But this attitude is changing. They feel they have given ample notice of their serious-ness' (unnamed source, quoted by Painton, 1983, p. 7). There has now developed in some quarters of Sweden a strong desire to hit back at the intruders. The feeling has been fuelled by a sense of military failure, the ignominy of adverse publicity and continuing sightings, and the steady erosion of the credibility of Sweden's neutrality (Dowden, 1983). Some governments would want to keep any foreign submarine sightings secret, because once they become public know-ledge there would be pressure on the authorities to act decisively. But this is not possible in the situation off Scandinavia: the matter is too important and too public to be ignored. Not surprisingly, the countries whose territorial seas are being violated have determined to resolve the ambiguities of the law by forceful naval practice.[3] In the case of Sweden the intrusions undermine one of the cornerstones of Swedish foreign and defence policy, namely, its commitment to neu-trality. From this viewpoint the intrusions must be stopped. 'The time may soon come', Richard Dowden writes, 'when the Swedes, who have scarcely fired a shot in anger for nearly two centuries, may find dead Russian sailors floating off their shores' (Dowden, 1983).

In addition to provoking the Scandinavian countries, the episodes have served to expose the difficulties of detecting and destroying submarines in even relatively restricted areas. For Sweden in parti-cular this problem has drawn attention to the low quality of their ASW practices and to their need for new ASW equipment. Consequently, in 1983 the Swedish parliament voted for $33 million to purchase new equipment (Fields, 1983; Dowden, 1983; Painton 1983, p. 7). By com-parison, it might be noted, the United States in 1983 appropriated $12 billion on ASW. The detection problem facing Sweden is increased by the fact that the intruders include not only conventional submarines, but also possibly one or more types of mini-submarines, some of which are tracked. These mini-subs may be used for underwater recovery or, more ominously, for the laying of navigational buoys on the seabed to guide other submarines through coastal defences. These are of obvious value in war, or near the outbreak of war.

In these episodes in the territorial waters of the Scandinavian countries, it is possible to see how the illegal naval activities of an alien power can provoke feelings about maritime territoriality, and so raise the political climate. Indeed, by undertaking these activities the Soviet Union has shown what Frederick Painton has called an 'almost contemptuous disregard' for the territorial waters of the Nordic countries (1983, p. 9). In one of the familiar patterns of diplomatic history, a great power has been disregarding international law when it thinks that its national interests require it, while its smaller neighbours show outrage at the intrusions on their sovereignty, take whatever countermeasures they can, and define and re-define their alliance roles or the meaning of their neutrality in the light of the great power's bullying.

Notes: Chapter 6

1   As was discussed earlier, there have been sporadic efforts to require warships to provide notice to coastal states for innocent passage through the territorial sea, or even to obtain coastal state consent for passage. The naval powers, throughout, have insisted that they could not accept any requirements for either prior notification or for consent for warship transit. UNCLOS III went along with this. In practice innocent passage has not proved to be a problem. The one recent exception occurred in August 1980, following a fire on board a Soviet nuclear-powered attack submarine. The Soviet authorities asked for permission to tow the disabled boat through Japanese waters, but they proceeded with their transit without waiting for formal clearance. The Japanese authorities denied permission for the boat's passage through territorial waters, for fear of possible radiation. This was ignored by the Soviet Union, and the violation took place. After a show of disapproval the Japanese recognized the transit as 'an instance of innocent passage' (IISS, 1981, p. 104; Adelman, 1981, p. 104).
2   Sweden's Submarine Defence Committee provided 'abundant technical and circumstantial evidence' to show that the Soviet Union had been responsible for the submarine incursions into Swedish waters. The committee report stated that 'No observation has been obtained indicating intrusion in Swedish territorial waters by NATO submarines' (Fields, 1983).
3   There were some suggestions in October 1982 that Sweden had allowed the submarine or submarines which had been detected to escape, to save themselves the embarrassment and danger of killing Russians. This has been firmly denied by the authorities (Dowden, 1983).

7

EEZs and Naval Diplomacy

At UNCLOS III the concept of the Exclusive Economic Zone, which gave coastal states functional but not territorial sovereignty over the exploitation of 32 per cent of ocean space, was recognised as being sui generis. Existing rights for naval activities in these areas seemed to be confirmed, but it is evident from earlier chapters that the long-term future of this vast area contains possibilities which are worrying to naval planners. Of particular interest are the implications for the future of naval diplomacy in those zones which were formerly high seas and therefore 'free', but which are now covered by a new range of functional sovereignties, and the threat (or promise) of more to come. The present chapter will speculate about these implications, both in respect of the 1982 Convention and the longer-term challenge posed by any increase in the restrictions on warships, either as a result of the development of customary international law or as a result of the outcome of UNCLOS, IV, V, etc.

Creeping Jurisdiction and Naval Diplomacy

The military implications of creeping jurisdiction on naval diplomacy arise from the problems of access, which, as was discussed in Chapter 3 and as MccGwire has explained, is the factor which gives the sea its essential strategic quality. In MccGwire's words, 'the strategic quality of a particular waterway will reflect some combination of the importance of the use to which it is put, the ease with which that use can be prevented, and the availability and cost of alternative routes' (1975, pp. 1060−1). Any threat to restrict this access seems to threaten to limit the utility of warships in their diplomatic roles.

The phrase 'naval diplomacy' refers to the use of warships in support of foreign policy, but by means of 'signalling' rather than shooting. It therefore involves employing them in different modes so as to communicate one's intentions, deploying them in order to nego-

137

tiate from strength in a crisis or more generally to provide bargaining counters, using them to increase one's influence-building options, or displaying them for supportive and representational tasks of various kinds (Booth, 1977, pp. 26–49).

There has been general agreement — though this is a view which will be questioned later — that any limitation on the access of warships to foreign EEZs will significantly diminish the usefulness of navies as instruments of policy short of war. This attitude led to the strong opposition of the superpowers to any such possibility during UNCLOS III (Janis, 1976, pp. 27, 33–4; Young and Sebek, 1978, p. 258; Richardson, 1980, p. 913). Without doubt, the immediate implications of a more restrictive EEZ regime would seem to degrade the potential utility of warships, for there would be less sea-room for free transit — and possibly none in some cases — and so journeys would be lengthier and more complicated. This would be the case, for example, if 'prior notification' arrangements came to be widely insisted upon, especially if they were tied to coastal state consent. If naval presence operations came to depend upon the discretion of coastal states as to which foreign warships could transit their EEZs, warship operations would come to have a 'patchwork' pattern, which would certainly not be to the liking of the naval powers. This would also be the case, but to a lesser extent, if 'free' access was allowed to EEZs, but only in designated sea lanes because of pollution or security requirements. Each of these possibilities, which would interfere with navigation in one way or another, would affect tactical arrangements and deployment prospects in a crisis. If, in an emergency, it was thought necessary to intrude into another's sea space without consent, then political and even military costs might have to be faced. If these costs were to be avoided by rerouting, then reaction-time would be increased. Even in non-crises, some have argued that the utility of presence forces would become degraded if they had to operate at longer distances from the shore — over 200 miles in the case of a more restrictive EEZ. The argument is sometimes heard that warships operating at such a distance from the shore would not be as visible as formerly, and so would not have the same diplomatic impact.

The problem of creeping jurisdiction does not only affect the future access of warships. Without doubt in the years to come, most states will be increasingly reluctant to allow foreign vessels to engage in scientific research in their coastal areas. Some scientific research, of course, will have military implications, and if coastal states do prevent 'marine scientific research' taking place, then some navies will be deprived of information, and to a degree their operational performance will be affected. All coastal states are sensitive to the presence of foreign intelligence-gathering ships, as the *Pueblo* incident showed in a particularly dramatic fashion in 1968. If the access of such vessels is denied in EEZs, then naval powers will be deprived of possibly valuable information of a military or even political kind. And in addition to limiting the access of ships, a more restrictive EEZ regime might grow to include restrictions on aircraft overflight. Chapter 5 discussed the importance of overflying rights with respect to international straits; the problems would be commensurately greater if approximately one-third of the air space above the sea became subject to restrictions (Reisman, 1980, p. 48).

As was discussed in Chapter 4, the 1982 Convention imposes no interference on military activities in EEZs. Consequently, for an indefinable future, there is little cause for legal apprehension on the part of naval officers. However, apprehension is justified in the longer term if the earlier arguments are valid regarding the growing sense of territoriality among the coastal state community, and the likelihood that this will be expressed in demands for greater control over foreign shipping, including naval vessels, in their own maritime backyards. If such demands grow, and are accompanied by demonstrations of political and military muscle, it would be difficult for the governments of the naval powers to avoid a growing sense of peacetime naval inhibition; if this came about there would be a decreasing readiness to deploy warships, particularly on 'marginal' issues. What was formerly no problem at all — the passage of warships beyond the territorial sea but within 200 miles of the shore — would now have become a potential issue in the bilateral relationships between coastal states and naval powers.[1]

The Scope for Naval Diplomacy

If the fears just discussed are valid, then the implications of greater restrictions in EEZs are clearly serious. But before we jump to the conclusion that creeping jurisdiction will lead to the end of naval diplomacy as we have known it, several cautionary remarks need to be made. First, not all manifestations of creeping jurisdiction will have direct military effects (Moore, 1980, p. 84). Secondly, it is predictable that inhibitions on distant water naval activity will continue to grow regardless of law of the sea developments. This is because of the changing balance of costs and benefits when it comes to the projection of military force by great powers in a post-imperial world of diffused military potential. Legal restrictions will add simply another problem to what is already an increasingly costly activity. Thirdly, as will be seen below, whatever the character of any future legal regime at sea, the scope for naval diplomacy will not only still exist, but will be offered new opportunities to find expression. The rest of this chapter will attempt to justify this assertion, by criticizing some of the assumptions of the conventional wisdom about the law of the sea and naval diplomacy, and by explaining some of the more subtle possibilities for naval diplomacy under a more restrictive regime.

Some of the navalist arguments against a restrictive EEZ regime can easily be exaggerated. While the pushing out of the claims of coastal states implies less sea-room for transit, for example, this is a trend which is already inherent in other developments. As a result of pollution and security considerations some coastal states have demonstrated their sensitivity towards the passage of foreign warships. Of more immediate practical significance for the naval powers themselves is the fact that tactics have been pushing warships further from coasts. The need for dispersal tactics has already made 'inconveniently large' the amount of sea space for the deployment of a sizeable and well-balanced task force (Brown, 1977, p. 179). A carrier task force is said to require an area of 200 square miles when deployed for action.[2] 'Moreover', Brown has argued, 'it is desirable to leave one or two hundred miles more between the task force perimeter and a hostile coastline and also to have several hundreds of miles extending in other directions to allow for tactical manoeuvre' (1977, p.179). The Falklands War was a clear demonstration of the desirability for warships to stay out of range of modern airpower whenever possible. It is important to remember that fourteen British warships were either sunk or damaged — the difference is of more significance to the survivors than to naval strategists — by the rather outdated 1950s-style aircraft of a Third World country, which were operating at the limit of their range and were using old-fashioned bombs of which only about one-half detonated (Connell, 1982).

If warships avoid transiting zones in which they are unwelcome, and in which hostile acts might take place, it is obvious that this will affect the timeliness with which they could act in a crisis. In practice a number of considerations complicate this simple proposition. The main point is that although the political costs of a deployment would be increased by intrusion into an unwelcome zone for the purpose of a rapid transit, the precise costs can only be discussed in each case; one could argue that this is such a scenario-dependent problem that the general proposition opening this paragraph is virtually meaningless. The problem cannot be fruitfully discussed without our knowing the parties concerned, the likely threat the transiting warships face, the time saved by intruding into potentially hostile sea space, the political trouble likely to be caused, the significance of the interests involved, the importance of timeliness, and so on. Few countries are likely to have the power to stop a major naval task force carrying out a mission, and may well keep quiet on that account. Parenthetically, it should be noted that a more restrictive EEZ regime would impose new burdens on coastal states, as well as upon naval powers: a more restrictive regime would put them on the spot, politically speaking, by obliging them to take sides in disputes in which they might have no direct interest. They would have to show their colours by the attitudes they adopted on warship transit and aircraft overflight. In many cases they would have no choice. In most crises, by definition, 'vital interests' are engaged, and this will mean that a naval power will be less willing to be solicitous towards third party sensibilities, though obviously the importance of particular bilateral relations will be greater in 'marginal' cases than in 'vital' ones, where 'necessity knows no law'.

The arguments above raise an important general point about the value of reactive naval deployments in crises. Criticism has sometimes been levelled against the posturing by US naval forces after the *Pueblo* incident in 1968 and during the 1971 Indo-Pakistan War. MccGwire's comments about the latter have a wider applicability:

> There is a suspicion that this type of deployment often represents action for its own sake and is an overly crude form of diplomatic signal. It also manages to combine the worst of two worlds. It lacks the type of influence that stems from the political commitment of a permanent presence, affords no possibility of precautionary deployments, and inevitably means a delay of several days before force can be brought to bear. Meanwhile, the high visibility of interocean deployment raises political expectations that are un-likely to be met. It can be argued that with regions as large as the Indian Ocean, one either maintains forces in the area or allows events to take their course, and that reactive (as opposed to per-iodic) deployments should only be ordered in exceptional cir-cumstances. (1975, p. 1075)

In short, when we discuss the timeliness of warship reaction, we tend to concentrate on the instrument to the exclusion of the political aim. This is a not unfamiliar phenomenon in the business of strategy, for too often strategists have failed to ask the fundamental question about war and politics, namely, 'What is it all about?' (Brodie, 1973, ch. 1).

The argument has sometimes been made that if warships come to be required to move in designated sea lanes through EEZs, this will greatly increase their vulnerability. But in practice the opposite might well be true. Standard operating patterns might have the effect not of increasing the chances of interdiction, but of increasing the opportun-ities for taking the enemy by surprise. The more predictable one's behaviour is believed to be by a potential enemy, the greater are one's chances of engineering a tactical surprise. The long history of intelli-gence failures attests to the extent that organizations nurture their cognitive consistency. Imaginative naval planners might decide to be content with designated routes in peacetime, while keeping fresh ideas for diversion and surprise in the event of war. In any case, as already happens, naval forces transiting archipelagos do tend to stay within predictable routes (Knight, 1977, p. 38).

Although the problem of the potential political costs involved in the transit of unfriendly EEZs cannot be avoided, they can be minimised. For example, were there to be a more restrictive regime it would be sensible for the naval powers to begin to negotiate bilateral and multilateral treaties to establish their rights of navigation in advance of a crisis (Knight, 1977, p. 39). However, this might be time-consuming diplomatically, sometimes difficult and probably costly.

There is another approach, which will seem heretical from the traditional viewpoint. This is to suggest that there might be a strategic if not a legal case for letting warship navigation rights through some EEZs lapse, in a de facto though not de jure sense. Such a move would increase the signalling potential of one's warships in a crisis. If one's warships are not regularly crossing the sea adjacent to a particular country, this will increase the meaning of any crossing which does actually take place. Such a pattern could mean that the coastal state concerned might be willing to accept a transit on the rare occasions when it was undertaken; and it might make easier the drawing up of special crisis arrangements. It could help to establish the basis for a working compromise between the coastal state's sensitivity about its maritime backyard in general, and the naval power's urgent requirements for transit on rare occasions. There is evidence to suggest that such compromises are possible. When the carrier USS *Enterprise* and its accompanying ships passed through the Malacca Strait on its way to the Bay of Bengal in 1971 the Indonesian government reaffirmed the right of littoral states to control such passage but reconciled this right with the US action by stating that the Command of the Seventh Fleet had given advance notice (Oliver, 1973, pp. 27–33). Subtle and quiet diplomacy should be able to make such arrangements common. Having said that, one would not expect any naval establishment to take the advice just offered, because of their enduring commitment to the belief that rights which are not exercised are apt to lapse. The alternative view is that the very fact of letting matters lapse in a de facto sense helps to create the conditions for more effective signalling in crises. If naval strategy is to succeed in its task, it requires the backing of diplomacy and an understanding of the relationship between the instrument and the aim. After all, their unity is the essence of Clausewitz's message, and a key to success in strategy.

There is another point to consider, and this arises from the tendency when discussing such matters to put too high a price on the new (or old) law of the sea. The law of the sea is important, of course, but it is certainly not always the most important thing for policy-makers to consider. Justice and legitimacy are also important considerations in

the making and execution of foreign policy, and they do not necessarily demand pedantic adherence to the law of the sea. In contemplating an exercise in naval diplomacy, the call of justice might be
stronger than that of the law of the sea. There is a body of universally
accepted rights, as well as rules, relating to the conduct of civilized
states. Among those rights are the right of self-defence (which may be
exercised in anticipation of an act of aggression), the right of humani-
tarian intervention (to protect one's own nationals) and the right
resulting from military necessity (which justifies the application of
regulated force to ensure the prompt submission of an enemy). In
addition, there is the right of collective self-defence deriving from
Article 51 of the UN Charter. Compared with these rights, one's duties
in terms of the law of the sea may be relatively unimportant. The main
point is that if a naval power's contemplated action at the crisis point
is seen to be legitimate, then it is likely that the necessary naval action
en route will be regarded accordingly. But if a state cannot justify its
naval actions on the basis of its rights in international law sufficient to
satisfy a significant portion of the international community, we might
conclude that the contemplated action probably is immoral or futile in
any case, and therefore better avoided. Sometimes, regardless of the
attitude of the international community, a naval power will decide
that it must act, even though costs will have to be paid in terms of
developing a reputation for illegitimate behaviour. We should never
underestimate the determination of great powers to have their way,
even if it means paying a heavy price.

Problems and Opportunities for Naval Presence

The 'presence' role of navies is the most difficult of all aspects of naval
strategy to analyse. There is a vagueness at the very heart of the
concept, which is its essence from the viewpoint of its strategic utility
but which is its curse from that of an analyst. When the implications of
the changing law of the sea are discussed in relation to naval presence,
few writers have given necessary credit to the subtleties of this
mission. From the first-order implications of the changing law of the
sea mentioned earlier, it appeared that creeping jurisdiction simply
threatened to undermine the future of the presence mission. The
discussion below will suggest that the territorialization of the sea
could have the opposite consequence.

The traditional and well-understood concept of naval presence has
been under challenge for a number of years. The US Navy had difficulty through the 1970s attempting to explain its utility to politicians
and the public in this regard, while at the same time Admiral

Gorshkov was deploying his limited literary skills to explain why a navy was needed by the Soviet Union for more than the limited purposes of the past. Everybody finds it difficult to determine with any accuracy the utility of naval presence, for while the costs are normally obvious, the pay-offs are often uncertain. Consequently, navies face major problems in explaining and justifying the mission to sceptical politicians and inward-looking publics. But political support is only one problem for the presence role. There are also problems in operating presences in such a way as to convey the appropriate signals to the right audience. There are tactical and technical problems arising out of the new array of threats which can be thrown against surface forces. There are problems arising out of the heavy economic costs involved in the development and upkeep of warships. And finally there are strategic problems arising out of the restricted useability of force in a more complex international environment. As a result of such considerations, it is clear that naval presence does not seem to offer the benefits of previous generations. Warships in forward deployment can still attempt many missions, but all the costs involved in discharging them are growing. This suggests that the utility of the historic concept of naval presence is in decline.

Having recognized the changing cost-benefit relationship of the presence mission, we must also recognize that superpowers will sometimes need to show a military interest in a particular distant region. Issues will arise on which they will not be dictated, and their armed forces are familiar with the problems of having to make the best of a bad job. Consequently, as long as warships represent the most efficient method by which they can bring flexible firepower to bear in distant regions, warships will retain a major strategic role. The problem is how to make them usable and effective. Changes in the law of the sea can be of assistance in this respect.

After a period in which the currency of naval diplomacy has been depreciating, a more restrictive law of the sea could help to revive it, by making naval diplomacy more selective and more salient. This would largely be the result of the growing significance which would be accorded to the EEZ. For the naval powers the legitimization and further development of the EEZ concept would mean a major new boundary to cross. This would give a new salience to any naval actions in the EEZs of foreign countries, and would likely produce a new selectivity in use. These effects should be welcome, since the market for naval diplomacy was on the point of becoming saturated in the 1970s. Changes in the law of the sea should help to alter that. Any new legal inhibitions which would be involved in sending warships off unfriendly coasts would be a discouragement to the knee-jerk naval diplomacy so characteristic of some periods of US strategy. The legal costs should discourage the ritualistic responses of the recent past, which tended to produce confused signals (as in the Indo-Pakistan War of 1971) or futile demonstrations of power which reduced precious prestige and credibility (the *Pueblo* affair). If, under a more restrictive law of the sea regime, it was decided to deploy naval forces, the very fact that a new boundary has to be crossed should help to make the action more salient in the eyes of adversaries, associates and onlookers.

In periods of knee-jerk naval diplomacy, familiarity tended to breed apathy. In contrast, the territorialization of the sea promises to make the exercise of naval diplomacy both more selective and more meaningful, because warships will have to intrude into waters over which coastal states will have greater interests and stronger feelings. For the first time since the Western powers stopped wielding the big stick without compunction or fear of retaliation, the sailing of a group of warships in distant waters will come to approach the symbolism of tanks at Checkpoint Charlie or aircraft buzzing over Berlin.

One of the assertions mentioned earlier about the impact of creeping jurisdiction on naval presence was that this aspect of naval diplomacy will lose its significance because, as it is sometimes put, 'the flag will not be as visible' as formerly. The latter fact is undeniable, for 'The flag, after all, is considerably more difficult to see at 200 than at 3 or 12 miles' (Janis, 1976, p. 8). But the matter is not as simple as that. There is more to strategy and diplomacy than optical truths. If one thinks of the subtleties of the presence mission, some of the weaknesses of the argument about 'visibility' will be revealed.

In practice, distance might actually help naval diplomacy. Distance helps withdrawability, which recent history suggests is sometimes more of a problem for the mighty than becoming involved in the first place. As the costs of commitment grow, the advantages of potential withdrawability might appear to be more telling to policy-makers than the advantages of timely involvement. There may also be advantages in a low profile. On the other hand, if a naval power does wish to make a hostile signal against a particular country, this can always be done by a mixture of declaratory and action policy, including movement into the EEZ of the relevant target country. For a naval power which wants a coastal country to feel unsettled, but does not intend to use force, there is a positive advantage in keeping one's head well below the horizon, in case it is decided to withdraw, and lose gracefully. Such a low profile can also be useful in relations between friendly states, where an overt and highly visible military commitment would be unacceptable. This was well exemplified in the early 1980s by the developing relationship between the United States and Saudi Arabia. As David Ottoway commented, 'an invisible American backup, whether it be "over the horizon" in the Indian Ocean or based in the United States, appears to be the closest kind of co-operation

with the United States the Saudis can presently afford politically'
(Ottoway, 1981).

Distance can therefore assist not only the naval power but also the
local country. It can even assist the general development of a moderate
international system. The greater the distance from which the naval
diplomacy is exercised, the smaller will be the escalatory steps before a
face-off. And if successful military *power* consists of achieving one's
objectives without having to use force, the opportunity to move in
small steps may be invaluable[3]. Small steps make it easier for the target
state to compromise, but also easier for the mightier power to accept
some loss. The smallness of the steps means that important questions
of 'face' and prestige are not engaged immediately. Instantaneous
face-to-face confrontations make it more difficult for the parties to
back down. In such circumstances some states might feel too weak to
compromise, and may prefer a defiant gesture to surrender. A hostile
warship just off one's shores might seem a tempting prize for a Third
World leader or group willing to take risks. Kamikaze attacks are conceivable in situations short of general war: they are an option for any
group with aircraft and explosives — and pilots who are deadly des-
perate. Warships can get countries into trouble, as well as out of it
(Booth, 1976, p. 12). Actually seeing a hostile warship might tempt
somebody to try to hit it. From the shore, with binoculars, warships
can look rather small, and hopelessly waterbound. Far out of sight
warships can be just as threatening and just as *politically* visible, but at
much less political and physical risk. The US warships standing off
Beirut in the late summer of 1983 were not only providing reassurance
to US troops and friendly Lebanese ashore, but were also offering
dangerous hostages to fortune in an overheated situation.

In most cases *actual* visibility is rarely the issue in naval diplomacy.
Instead, what really matters is the *political* visibility of warships. In
this respect Knight has properly pointed out that

> public perceptions of naval power are largely irrelevant in most
> Third World nations because of their totalitarian forms of govern-
> ment. The head of state knows what vessels are situated where
> and probably has his copy of *Jane's Fighting Ships* (or a know-
> ledgeable admiral) nearby to tell him the nature of the threat
> posed. Credibility of the threat becomes the critical factor at that
> stage, and whether the public can actually see the vessels would
> seem to be of relatively minor importance (1977, pp. 35—6).

These comments are also pertinent to those countries which do not
have 'totalitarian' forms of government. Clearly, in a naval presence
mission 'the flag' does not actually have to be seen. In the Indo-
Pakistan War of 1971, for example, the main superpower naval diplo-

macy took place well over 100 miles from the coast of India (Jackson, 1975, pp. 229–30; Zumwalt, 1976, pp. 367–8). The task forces were not actually visible to observers ashore, but nobody could say that the Soviet and US warships were not *politically* visible. Indeed, they were embarrassingly 'visible' in the case of the US task force, since the signals being transmitted by the deployment appeared confused. This was more the responsibility of the White House than the Chief of Naval Operations. The problem was one of vague aims rather than dimly visible ships.

In practice, naval diplomacy and naval presence rarely take place within sight of land. Some of our images are too strongly affected by the heyday of gunboat diplomacy, kept alive by the fashion for Victorian prints of British gunboats off Chingwangtao, or of cruisers lying at anchor off West African towns. Port visits apart, it is a long time since naval diplomacy invariably involved the parading of warships in sight of land.

Naval diplomacy in the Mediterranean, a region which is both strategically important and physically confined, gives some illustrations of the points above. In the Suez crisis of 1956 the Commander of the Sixth Fleet took his main force and 'operated idly' midway between Suez and Cyprus, that is, over 100 miles from Suez, where the main action was (Wylie, 1969, p. 56). The Commander kept his destroyer screens out and his combat air patrols up, but 'he took no action, even though he was obviously ready and everyone, on both sides, knew he was ready'. One might note that in the intervening twenty years surveillance and communications systems have improved markedly, such that what could be seen then will be even more visible today. It was the verdict of J.C. Wylie (a former Deputy Commander-in-Chief of US Naval Forces in Europe) that this distant readiness of the Sixth Fleet exerted a stabilizing influence on the situation, as did the alerting of even more distant US warships. He commented: 'a major stabilising element in the international situation at this time was that, except for the ships in the eastern Mediterranean, *no one knew where the American fleets* were. It was only known that they had left their usual operating areas' (Wylie, 1969, p. 56; emphasis added). So much for the disadvantage of not seeing the flag. Diplomatic messages are various, and so are the types of naval signals which can be used to transmit them.

The tendency for naval demonstrations to take place at some distance from the coast can be a matter of military as well as diplomatic tactics. The closer the warships are to the shore, the more vulnerable they will be to 'bee-sting attacks' from the small, fast but powerfully armed warships of coastal states and also to their shore-based aircraft. To be out of range of fighter-aircraft was the reason the US Navy wanted to push the blockade of Cuba further from the island than President

147

Kennedy thought desirable, in view of his hope of giving Khrushchev the maximum time to think and stop his ships. It was similar reasoning which in 1971 led Admiral Zumwalt, at that time CNO, to question the President's orders relating to the stationing of Task Group 74 during the Indo-Pakistan War. In Admiral Zumwalt's words:

> The first orders to TG 74 had been to go on station in the Bay of Bengal, off the East Bengal coast. I argued against stationing the ships there. I felt it was taking an unnecessary risk to put a task group without a stated mision in precisely the place where harm was most likely to befall it. I won my argument, and the group was sent south of Ceylon, where the Russians, when they arrived, promptly began trailing it. (1976, p. 368)

In view of the earlier comments about the ritualistic character of much contemporary naval diplomacy, we should not leave this episode without quoting some of Zumwalt's later remarks. For the first week or so of 1972, he records, 'the American and Russian ships circled around each other warily, much as their counterparts had been doing in the Mediterranean for years. Then, on 8 January, Task Group 74 was ordered out of the Indian Ocean as mysteriously as it had been ordered in.' What signal was being sent? Evidently Zumwalt, the CNO, was not sure. This suggests, again, that the nagging little question, 'what is it all about?' was either not asked, or not clearly answered in the White House. In addition, those who fear that creeping jurisdiction will significantly affect the timeliness of naval responses might note Zumwalt's observation that the US task group was not formed until the outcome in East Bengal was already apparent. Even in the recent past, timeliness has not necessarily been an important attribute of naval diplomacy.

Naval diplomacy can give confused signals, but it can also be used to make clear political points (Booth, 1977, ch. 2). Naturally, the signal one wants to transmit will affect the character of the naval deployment, in terms of location, force structure, behaviour, and so on. It was argued earlier that one can signal involvement without actual visibility. It is to be expected, therefore, that one can transmit a signal of aloofness and non-commitment even more effectively by avoiding actual visibility off the coasts of the crisis area. The actions of the Sixth Fleet during the Middle Eastern crisis of 1967 again provides some useful illustrations (Wylie, 1969, pp. 58–9). Any strengthening of psycho-legal boundaries at sea will help the transmission of signals of non-involvement: by not crossing particular lines, one will the more effectively transmit a message of one's desire to avoid military involvement in a situation.

In 1967 US policy for the Middle East was of a dual nature. On the one hand it was to stand aloof from military involvement if possible and to play the military role in a low key fashion in order to give maximum scope for diplomatic manoeuvre; on the other hand it was intended to be within striking distance in case circumstances changed and dictated direct naval involvement. A variety of naval actions were carried out in support of this two-sided policy. First, there were no premature departures of US warships from any port. No scheduled visits to Mediterranean ports were interrupted or shortened. The amphibious forces were deliberately and visibly maintained in the central Mediterranean, between Naples and Malta. As Wylie explained, 'This put them where everyone could see them and knew exactly where they were — a thousand miles away from the south-east corner of the Mediterranean. This signal . . . was promptly received and noted.' Finally, the main body of the Sixth Fleet was purposefully retained south of Crete, and well clear of the crisis area: 'They were over three hundred miles from Suez and at least two hundred miles from Egypt's western desert.' However, because of the role played by American newsmen and the presence of escorting Soviet ships, 'American whereabouts and actions, or lack of action, were known to all interested parties'. In these various ways, therefore, the move to readiness by US forces in the Arab-Israeli mobilization period had a variety of careful signals built into it, in which maintaining distance from the flash-point was a help in demonstrating the wish of the US government to keep aloof (Wylie, 1969, pp. 58—9).

One might conclude from the above episode that in the prosecution of a diplomatic mission by a US task force, the presence of American newsmen is more important in ensuring the *political* visibility of US warships than is any eye contact by observers in coastal states. More recently *Time* magazine published a photograph of three US carriers steaming in line abreast in the Mediterranean. It made a good picture and they looked an impressive force. But they were together in this formation for photographic reasons rather than tactical ones. When it comes to the effective employment of military power, what is needed is the subtle or not so subtle manipulation of images, and for this actual visibility is not necessary. In politics 'reality' is in the eye of the beholder.

Another argument about naval diplomacy which needs to be reconsidered is that which claims that greater restrictions in EEZs will degrade the 'presence' utility of naval forces by imposing a patchwork character on deployment patterns. This might not be such a significant or adverse development as it immediately appears. First, some operations already have a patchwork character by choice, as was evident in some of the operations described earlier (for the Baltic see Young and Sebek, 1978, p. 257). Patterns can be devised to make the appropriate diplomatic points. Secondly, if the adoption of a patchwork deployment pattern means that a collection of warships such as the Sixth Fleet could operate in some sea areas (those of its allies) from which Soviet forces would be excluded (as under a more restrictive law of the sea regime) then this would give sanctuaries from the continual presence of the shadower. Thirdly, if deployment in some zones is left to the discretion of local countries, this adds another quiver to the bow of naval diplomacy. Another boundary might inhibit, but it also adds another rung to the escalation ladder, and hence increases the flexibility of the instrument (warships) able to move up that ladder. The potential patchwork character of naval diplomacy does not therefore have fundamental implications for naval diplomacy. It does lead one, however, to consider the uses of naval arms control schemes as instruments of strategy; this will be discussed in the following chapter.

Some of the problems of warship and aircraft reaction-time in crises were discussed earlier in relation to straits. If reaction-time is thought to be all-important in a particular situation, actions should presumably be taken in advance of a crisis. Reaction-time can always be cut by keeping more forces deployed fully forward, thereby avoiding the type of delay in reinforcement which took place in the 1970 Jordanian crisis (Zumwalt, 1976, p. 298). An augmentation of forces might seem unthinkable in advance of a crisis, because of economic and other constraints, but in a more troubled world, especially one where access to resources might become more critical (Kemp, 1978, pp. 396–414), perceptions of what costs are affordable, and when, might quickly change. The oil crisis of 1973, the troubles faced by Western economies and the image of Soviet imperialism in the Third World all served to make the late 1970s and early 1980s rather more hard-nosed in the West than seemed likely a decade earlier. This change of attitude released some of the constraints on defence spending in the United States, though feelings about intervention are still affected in some quarters – but by no means all – by the sceptical attitudes left over from the Vietnam period.

As was already mentioned in relation to straits, the territorialization of the sea will help serve as a fail-safe device for naval powers. This should improve the rationality of naval diplomacy, an outcome which is important for the United States in particular and the West in general. To a degree the diplomatic potential of warships has been threatened in recent years as a result of a variety of political and economic trends (Booth, 1978, pp. 12–20). It can be argued that US warships have been used too much rather than too little and that consequently the diplomatic market has been saturated; that the credibility of US forces has been called into question by their deployment in 'unusable' situations; that their prestige has been frittered away by futile gestures; and, finally, that their employment has been ritualistic rather than relevant to the subtleties required by US foreign policy.

The use of US warships has sometimes appeared to be not so much a continuation of politics, but more the knee-jerk reaction of a *macho* leadership, what might be called the 'have-gunship-will-travel' syndrome. This habit was somewhat neglected during the Carter administration, but it was thoroughly revived by President Reagan, notably with the dispatch of the battleship *New Jersey* to the eastern Mediterranean in the crisis of September 1983. The spruced-up but aged battleship thundering at the edge of the crisis, but probably incapable of helping to resolve the historic conflict in that strife-torn land, seemed a fitting symbol of the President's own position in the crisis. Once more, the articulation of the actual political interests of the United States in the crisis, or its medium-term objectives, was not as clear or strong as its determination to exercise its authority by military demonstration. But presidents are in a difficult predicament at such times. Doing nothing is rarely a vote winner. Consequently the pressure to act is considerable. As President Ford put it after the *Mayaguez* incident, 'To do something was at least an expression of effort' (quoted by Rowan, 1975, pp. 142–3).

The knee-jerk syndrome (and reputation) has had a deleterious effect on the diplomatic prestige of the US Navy. This is of some importance for Western security at this juncture of world politics, for, despite the growing problems they face, warships still retain unique qualities in terms of furnishing the United States with flexible military options in distant areas. This should put a premium on selectivity and appropriateness of usage, in order to nurture credibility and prestige. The territorialization of the sea could assist this task by intruding a fail-safe mechanism into the decision-making process. It should encourage decision-makers to stop and think, to clarify their interests and objectives before allowing the availability of the instrument to shape the will to find it employment. In an over-armed world, with numerous wars looking for excuses to happen, no task is more important for strategists than that of asking what can and should be achieved by military force in a situation, before troops are actually committed.

Careful deliberation about objectives should guard against two possible pitfalls. First, as suggested, it should discourage the instrument from shaping the will. If a government has a powerful instrument on hand, there is always a tendency to use it, to let the instrument shape the will rather than let the aim determine the instrument (Booth, 1977, pp. 100–3). In this respect some of Admiral Zumwalt's criticisms of the White House in 1971–2 are very relevant (1976, pp. 367–8). Useful as warships are, they cannot do everything. They are no substitute for an intelligent foreign policy, nor can they always be relied upon to compensate for a bad one. Secondly, more deliberation should discourage the futile employment of one's forces;

the latter loses prestige, one of the major assets of any military service. Because of the new constraints on using force, maintaining military credibility is more difficult than the free-for-all past, when it was relatively easy to keep one's credibility up to date. In contemporary circumstances, each naval-diplomatic 'shot' must be made to count. The overall game is always bigger than the next small play, and so a navy's prestige should not be sacrificed on the altar of the perceived need, as former-President Ford might have put it, simply to 'express effort'.[4] If the usability and credibility of superpower naval forces are being questioned by sceptical taxpayers and inward-looking politicians, it is all the more important that their diplomatic potential be carefully nurtured. This is vital, because there are some functions which warships alone can perform; it is imperative that they have maximum credibility and hence impact when their political masters do really mean business. This calls for the exercise of some restraint on use in othe circumstances.

The trend towards the territorialization of bigger parcels of the sea should have the effect of forcing the naval powers to be more deliberate about what they do. From both a national and international point of view, any additional inducement to rationality is surely a development to be welcomed. The global ammunition dump might not be able to withstand the alternative.

If the political implications of creeping jurisdiction on naval diplomacy can be easily exaggerated, some of the problems of naval presence in a more restrictive law of the sea regime might be eased by various technical developments. Improvements in surveillance mean that the whereabouts of ships will be better known, however distant, and this should help signalling. Improvements in weapons range mean that it will not be necessary to operate near to shore in order to pose an offensive threat. Improvements in the speed of some types of warships may help reduce the problems of reaction-time, at least where a small force will suffice.

The new patchwork pattern of maritime jurisdiction, and its associated feelings of territoriality, will give more scope for naval forces to be used to show their support of friendly countries, traditionally an important diplomatic usage of warships. New maritime boundaries and the task of policing them will give new opportunities for practical as well as the symbolic employment of warships in supportive roles. The West African Patrol of Soviet warships is a harbinger of this possibility (Dismukes and McConnell, 1979, pp. 130–3).

When commentators discuss the visibility of the flag, the tendency is always to consider the naval flag. But states can show a maritime presence in other ways. Historically, the British merchant marine helped to show the British flag in many parts of the world, and on a daily basis it was a more regular and visible symbol of British greatness than the Royal Navy. A similar argument could be put for the Soviet Union today. With our attention distracted by their rakish warships, there is a tendency to overlook the use and utility of the Soviet merchant marine as an instrument by which they attempt to win friends and influence people (Dismukes and McConnell, 1979, pp. 317–35; MccGwire, 1981, pp. 166–7). A country's interest and presence is created by more than simply the ready availability of its warships.

In sum, this section has attempted to show that several of the intuitive expectations regarding the impact of creeping jurisdiction on naval diplomacy and naval presence are questionable, and that in some respects a more restrictive legal regime at sea might have at least neutral or possibly even beneficial effects on this instrument of policy. In the section following the argument will be pushed further, and show how the territorialization of oceans can strengthen the impact of demonstrations of naval power.

Charging the International Atmosphere

Chapter 3 introduced the idea of 'psycho-legal' boundaries at sea, the idea that UNCLOS III had shaped feelings and attitudes, as well as national claims to larger areas of the ocean. It was suggested that unilateralist drives to parcel up parts of the ocean will be legitimized by the territorialist mood of the majority of the international community; and that as state control expands over the sea, more meaning will be attached to the boundaries which will accompany the process. Nations will feel protective and sensitive − indeed patriotic − about these areas of ocean. Inevitably, this process will have an effect on the use of the sea as an arena for the demonstration of military power.

Feelings are important in international politics, though they are often ignored by policy-makers and analysts alike. At the end of August 1983 the government of Nicaragua protested to the United States against the presence of a US frigate and three destroyers close to its coast. A communiqué issued by the Nicaraguan Ministry of Defence said that the vessels were 15 miles off the Nicaraguan coast and described their presence as a sign of 'the aggressive policies of the US against the Sandinist revolution' (*Guardian*, 1 September 1983). Having the warships of another nation in areas of sea which one considers to belong to oneself, especially when relations are tense, inevitably affects national feelings, and these, in turn, will have political consequences. Herein lie the opportunities for a new era of naval diplomacy.

The role and importance of naval diplomacy is of particular relevance because the contemporary strategic era is one in which the instruments of military power tend to be manipulated by the great powers in peacetime rather than used in wartime. Strategists – in the major powers at least – are no longer preoccupied by the planning of victory in war, but by the use of the military instrument for coercion, intimidation and deterrence. 'Military strategy', in Schelling's famous formulation, 'has become the diplomacy of violence' (1966, p. 34). Or, as Robert McNamara put it shortly after the Cuban missile crisis, 'There is no longer any such thing as strategy, only crisis management' (quoted by Bell, 1971, p. 2). In this era of 'tough bargaining', 'manipulating the shared risk of war' and 'the diplomacy of violence', the naval instrument of power will be assisted by the territorialist mood of the international community, and the psycho-legal boundaries which result. The fact that warships will have to cross these boundaries as they go about their business, even though these boundaries will always be more permeable than those on land, will help to enhance the symbolism of naval diplomacy. Symbols are only important if people think they are, and as was argued earlier, we have entered a period in which a range of factors is making nations more responsive to all developments at sea, including the symbolism of boundaries.

This heightened sense of responsiveness should assist in both the supportive and coercive aspects of naval diplomacy. When warships carry out supportive tasks in the waters of friendly powers their presence will have been explicitly welcomed, and so there is little problem for the future of this type of presence mission. The definition of 'friendly waters' will be stronger. Equally, although the problems of deployment will be greater, the impact of a coercive gesture will be enhanced in waters in which the warships are definitely not welcomed. But since coercive naval diplomacy is designed to send a disturbing message to the coastal state or its associates, trespassing into 'unfriendly waters' will only strengthen the signal which it is hoped to transmit. In the case of both supportive and coercive gestures, the fact that there will be new and salient psycho-legal boundaries at sea will make the crossing of them by warships of another state all the more significant. And this significance will grow, as and when the feeling of ownership over particular parts of the ocean increases. Meaningful threats and strong commitments cannot be transmitted solely by verbal means. An 'action language' is required, for actions speak louder than words. Warships and psycho-legal boundaries can provide part of the grammar for this form of communication.

Rather than marking the end of naval diplomacy, therefore, the territorialization of the sea will only open up a new and more complex era. One positive change should be a decline of the ritualistic quality of much of naval diplomacy mentioned earlier. 'When in doubt send a gunboat' might have been good advice in an earlier period, when coastal states possessed a strong expectation that the weapon would be used unless some condition was met. But sending a gunboat, or its modern equivalent, has become less effecive in the course of time because coastal states are militarily stronger, the international milieu has changed somewhat and in some circumstances great power force is less 'usable'.[5] The expectation of the Argentine junta that Britain would not employ its task force to bring a bloody conclusion in the Falkland Islands conflict in 1982 was an example of this reduced expectation of violence. Britain's military signals were not powerful enough for Argentina's antennae, and both nations had to pay a heavy price as a result. As this and other costly episodes show, it is imperative to transmit the correct signals for the particular audience concerned. George Will has explained that Lyndon Johnson's administration conducted a war of subtle 'signals' against Hanoi, including 'finely calibrated escalations and "pauses"', although they were 'unintelligible, or perhaps just ludicrous' to the other side (Will, 1980). It takes two to make a military-diplomatic signal work.

At a time when the constraints on the use of force by the great powers seems to be greater than in earlier periods, the problem of devising tactics and signals by which to register commitment and displeasure have grown commensurately. However, by placing new legal boundaries across the paths of the warships of the naval powers — boundaries which are inevitably going to become more politically sensitive — UNCLOS III has begun a process which will provide warships with an opportunity to increase the salience of their diplomatic role. Sending a warship across a politically sensitive maritime boundary obviously falls far short of sending an army to trample over or occupy a patch of land, but it does promise to add new significance to the movement of warships.

Naval diplomacy, like all forms of deterrence, compellence, or reassurance, is essentially a psychological phenomenon. Naval diplomacy attempts to translate military movement into diplomatic influence by changes in the location, force-structure and weapons-display of warships; it is hoped that such changes will affect the perceptions of those onlookers it is intended to impress (Cable, 1971; Luttwak, 1974; Booth, 1977). At its more coercive end, naval diplomacy can be conceived as 'competition in risk-taking', to borrow Thomas Schelling's noteworthy phrase and set of ideas (1966, pp. 91–6). Coercive naval diplomacy involves the creation of an uncertainty in the minds of target governments as to where the adversary's naval activity might ultimately lead if certain steps are not undertaken. What matters is not so much the actual military significance of the action undertaken, but how it is construed by the target onlookers.

When a naval power places its warships in danger spots it creates a risk of war (however distant) through a process of commitment whose outcome is unpredictable. The naval power deliberately decides to lose some control of the situation, by exposing its warships in a relatively vulnerable position. A signal is projected that the naval power is at least willing to take one step on the escalation ladder. This might be necessary even if 'peace' is the objective, since a reputation for constant moderation might not in itself guarantee peace (Schelling, 1966, p. 41). If moderation is perceived as passivity, it might well tempt the aggressive. Feeding temptations to the ambitious does not serve the cause of peace.

Warships off hostile shores represent 'threats which leave something to chance', to borrow an earlier Schelling formulation (1960, ch. 8). Naval diplomacy is therefore a test of nerve rather than of force, with naval powers seeking to achieve their objectives by demonstrating a willingness to embark upon risky actions which could develop a momentum of their own; they risk escalating out of control. Such risk-taking makes no sense if it leads directly to general war: but likewise it makes no sense if it is completely without danger (Schelling, 1966, p. 96). By increasing the risks in these ways coercive naval diplomacy rocks the diplomatic boat; it creates a sense of uncertainty which is fraught with the danger of war. Warships thereby *charge* the diplomatic atmosphere in ways which the naval power hopes will be politically exploitable.

The symbolism of naval diplomacy can still be particularly strong in Third World confrontations, where traditional attitudes to the use of force still pertain and where there are greater expectations about the usability of force. After all, in the past these countries were frequently the victims of the naval powers. A clear example of a superpower seeking to charge the atmosphere of the international politics of a particular region was the series of naval operations which were carried out by US warships off the coasts of Nicaragua in the summer of 1983; they were the latest in a series of major US exercises in the Caribbean designed to demonstrate and hone US military power in an important and edgy region.[6] Similar activities, though on a smaller scale and in a less unstable region, were carried out by Soviet forces, including naval units, in the north Pacific in the middle of 1978. These 'war games' were seen, and presumably were meant, as a veiled threat to Japan's moves to resume peace treaty negotiations with China — a development which Moscow saw as the crystallizing of a potential anti-Soviet alliance (Whymant, 1978).[7]

An earlier illustration of the way in which naval demonstrations can charge the international atmosphere could be seen in the uncertainty which seems to have been created, for better or worse, in the minds of Iranian students as a result of US naval and military moves shortly after the hostages crisis erupted at the end of 1979. Earlier still, in 1971, some Indians seem to have become so edgy as a result of US naval preparations that there were rumours that Indian pilots had offered to fly kamikaze missions against the centre-piece of the US naval task force, the USS *Enterprise*. A more recent example, to be discussed at more length in the next chapter, was the US decision to provoke an incident with Libya in the Gulf of Sirte in August 1981. Colonel Gadafy had long represented the devil incarnate to the Reagan administration, but nothing conveyed the possible implications of that message to the Libyan leader as effectively as the conduct of war games by the Sixth Fleet off the Libyan coast, in water claimed to belong to Libya. There could be no doubt about the US message: it was written by the smoke from the burning remains of two Libyan aircraft shot down by US fighters.

In ways such as those just described, naval diplomacy charges the diplomatic atmosphere with threat, in the hope that favourable outcomes will result for the demonstrating power. In the Iranian and Indian cases it did not; and in the Libyan it is probably too soon to say. But in the former cases the US naval demonstrations seem to have provoked passions rather than to have deterred. In the case of Iran the Ayatollah Khomeini grandiloquently declared that 'The US may destroy us, but not our revolution . . . Listen to the people's slogans. For instance, AIRCRAFT CARRIERS IMPRESS NO ONE. CARTER DOESN'T KNOW ABOUT THE LOGIC OF MARTYRDOM . . . In this spirit we will solve all the problems of Iran' (*Time* magazine, 7 January 1980). Other placards had announced: 'WE WILL SINK THE US NAVY IN BLOOD' (*Time* magazine, 10 December 1979). When a naval power's bluff is called, it has the choice of escalation or frustrated impotence. President Carter, wisely, chose the latter on this occasion. Even if the deployment of warships failed to impress the Ayatollah and his frenzied supporters, it may have had a cathartic effect on American opinion.

For the most part, superpower naval behaviour in the 1960s and 1970s was very controlled. Indeed, there was so much control that superpower naval diplomacy almost became a ritual rather than a test of nerve, and still less of force. As a result of a desire to maintain crisis control – the echoes of the Cuban missile crisis are still loud – US governments have tended to neglect their opportunities to exploit crises to their advantage. Control is more important than winning. The White House rejected the possibility of a countervailing naval demonstration at the time when the Soviet Union was helping the MPLA to victory in Angola in 1975 for example. But in this as in other cases, the problem is always in knowing which crisis to exploit and which to ignore, which to simply control and which to seek to win. It is no easy matter getting the answers right, while the consequences of making the wrong choice can be costly indeed. But sometimes risks have to be taken, and the greater the degree of control and restraint involved in a superpower's naval behaviour in crises – in short, the more ritualistic it is – the less will be the diplomatic impact of that behaviour. It will merely be seen as a routine expression of interest. Obviously, it will be undesirable for the naval powers concerned if demonstrations of naval power directly lead to war: they will have failed in their purpose if they do. But they are also likely to fail in their purpose if they do not convey the idea that there is some risk of war. For unless the diplomatic atmosphere is charged with at least some prospect of violence, the episode will not provide any politically exploitable uncertainty; and so an opportunity will be missed. Crises, it should be remembered, are moments of opportunity as well as danger.

The diplomatic utility of such competition in risk-taking has sometimes been evident in relations between the superpowers, despite what was said earlier about their general record of prudence. The aggressive tactical behaviour of Soviet warships at the turn of the 1960s and 1970s led to the Incidents at Sea Agreement in May 1972 which formed part of the SALT I package. In the years leading up to the agreement, Soviet warships frequently violated the 'rules of the road' when they were operating in the vicinity of US warships. This resulted in several collisions and many more near collisions. It was a deliberate policy on the part of the Soviet Navy, and not the result of the whims of individual commanders or professional incompetence. The aim, presumably, was to charge the atmosphere and subtly change the psychological relationship between the two countries on naval matters. It worked. It was a great success on the Soviet Navy's part, for just as the missile agreements had the effect of establishing a picture of superpower 'parity' in that aspect of the military balance, so the Soviets did something to create an image of naval parity. To the extent it was achieved, it was the result of assertive Soviet naval diplomacy over the preceding years rather than any parity of capability.

If control and ritual are always allowed to predominate over the testing of nerve in superpower naval diplomacy, then the diplomatic impact of naval manouevring will decline. To restore its impact, a naval power must be prepared sometimes to behave more aggressively, and to be seen to be willing to lose a little control. This could obviously be dangerous, for it entails the risk of letting matters get 'out of hand'. And although naval diplomacy is a flexible and relatively controllable instrument, it is well to remember the occasions when the United States has become embroiled in war, by chance or circumstance, as a result of attacks on its ships. Ships in exposed positions have played a part in all but one of the major wars in which the United States has been involved in the last century (Booth, 1976, p. 12). But risks can never be totally avoided in international life, and increased tactical assertiveness may have to be undertaken in some circumstances in order to increase the potential impact of naval diplomacy. And as was suggested earlier, such an outcome will be helped by the proliferation of new psycho-legal boundaries, which will give more meaning to both supportive and coercive gestures of naval diplomacy. They will provide another rung on the escalation ladder, but without the high drama and awful consequences of failure which exist on land. They will assist in the transmission of signals, one of the greatest problems facing those wanting to engage in naval diplomacy.

The most drastic naval signal of recent years, and surely the most dramatic illustration of the interplay between naval demonstrations and psycho-legal boundaries, was the sinking of the Argentinian cruiser the *General Belgrano* by a British submarine on 2 May 1982. Although the British action exceeded the bounds of what is normally understood by the phase 'naval diplomacy', without doubt it charged the atmosphere more effectively than is conceivable by any other means, though some have questioned whether it was justified or successful from a political point of view.

Shortly after the Argentinian invasion of the Falkland Islands the British government announced it was establishing a 200-mile Maritime Exclusion Zone (MEZ) around the islands. Any Argentinian warships or naval auxiliaries found within the MEZ would be treated as hostile and would be liable to be attacked by British forces. The announcement was followed by reports that a British nuclear submarine was patrolling the area; whether one was or was not, and it now seems improbable, the reports had the effect of curtailing the activities of the Argentinian Navy. The signals of naval strategy are many and various, and what matters is not objective reality but what the target state or states believe to be true. In response, the government of Argentina used words rather than actions: it shepherded its ships to its coasts and announced the establishment of its own 200-mile defence zone off its shore and around the Falklands. It is interesting to note, parenthetically, the pull of the 200-mile limit in both cases. This precise figure seems to have been hit upon for other than tactical reasons, but the effect has been to strengthen the identification of security considerations with 200-mile zones. This has important implications for the future of EEZs. Much to the chagrin of those naval officers who are sensitive to the legal dimensions of naval strategy, the 200-mile exclusion zones in the South Atlantic have set a precedent. They have increased the prospect of 200-mile zones for security functions, and will play a part in whatever trend there is towards 200-mile territorial seas.

Just over two weeks after the MEZ was announced, the British government turned the screw more tightly. Over a period of about a week the list of prescribed activities grew, until the MEZ became a Total Exclusion Zone (TEZ); any ships or aircraft now found within the 200-mile zone would be treated as hostile. On 2 May, following the announcement of the TEZ a few days earlier, the Argentinian cruiser the *General Belgrano* was sunk by a British nuclear submarine with the loss of 368 lives (Hastings and Jenkins, 1983, pp. 148–50). Soon afterwards, Argentina took its revenge against *HMS Sheffield*. The British further turned the maritime screw by extending its war zone into a blockade of the Argentinian coast (to a distance of 12 miles). The sinking of the *General Belgrano*, with its various military and political repercussions, provoked considerable controversy, particularly in Britain itself. But whatever the rights or wrongs of the action, it undoubtedly illustrates a variety of the problems, utilities and dangers which exist on the boundary separating the exercise of naval power and the use of naval force.

The declaration of the exclusion zones and then the sinking of the *Belgrano* dramatically charged the atmosphere in the South Atlantic. The lines drawn on the map, and the actions taken in relation to them, shaped attitudes and perceptions. The British government's 'action language' demonstrated its determination far more effectively than words could ever have done. The British government showed its willingness to escalate, and so told the Argentinian junta in an unmistakable fashion that it was serious about seeing the matter through to a conclusion. Undoubtedly this determination backed by evident power contributed to the sense of fatalism which seems to have affected the Argentinian leaders and forces.

The strength of Britain's hostile signal was related to the actual line of the TEZ. It is now generally agreed that the *General Belgrano* was 35–40 miles outside the TEZ when it was sunk. This in itself carried an important message, for it seemed to tell all onlookers how ruthless Britain intended to be. If even moderate Britain could act so 'unfairly', people thought there could be no doubting its resolve. Subsequently, and as a result, the Argentinian fleet dared not sortie out of its territorial waters. Instead, it attempted to maintain some vestige of self-respect by claiming that its aircraft carrier the *Vientecinco de Mayo* needed repair.[8] Following the sinking of the *General Belgrano*, therefore, the threat to the British task force came almost exclusively from Argentinian aircraft, not warships. As a result, the commander of the British submarine which had sunk the *General Belgrano* felt justified in claiming that in the long run his attack had helped to save lives: 'Sink one and you've sunk the lot' were the words of one US defence expert (quoted by Eddy *et al.*, 1982, p. 159). He seems to have been proved right.

By sinking the *Belgrano* outside the TEZ, it has been claimed, the British government failed to get law and policy into accord, thereby risking a loss to British prestige. The basis of this argument is that there was no point in the British government declaring a TEZ if it did not intend to adhere to it. By declaring a TEZ and then seeming to violate it, Britain was damaging its reputation as an upholder of international law, and this threatened its standing in the international community. The latter was a not insignificant consideration, since the perception which other nations had of the legitimacy of the British cause was presumably related to the amount of assistance or resistance it could expect from third parties. Such perceptions are of material significance for medium powers. The counter to this argument is that when the British government announced the TEZ, it also reserved the right to take 'whatever additional measures' might be needed to carry out self-defence under Article 51 of the UN Charter. By adding this point, the British government was saying — though apparently not in words which were clear to the Argentinians — that it did not necessarily intend to confer immunity on threatening Argentinian warships outside the TEZ.

The Argentinian Navy did not give sufficient attention to the small print of the British announcement. If the Argentinian commanders believed that they were immune from attack as long as they were outside the TEZ, then they were guilty of gross incompetence, for the British declaration had not ruled out an attack on the high seas if required by self-defence. Unfortunately, the increasing range of weaponry — and it was known that the *Belgrano* had Exocet missiles — means that the area in which one might justify self-defensive actions is getting larger and larger. The Argentinian commanders should have appreciated that.

British action against the *Belgrano* has sometimes been justified according to the dictum that 'necessity knows no law'. Whatever the legal considerations involved in the sinking of the *General Belgrano*, the overwhelming factor in the minds of the British War Cabinet and its advisers must have been the military necessity of stopping a major threat to its precariously poised task force. At that stage in the war, all could have been lost for Britain had there been a major naval disaster. In the light of the dynamics of the situation, therefore, 'irrespective of the *Belgrano*'s course or destination on 2 May, it would have been militarily irresponsible not to have put out of action so substantial a part of the enemy's arsenal' (Jenkins, 1983).

Although the sinking of the *General Belgrano* might be considered to have been a military success from the British viewpoint, since it kept the Argentinian Navy at base, several voices have been raised arguing that it contributed to a major political failure. The basis of this argument is that the sinking was such a decisive and bloody act that it put an end to all possibility of a peaceful resolution of the conflict. This must obviously remain an open issue until much more is known about the state of decision-making in the two capitals and in the various locations where conciliation was being attempted. Only future his-

torians can settle with any authority whether the chances for settlement were better one week before the sinking of the Argentinian
cruiser, or one week after. With only a little hindsight, however, it
seems that it was already too late; conciliation had lost, and the
Belgrano made no difference. By 2 May, both governments had already
relearned the tragic lesson that it always seems easier to fight than to
terminate hostilities by negotiation.

Escalation can be profitable, but it is always dangerous. Although
the British government skilfully handled the interplay between diplomacy and force during the Falklands War, it was attended by good
fortune, including the presence of a rather cautious and fatalistic
adversary. Despite this, there were a few moments when some people
rightly feared that events might slip out of control, with the war
becoming more destructive than was rational for either party. The
sinking of the *General Belgrano* could well have been followed by such
a furious attack on the British task force, and such a decisive loss of life
and ships, that the British government would have felt compelled to
carry the war to the Argentinian mainland, unless it was willing to
accept surrender. But surrender was no part of the character of the
Thatcher government, and so pressing on would have been more
likely. But if this had occurred, where would it have ended? When
national passions are roused, and when the logic of events is increasingly determined by military rather than political imperatives, proportion, control and a proper sense of political objectives can be lost.
In a revealing interview a few months after the war had ended, the
British Minister of Defence, John Nott, told a reporter:

> Well, we couldn't have lost it. I mean, I knew that in the end we
> would win because we had to win. There was no way in which in
> the end we could afford to lose this. Once we had set out, once the
> task force had set sail, it was inconceivable that it could turn back,
> and it was inconceivable we could lose . . . We never doubted that
> there'd be a victory, but I confess to you that I thought we'd lose
> more ships and men than we did (Coleman, 1982).

Clearly, if this statement is to be believed, 'victory' had come to be
more important than the value of what was being fought over. In the
psychological dynamics which led to such thinking in the case of the
fight for the Falklands one hears echoes of the First World War, and
dimly perceives scenarios for the escalation of local crises into the
Third World War.

Essentially the sinking of the *General Belgrano* should be seen not as
a success for British arms, but a token of earlier failures in British
strategy. Except for the pathologically violent, force is only used in
international politics when one's own military power has not proved

credible or efficacious to achieve its objectives by deterrence or compellence. In 1982 British strategy in the south Atlantic was found wanting. Before the war, it appears that the British Foreign Office had considered that it would be too provocative to send two frigates to the Falklands in the light of its negotiations with Argentina. Provocative or not, however, the demonstration of such a commitment by 'action language' might have deterred the calamity which followed, and forestalled the need to send a whole task force. Deterrence is always costly, and can sometimes be criticized for being 'provocative' or 'intimidating', but it is always less costly than tempting aggression by impotence, and then having to try to retrieve the situation by force. Deterrence needs not only to be thought about, it also needs to be seen to be thought about. It needs not only to be done, it needs also to be seen to be done.

Among other lessons, the *Belgrano* incident showed how the spread of pyscho-legal boundaries (albeit of an ad hoc nature in the case of the TEZ) can shape diplomatic and military perceptions. Boundaries, of one sort or another, imply costs, and these very costs should, in turn, encourage deeper thought on the part of the governments concerned before task forces and naval presences are dispatched. Objectively, therefore, the increased costs should not be feared but rather should be appreciated as something which might lead to the more rational employment of warships, with more selectivity in use and fewer knee-jerk responses. As a result, the market for naval diplomacy will not become saturated, and the symbolic value of warship demonstrations will not be reduced by over-use. Any developments which discourage hasty military employment is to be welcomed, given the awesome possibilities of crises escalating in a world where military power, including nuclear power, is expected to continue to proliferate. In such circumstances, as George Kennan once put it, what the system needs is less militancy and more gardening.

From the perspective of individual states, the need is for military power to count when it is employed. The territorialization of the sea will help in this regard. By surging across boundaries into unwelcome areas, naval powers can demonstrate their commitment on an issue with rather more effect than has hitherto been possible; and this potential will increase, as the feeling of territoriality over EEZs grows. However, because of the flexibility of warships and what might be called the 'penetrability' of EEZs, withdrawal will always remain a relatively easy matter. The prospect is thus offered of more flexible escalation and de-escalation strategies. Backing down can be faced with more equanimity than if the government concerned had made a specific threat to carry out a specific action. Anything which encourages the number of steps involved in military escalation should be a moderating factor in international relations, especially since such a process should make it relatively easier for great powers occasionally to back down.

Despite the admitted problems for naval mobility which the territorialization of the sea will bring about, the relative advantages favour the West over the Soviet Union. A combination of creeping jurisdiction and maritime geography places even more disadvantages across the path of Soviet naval mobility than it does across the Western nations. This is some comfort for those who believe that the economic development and future of the Third World, as well as Western Europe, is intimately tied up with US foreign policy, and hence in the success of US strategy. Not only will the Soviet Union be relatively disadvantaged, but the process of territorialization should help nurture the credibility and prestige of the US Navy. This will be achieved by rational employment and selectivity rather than over-use; the spread of psycho-legal boundaries, which can be seen as political thresholds, will assist this outcome. Such a prospect is all the more welcome to US allies at a time when the United States appears to be on the brink of one of those bouts of interventionism which have periodically characterized its international behaviour.

LOS and the Future of Naval Diplomacy

Since the mid-1960s a number of factors have converged to focus attention on naval diplomacy. These include the expansion of Soviet naval activity, the perceived advantages of a 'blue water' strategy for the United States in the light of the Nixon doctrine, the expanded naval programme of the Reagan administration and the occurrence of a succession of regional problems tempting superpower attention short of war. The potential benefits of naval diplomacy have been evident, but at the same time the costs of exercising naval power in somebody else's maritime backyard have been growing. These costs were evident before the law of the sea raised its head in the late 1960s. The 1982 Convention has not directly added to the legal problems of naval diplomacy, though the process of UNCLOS III does promise a significant increase of problems in the long term as a result of legitimizing territorialist trends in the international community. These trends, it has been argued, pose new problems for the naval powers, but they also provide new challenges and opportunities for those who might wish to use warships for diplomatic purposes.

Without doubt, further changes in the law of the sea in a territorialist direction would complicate the execution of naval strategy. But two groups have argued that the implications of change would go beyond mere complication. One group consists of the navalist alarmists, who prophesy that a traditional and favoured instrument is about to be blunted. The other group is the anti-strategist wishful-thinkers, who see in the possible horning-in of warships a blow against the use of force in general. Those who make such claims do so partly because they pitch their argument at too high a level of generalization. Certainly the problems involved in the use and management of all kinds of military power have appeared to grow since the 1950s, but we still live in a troubled world of independent sovereign states with multiple instabilities matched by, and sometimes caused by, a proliferation of modern weaponry and military manpower. And against this background the sea is becoming a more significant political arena. One would hardly think that there is any reason to suppose that warships are about to go out of business in the foreseeable future, even were there to be a paradigm shift of the kind envisaged in Chapter 4. The problem is, what exactly is the business of warships to be? This question has placed severe demands on the intellectual and political resources of the major navies of the world, as well as aspiring or struggling medium-power navies.

By concentrating on change it is easy to overlook continuity in naval affairs; and in thinking about the break-up of an old order at sea, based on 'freedom' (for some), we risk overlooking the extent to which the years ahead will remain permissive in so far as the legal dimension of naval activity is concerned. And policy-makers and naval establishments should look at possible changes in a territorialist direction not simply as potential inhibitions on naval mobility, but also as opportunities for maximizing the diplomatic potential of warships. As was explained earlier, deployments near to foreign coasts will have more meaning, whether of a supportive or coercive character, because of the greater symbolism invested in the seaward extension of the national entity. This outcome is the logical implication of the creep of national jurisdiction over areas that were formerly international. The question is not whether the opportunities exist, but whether governments will attempt to exploit them by supplying the necessary hardware and strategic guidance.

We can take for granted that the occasion for supportive and coercive naval demonstrations will arise. And we can expect that some governments will seek to exploit the opportunities presented. In the case of the superpowers this may occasionally be for no other reason than that they already possess impressive navies which need employment. As it happens, both superpower navies have continued to do well in appropriations in recent years. Consequently, it is difficult to imagine major crises in coastal states in the decades ahead which will not have some warship involvement by one or both superpowers, however limited. At the very moment this book is being written, US warships off Beirut have moved from demonstration to bombardment, while naval 'exercises' continue to take place off Central

America in the hope of deterring further Cuban and Soviet involvement in the region. In addition to the activities of superpower navies, we must not allow the relative decline of the Western European navies to obscure the emerging navalism of regional naval powers elsewhere, and the general proliferation of modern maritime weapons systems to countries hitherto lacking any naval punch. Taken as a whole, this means that not only the opportunities for the exercise of power at sea will be present, but also the hardware; the necessary, if not sufficient, conditions objectively exist for a significant era of naval diplomacy.

The sufficient conditions for enhanced naval diplomacy will be completed by the peculiar characteristics of the disputes and conflicts which will inevitably arise in the Third World, and by the interplay of forces impinging on the decision-makers in Washington and Moscow. In this respect the prospects for long-term 'meaningful' detente appear to be slim. It will be 'peace and ill-will' rather than 'peace and good-will' (Vigor, 1975, ch. 3). Consequently the likelihood of continued jostling for position will be high.

Despite the forecast above, it may happen that the political masters of naval power will not take advantage of the opportunities offered for a more selective and salient naval diplomacy. It may be, as some have argued, that the new boundaries will impose 'psychological inhibitions' on the exercise of naval power. This is a point on which there is much scope for discussion, not least about the meaning of 'psychological inhibition'. Presumably what is meant is not an emotional reflex-action, but rather the weighing of costs by decision-makers and the decision that in some cases it will not be worth intruding into the coastal zones of particular states. But this already happens sometimes, and especially in the case of security zones. It would not be unreasonable to expect it to occur more frequently in future. The more careful weighing of costs by decision-makers, before they deploy their military assets, would not be an unwelcome development in the international arena.

In the mid-1970s Elizabeth Young prophesised the demise of naval diplomacy. As a result of the evolution of the law of the sea she foresaw that naval presence operations would be performed 'only in the territorial waters of already friendly and aligned states, others — members perhaps of a regional body like the Organisation of African States [*sic*] — being no more willing to welcome a naval contingent than Switzerland or Sweden would be to greet a regiment of Soviet tanks or a wing of B-52s' (1974, p. 262). This beguiling and much-quoted piece of writing, which implies the decreased usefulness of warships, is an important statement, but it is misleading in a number of ways.

First, while appearing to be sounding the death-knell of naval diplomacy Young's quotation actually admits the continuing value of presence forces in a supportive role. This role, in fact, was a notable one throughout the 1960s and 1970s. We need only consider the Sixth Fleet, described by one prominent Israeli as Israel's strategic reserve (Heikal, 1975, pp. 47–8), and the various supportive deployments undertaken by Soviet warships in Egyptian and Guinean waters (Dismukes and McConnell, 1979, pp. 71–2, 108–12, 130–3). We can certainly expect there to be many calls for supportive deployments in future for, as Inis Claude has argued, many of the problems of the Third World arise out of *weakness* rather than *strength*, out of *incapacity* rather than *power* and out of *helplessness* rather than *arrogance* (John, 1975, ch. 1). The weak, like the poor, are likely always to be with us, and both can either be exploited or helped. The ability of the superpowers to project military power at great distances opens up both options.

Elizabeth Young's apparent doubts about the future of the presence mission underlines the utility of warships rather than the opposite. If the supportive value of warships to 'friendly' states is accepted, the obvious inference is that the supported nation has security problems (against somebody) for which friendly warships can offer some assistance, either symbolic or practical. If this is the case, it is impossible to give credit to Young's later assertion that presence forces therefore may become a 'mere folkloristic manifestation'. Providing support to one's friends or allies against potential adversaries is hardly a manifestation of an outworn belief; it is an activity at the very heart of high politics. And it will be no less important in future than it has ever been.

Elizabeth Young's reference to the Organization of African Unity misleads by its generality and by its comparison with Sweden and Switzerland. Certainly the OAU might not 'welcome' a naval contingent, but Guinea or Angola or Ethiopia might. In fact they have. In 1978 Zaïre welcomed an intervention by Western airborne forces. The behaviour of individual nations cannot be predicted on the basis of the rhetoric of the international organizations to which they belong. Governments on the whole are far more pragmatic. The gap between the theology of the United Nations and the self-interested behaviour of its members is a regular reminder of this. Furthermore, when contemplating the future of naval diplomacy, it is not helpful to compare the political and security interests and aspirations of the members of the OAU, which belong to a fractured and unstable continent, with Sweden and Switzerland, the secure and archetypal European neutral states.

There is also a logical problem in Young's forecast about naval presence. If warships are carrying out supportive tasks in the waters of 'friendly and aligned states', they have already been 'welcomed'. There is, therefore, no problem for this type of presence mission. If on the other hand, warships are carrying out a presence mission in waters in which they are not 'welcomed', that was presumably the point and expectation of the demonstration. The action was carried out as a method of demonstrating support to an alternative position. Whether or not the warships are 'welcome' is not the issue, for it is in the nature of their business that they are sometimes not 'welcome'. The main task is to ensure that the proper diplomatic message is transmitted and understood, and as was argued earlier, restrictive trends in the law of the sea should assist in this respect. So, whether warships are 'welcomed' by coastal states or not, there will still be ample room for naval diplimacy, even under a more restrictive law of the sea regime.

There is a further important point. Regional bodies like the OAU are by no means necessarily hostile to the naval forces of the superpowers. The South American states helped to legitimize what some regarded as the illegal US blockade of Cuba in 1962, while the Arab states in 1967 and 1973 welcomed the naval support given them by the Soviet Union. And what of the OAU? Did it speak out against the Soviet warships helping Angola in 1975? And has it spoken out against the Soviet naval presence off Guinea? Would it speak out against a naval blockade of South Africa? (It certainly welcomed the British blockade of Beira aimed at ending Rhodesia's flirtation with independence.) In short, the members of the OAU and other regional bodies will always be willing to welcome external support against their local adversaries. South Africas may come and go, but regional pariahs will go on for ever.

The criticisms just listed conclude the examination in this chapter of the major arguments regarding the implications for the future of naval diplomacy of a more restrictive coastal regime. It has been seen that most of the arguments foreseeing the early demise of warships have weaknesses. Naval diplomacy would not in fact come to an end: it would only become more complicated. The maritime 'territorial imperative', and its concomitant psycho-legal boundaries at sea, will always be less immediately sensitive and further from the national nerve-endings than those on land. But this is not a disadvantage from the viewpoint of naval diplomacy. The nature of these boundaries is such that it will always be that much easier both to play chicken and to swerve away without too much loss of prestige. It will allow a face-off, as at Checkpoint Charlie, but without the same high drama and awful consequences of failure. By adding new rungs on the escalation ladder and by encouraging more rational decision-making, the new milieu of naval diplomacy should help diplomatic flexibility. It should be somewhat easier for great powers to withdraw and accept a loss, rather than seeing no alternative to pressing on. All this is to be welcomed both by the possessors of naval power and the supporters of a moderate international system.

Notes: Chapter 7

1   The potential problems in bilateral relations arising from the territorialization of the EEZ are not only 'military' or 'scientific'. Note the possibility of a paradigm shift in the economic dimension, referred to in Chapter 4, in which some states might charge tolls for the passage of merchant ships through their coastal waters, and especially choke points. From the viewpoint of international trade and harmony, there would seem to be nothing at all to commend such a trend.

2   Carriers need a considerable depth of sea, as well as width. They are generally said to need at least 60 feet of water.

3   The distinction between military 'power' and 'force' is discussed by Schelling, 1966, ch. 1.

4   To be fair to President Ford, he was aware that there was more at stake than merely the *Mayaguez*. He knew that he was also involved in a 'supergame'. His full remarks on 14 May 1975 were as follows: 'Subjectively, I was having thoughts like this: If it failed and I did nothing, the consequences would be very, very bad, not only in failing to meet that problem, but the implications on the broader international scale. To do something was at least an expression of effort, so I felt it would be far better to take strong action even though the odds might be against us. It was far better than failing and doing nothing' (Rowan, 1975, pp. 142–3).

5   The more ritualistic the response, the less its effectiveness tends to be. Mao Tse-tung, in his earthy way, put it to Edgar Snow as follows: 'Sometimes we [Chinese] have only to fart to stir Americans into moving a battleship or two or even a whole fleet.' Diplomatic impact is not enhanced by predictable responses (Booth, 1978, pp. 14–15).

6   A convenient list of such exercises was published in *Time* magazine, 8 August 1983.

7   The most comprehensive listing and analysis of the display of naval power by the Soviet Union is Dismukes and McConnell, 1979.

8   A personal note. In 1980 the Naval Institute of the Argentinian Navy published a Spanish translation of my book *Navies and Foreign Policy*. In their Foreward to this edition The Council of Directors of the Institute chose of pick out half a dozen sentences for the special attention of its readers. They were a revealing and self-effacing choice. It is difficult to imagine that a navy through which ran the blood of a Nelson would have picked out 'for second reading' my throw-away observation that warship repairs could be used as an excuse to stay on the side-lines of a dispute in the same way that diplomats use 'headaches'; or my aside that retreat and defeat are not necessarily detrimental to a government's prestige (a point which needs to be understood in context); or my adaption of Napoleon's adage to the effect that while the only thing that cannot be done with bayonets is to sit on them, this is not the case with ships, since they can be sat upon for days upon end, with the crew always busy, while the ships watch and wait to see what materialises (Booth, 1980, 'Prologo' by El Consejo Directivo). In the 1930s Liddell Hart provided an intellectual framework for a deadly aggressive strategy on the part of Britain's major enemy. I am content to think that my only direct contribution to real world strategy may have been to have provided some sort of intellectual rationalization for the exceptional restraint shown by the Argentinian Navy in the Falklands war. Argentina was not an 'enemy' of Britain's, but in 1982, inebriated by miscalculation, its military junta precipitated an unnecessary war against us. Restraint is even more precious in unneccessary wars than in those where there is no alternative but to fight.

8
The Utility of Warships

The successful pursuit of vital interests by any state is in part related to its capability and will threaten and use force, and by the way these are perceived by adversaries, allies and third parties. Real success lies in so managing one's military and non-military capabilities that one achieves one's objectives without the risks and costs of fighting. Earlier chapters have suggested that while there is no prospect of a revival of the sort of gunboat diplomacy which characterized the age of imperialism in the last century, warships will remain instruments of diplomacy for several countries, and defenders of the maritime sovereignty of many more. Before general conclusions are drawn regarding the future utility of warships, it is necessary to examine the possible implications of the changing law of the sea on three particular areas of strategic life, namely, maritime conflicts, intervention and arms control.

Maritime Sources of Conflict

Midway through the life of UNCLOS III an editorial in *The Economist* declared bluntly: 'Give men something new that they can quarrel about, and they will. The map of the world has been shaped by their quarrels: nearly all the frontiers on it were fixed by war, or by threats of war' (*The Economist*, 23 July 1977). At the stage at which UNCLOS III had reached when these words were written, the new frontiers being proposed for the sea (EEZs, and so on) were ahead of the law. Six years later, with the Convention produced by UNCLOS III hovering between widespread signing but uncertain ratification, these same frontiers now accord with the law — by custom if not by treaty. In many parts of the world the new boundaries have been settled amicably; but there have been and will be problems in other parts. And in some circumstances force and the threat of force will be used to settle them. In unglorious miniature, the Falklands War showed how badly states can treat other states, how sovereignty issues can inflame emotions, how flimsy can be the image of 'amity' between nations and how limited is the trust which states can afford to place in international law.

The range of disputes and conflicts arising from maritime causes has been thoroughly explored by a number of writers (Buzan, 1978; Osgood, 1976). It is therefore unnecessary to examine the matter in detail. It is important only to appreciate the extent and character of possible disputes and conflicts, since these might have implications for navies, ranging from the precipitating of local arms races to the shaping of the direction of procurement. Nothing concentrates the military mind so much as the possibility of conflict.

Maritime sources of conflict can be categorized in several ways:

Regionally

An area-by-area survey of disputes and conflicts relating to the law of the sea formed the bulk of Barry Buzan's invaluable monograph *A Sea of Troubles?* This survey made it clear that no continent during the life of UNCLOS III was free from fishing or demarcation disputes of one sort or another.

By issue areas[1]

Maritime sources of conflict were classified by Buzan under four main headings: disputes over national boundaries; disputes over rights within national boundaries; disputes over rights in the ocean area beyond national jurisdiction; and disputes arising from non-ocean sources. Robert Osgood, in his survey, classified the main issue areas as economic zones, commercial boundaries, straits, security matters, superpower naval interests and the deep seabed. According to Lewis Alexander, the main impact of jurisdictional claims on ocean use can be classified as follows: the use of living marine resources: continental shelf resources; deep seabed minerals; international navigation; military uses; and marine scientific research (1983, pp. 577–88). In one computation, there were approximately 331 potential boundary disputes resulting from the universal claim to 200-mile zones alone (Alexander, 1983, p. 579).

By the actors involved

Less usefully than the other approaches, Osgood categorized the possible contenders in maritime disputes and conflicts. His simple classification looked at the problem in terms of major powers versus major powers, big states versus small states and small states versus small states (Osgood, 1976, pp. 12–14).

Disputes of various type and intensity therefore abound at sea, and the international community should not be surprised if they sometimes spill over into violent conflicts. This is particularly likely when the disputes involve the ownership of valuable resources. Fish and oil are resources which are of immediate value and exploitability, and hence have and will figure prominently as sources of maritime disputes.

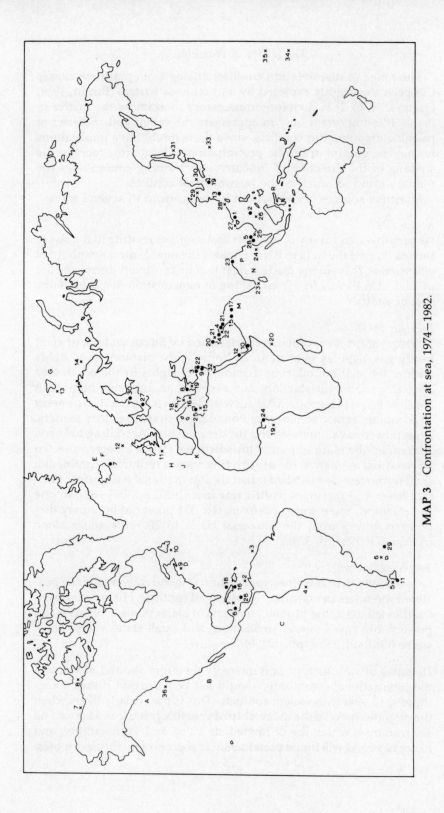

MAP 3 Confrontation at sea, 1974–1982.

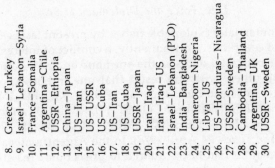

Major demarcation disputes
Key = x

1. US–Colombia–Nicaragua
2. Venezuela–Colombia
3. Guyana–Venezuela
4. Bolivia–Peru–Chile
5. Chile–Argentina
6. UK–Argentina
7. US–Canada
8. US–Canada
9. US–Canada
10. Canada–France
11. UK–France
12. UK–Denmark
13. Norway–USSR
14. Norway–USSR
15. Libya–Tunisia
16. Albania–Greece
17. Albania–Yugoslavia
18. Italy–Yugoslavia
19. Equatorial Guinea–Gabon
20. Somalia–Kenya

21. Iran–Iraq/Iraq–Kuwait
22. Iran–UAE
23. India–Sri Lanka
24. Thailand–Kampuchea
25. Vietnam–Kampuchea
26. China–Vietnam
27. Chian–Vietnam
28. China–Taiwan
29. North Korea–South Korea
30. North Korea–South Korea
31. USSR–Japan
32. Israel–Egypt
33. Japan–US
34. New Zealand–US
35. US–UK
36. US–Canada

Major fishing disputes

A US–Canada
B US–Panama
C US–Peru
D US–Canada

8. Greece–Turkey
9. Israel–Lebanon–Syria
10. France–Somalia
11. Argentina–Chile
12. USSR–Ethiopia
13. China–Japan
14. US–Iran
15. US–USSR
16. US–Cuba
17. US–Iran
18. US–Cuba
19. USSR–Japan
20. Iran–Iraq
21. Iran–Iraq–US
22. Israel–Lebanon (PLO)
23. India–Bangladesh
24. Cameroon–Nigeria
25. Libya–US
26. US–Honduras–Nicaragua
27. USSR–Sweden
28. Cambodia–Thailand
29. Argentina–UK
30. USSR–Sweden

E Iceland–UK
F Iceland–Norway
G USSR–Norway
H Spain–EEC
J Spain–Portugal
K Spain–Morocco
L Cameroon–Nigeria
M India–Taiwan
N India–Japan/USSR
P Thailand–Taiwan
R Taiwan–Indonesia

Serious naval operations
Key = ●

1. China–Vietnam
2. China–Vietnam–Philippines
3. Turkey–Cyprus–Greece
4. US–Arab states
5. US–Kampuchea
6. UK–Guatemala
7. UK–Iceland

Most commercially exploitable fish — by present tastes — lie within 200 miles of coastlines. Consequently, a conflict of interests will continue between coastal states on the one hand and non-national fishermen on the other, with the result that one might expect to see a continuation of headlines such as 'FOUR KILLED IN FISHING "WAR" OFF ARGENTINIAN COAST' (*The Times*, 3 October 1977) or 'CANARY ISLANDS FISHING CREW MAY BE IN POLISARIO HANDS' (*The Times*, 24 April 1978). In the Argentinian case the local naval commander had been ordered to press home his attack on the Eastern European trawlers fishing within 200 miles of the Argentinian coast 'to the ultimate consequences, because the defence of our sovereignty is at stake'. A navy spokesman said that this meant firing on the trawlers and then 'rescuing as many survivors as possible if they were sunk'. In the other case, the Polisario (the Saharan Liberation Front) had stated several times that it considered the waters off the coast of the Western Sahara to be part of the territory of the Saharan nation, and that it would take action to support its claim. It did. Despite the theories of a prominent group of academic writers about international politics in the 1970s, sovereignty is not going out of fashion. In coastal seas it will be the order of the day.

Population pressures (and climatic disasters) will increase the demand for the exploitation of fish. In the case of oil resources at sea one might expect disputes to grow alongside the depletion of the world's stocks of fossil fuels. This means, among other things, that small countries with claims on oil resources should not be surprised if they are leaned upon by their more powerful neighbours. Symptomatic of this problem was the way the Chinese government in early 1983 stepped up its own claims to the Spratley islands, which are situated about 600 miles from the Chinese mainland, and some of which are occupied by Vietnam and the Philippines (*Guardian*, 9 May 1983). These islands — called by the Chinese the 'Southern Sands Archipelago' — were said to form part of China's sacred territory; and the question of sovereignty was said to be 'non-negotiable'. As yet, China probably does not possess the requisite air and naval forces to take the islands quickly and without trouble, but some observers have suggested that the Chinese government's earlier interest in Britain's Harrier jump-jets might be seen in the context of the limited use of force to the south, rather than in relation to meeting the threat posed by China's northern neighbour (*Guardian*, 1 March 1979).

Even if China presently lacks the power to take the Spratley islands, its claim should not be dismissed as mere rhetoric, for as Sir James Cable has been warning for some years, 'the fashionable trend of the past decade has been island grabbing' (*Daily Telegraph*, 5 May 1982). One interesting version of this 'fashionable trend' was the suggestion by *The Economist* at the time of the hostages crisis in Tehran that the

United States should capture several Iranian-owned islands (Abu Musa and the Tumbs) as bargaining chips in their negotiation over the release of the hostages. Because of the difficulties and dangers which would be involved in any direct US military action which attempted to free the hostages, *The Economist* sought the advantages of indirect action. By capturing something of value, it argued, the United States would show the Iranian leaders that their actions were not cost free (*The Economist*, 24 November 1979, 'Our people, your islands'). For better or worse, the suggestion was not taken up; but it did underscore Cable's point. Looking to the future rather than the 1970s, it does appear that the world does not possess very many islands that are available for grabbing, that is, islands of the size, defencelessness and yet importance to make the risks of invasion worthwhile. Nevertheless, Cable's warning remains valid. Small islands do appear to be promising targets for ambitious (or insecure) superpowers and regional powers in the years ahead. Those presently with sovereignty over them should be warned. They would be well advised to look to their security.

Although resource issues seem to provide the likely cause for the most serious maritime disputes and conflicts in future, the most dramatic actual incident in the early 1980s arose over the issue of navigation rights, at least ostensibly. This incident was the shooting down of two Libyan aircraft in the Gulf of Sirte (or Sidra) in August 1981. Ironically, the incident occurred at just the time when UNCLOS III itself was going through a stormy passage in its efforts to establish a system which would try to avoid the need for such incidents.

The Gulf of Sirte incident arose out of the claim which had been made by Libya since 1973 that the Gulf consitituted 'historic Libyan waters'. These waters, which are approximately 280 miles wide and 150 miles from north to south, were generally thought by law of the sea experts to have been too extensive to justify the Libyan claim (Guest, 1981). However, foreign opinion has rarely determined Colonel Gadafy's attitudes, and Libya persisted with its claim. This was particularly unacceptable to the US government, which would not concede navigation rights in the Gulf of Sirte. Throughout the 1970s, it had been the aim of US policy to contest such unacceptable legal claims, and even during the Carter administration various countries were singled out for trials of strength; the most important of these were Argentina, Burma and Libya (*Guardian*, 20 August 1981). But in 1980 President Carter issued orders to the Sixth Fleet to avoid sailing south of the line claimed by Libya in the Gulf of Sirte, in order to avoid further Middle Eastern complications while the hostages crisis was being played out in Tehran (Winchester, 1981). The end of the hostages crisis and the arrival of President Reagan changed matters. And in August 1981 the administration decided to challenge Libya's claim to the Gulf. This decision, it can be seen, did not represent a radical change in US policy; it was only a shift from the temporarily passive position adopted by President Carter as a result of the inordinate importance which he had given to the hostages crisis.

During the course of 1981 the Reagan administration became concerned that Libya's claim to the Gulf of Sirte would become legitimized by default. If navigation rights were not exercised, they might lapse. This concern was naturally strongly supported by the Sixth Fleet command. An additional and very sharp edge to the attitude of the White House was given by the intense hostility felt by President Reagan and his entourage towards the Libyan leader, Colonel Gadafy. At that point, Gadafy was being called 'the most dangerous man in the world' (Winchester, 1981). The outcome of the administration's feelings and calculations about Libya's claim to the Gulf of Sirte was a decision to challenge Gadafy, and at the same time perhaps cut down to size those of Libya's foreign policy pretentions which the White House found so irritating. Accordingly, in mid-August 1981, a powerful force of US aircraft and ships entered the Gulf of Sirte, having given the proper 'Notice to Mariners' that a military exercise was about to take place (Winchester, 1981). The force itself had instructions to shoot back if fired upon. During the first few days of the exercise it was reported that Libyan aircraft had approached the Sixth Fleet on no less than seventy-two occasions, before being warned off by US fighters. Finally, two Libyan pilots 'believed − or were lured into believing' that they had caught two US aircraft napping. They were wrong, and the ensuing dogfight was no contest. The US F-14s quickly shot the Soviet-built Libyan SU-22s into the sea, 60 miles from the coast according to US sources, 30 according to the Libyans.

To many observers, probably most, the incident appeared to have been a well-engineered trap on the part of the White House, though some in Washington later argued that the Libyans had deliberately sacrificed their aircraft in order to have the opportunity to brand the United States as the 'arch aggressor' (Winchester, 1981). President Reagan himself insisted that it had not been the US intention to be provocative; he said that US warships had simply been doing what had been done elsewhere, and what was normally done by the warships of other nations, namely, assuring that 'everyone is observing international waters and the rules pertaining to them' (*Guardian*, 22 August 1981). A Libyan spokesman denounced such explanations. He stressed that the United States had been the aggressor, and that the presence of the Sixth Fleet in the Gulf of Sirte represented 'a great violation of our sovereignty'.

Violence had obviously been expected by the Sixth Fleet, and it had occurred. A week before the incident *Newsweek* magazine had reported that the Sixth Fleet had been ordered by President Reagan to conduct manoeuvres in the Gulf in order to test Colonel Gadafy's response. Britain, together with other US allies, had been briefed about the Sixth Fleet manoeuvres but not about the other, violent, possibilities which might arise. Like the United States and others, the British government rejected the Libyan claim to the Gulf. The Foreign Office commented that the incident appeared to have been an unprovoked attack by Libyan aircraft over what were generally recognized to be international waters. It was clearly not 'unprovoked'. By sailing into the Gulf of Sirte in August 1981 US warships were throwing down a deliberate challenge to Libya. And Libya, or some Libyans, unwisely responded. But the main fact is that the US action had been provoked in the first place by Libya's unilateral interpretation of the law of the sea. It needed to be tested, if necessary by force.

As a result of the Sirte incident the US interpretation of the law of the sea appeared to be vindicated (Neutze, 1982, pp. 26–31). Perhaps, also, Colonel Gadafy was chastened with regard to his foreign activities in general, though his policy in Chad in the following two years did not suggest that the sobering effect of the incident lasted long. But it should be said that Gadafy has always been a more pragmatic leader than is generally thought. Although in August 1981 there was some risk of a break in the export of Libyan oil to the United States, or of wider repercussions in US relations with the Arab world, these were not allowed to materialize. More to the point, in February 1983, when Libyan aircraft again approached the US carrier *Nimitz* in approximately the same area of the Gulf of Sirte as that in which the 1981 incident had taken place, they turned tail without a shot having to be fired (*Guardian*, 19 February 1983). The 1981 incident seemed to show that assertive naval behaviour can be expected against those who challenge superpower interpretations of the law of the sea, that law of the sea issues can be relatively compartmentalized and that order at sea is a widely valued norm among the international community.

If the confrontation in the Gulf of Sirte was the most dramatic manifestation of legal disputes over navigation rights in the early 1980s, the most serious actual threat to international navigation occurred in the Strait of Hormuz as a result of the Iran-Iraq War, which had dragged on, with great loss of life, since 1980. The Strait of Hormuz has often been seen as one of those flashpoints of world politics which could produce a conflagration spreading far beyond the geographical focus of conflict.

The immediate source of the danger to shipping in the Gulf arises from the repeated Iraqi threat to attack Iran's oil installations at the head of the Gulf. If these were to be destroyed, Iran has threatened to close the Strait of Hormuz in retaliation, and as was mentioned in Chapter 5, the Strait is an international waterway through which considerable amounts of oil flow to Japan, Western Europe and the

United States. While the Western dependence on Gulf oil has declined since the early 1970s — it now represents only about one-fifth of overall supplies — the amount involved is still very significant, and some countries within the Western world would be much more seriously hit than others (Japan would be much more hurt than the United States, and France more so than Britain). In addition, the closing of the Strait would breach the important principle of free international navigation. It is therefore seen to be in the general interest to maintain the passage of ships and goods through this major commercial artery.

In practice, Iran's threat to close the Strait is easier said than done. Over 21 miles wide, like the English Channel, the Strait would be difficult to block by physical obstacles, while mining or a naval blockade would be difficult against the determined opposition of the major naval powers. A more conceivable challenge, therefore, is the possibility of Iran threatening or attacking tankers in order to create an atmosphere in which their owners would be scared off. It would be difficult for the naval powers to offer such a degree of protection to shipping through convoys and other means that every merchant ship would be safe. So although there can be no doubt that the naval powers would try to keep open the Gulf to international shipping, the important question would be the degree of loss which the business community could stand before being scared off.

For the purpose of protecting shipping in the Gulf, the United States has powerful ships and aircraft in the area, while Britain and France could provide at least a token force. It would seem sensible for the naval powers to share the burden. Given the major interests of the Western Europeans and Japan in the region, there is a good case for internationalizing any attempt to keep the Strait open. And warships are not a difficult means by which a group of nations can both do a good job and demonstrate collective resolve on a general principle. Any warships used must be deployed effectively, but the naval powers should not limit their response solely to military actions; it would also be important that they legitimized their actions through the United Nations and through local institutions, notably the Gulf Co-operation Council.

In the years ahead the Strait of Hormuz will remain one of those potential flashpoints which could set the world ablaze. But it need not, if people calculate their interests carefully, use force as a last resort and place more emphasis on tolerance than dramaturgy. But such behaviour can never be guaranteed in international politics, and not least in the Middle East: the history of this region shows that the situation there is never so bad that it cannot get worse.

Trouble at sea in the Gulf would be the result of the spilling over or escalation of a bitter war on land: it would not therefore primarily be a 'law of the sea' dispute. Regarding the latter category, there now seems to be fairly general agreement that the process of regime change initiated by UNCLOS III will not result in 'chaos' at sea, involving widespread violence: the consensus is that the prospects for armed conflict are limited. Isolated acts are always possible, but large-scale conflicts are not thought to be likely. The optimism is well justified, for although the post-UNCLOS III law of the sea could be the source of disputes and conflicts over rights, there are various factors making for stability at sea. Barry Buzan has listed them as follows: crystallizing norms, the limited naval capabilities of the most states, the fact that the issues involved will rarely carry politically important emotional appeal, the relative remoteness of most disputes (which will help their encapsulation and provide various options for settlement) and, finally, the fact that few of the disputes will have immediate and significant strategic implications for the countries concerned (1976, pp. 45–8).

There are some exceptions, and these are potentially dangerous. Among the maritime disputes with serious strategic implications, those between the Soviet Union and Norway and the Soviet Union and Japan seem to be the most dangerous. In addition, the Greek-Turkish dispute over the Aegean Sea seems the most likely national confrontation which might take on a maritime dimension; it is certainly one of the most complex disputes to resolve. In this dispute, as in others, it can be argued that if the states concerned are rational, then they will use non-violent methods by which to solve their differences. It hardly needs adding that behaviour in international politics is often propelled by other than a cool calculation of interests, and the location of each of the disputes mentioned is sensitive and the parties are somewhat nervous. Following the pitiful miscalculations on the part of the British and Argentinian governments which led them into war in 1982, and the bizarre set of incidents which provided the occasion for the fight, who can feel entirely confident about a future trouble-free sea?

It would be surprising if the post-UNCLOS III world failed to produce at least several crises at sea, together with a slight increase in the hitherto thankfully low level of naval violence. This will require effective deterrence, as well as self-restraint. Governments will have to show that they intend to defend their rights in what they regard as their own patches of sea, if not beyond, and there is no more effective way of doing this than deploying warships. Warships are badges of sovereignty. As a youthful Mr Begin is supposed to have put it during the birth pangs of the state of Israel, 'I fight therefore I am'.

We cannot predict whether particular maritime disputes will take on a military character, but we would be excessively optimistic if we believed that no clashes would ever occur. The ingredients are present in many areas, in terms of interest and capability; all that is required is a triggering event. The history of international conflict shows that these are always the most difficult things to predict; one can only be sure that international politics will throw up such occasions, especially in periods of uncertainty. 'Pleikus are streetcars', McGeorge Bundy said in explaining how the Vietcong attack on an American base had provided the occasion for the US decision to bomb North Vietnam. 'If you wait long enough, one will come along' (quoted in Hoopes, 1969, p. 30).

Intervention from the Sea

Once fighting has been enjoined, one of the traditional tasks of warships has been that of projecting military power ashore in the form of amphibious operations, or, more simply, carrying interventionary forces to unopposed landings. But since the mid−1960s there has been an extensive literature pointing to the declining utility of great power intervention (Knorr, 1966 and 1977). Expressed simply, the argument is that the political, economic and military costs of intervention have risen, while the purpose for which intervention frequently proved useful in the past (bases, the control of markets and raw materials, and so on) are no longer relevant for the foreign policies of the developed world. The direction foreseen for the law of the sea appears to add yet another weight to the cost side of this argument.

Running parallel with the secular trend against great power intervention, there have been a number of contributory maritime developments. MccGwire has listed these as follows: (i) *Advances in weapons technology*. As the specialized demands of naval war have grown, so have warships become less flexible. This, he claims, makes them less readily usable as instruments of intervention. (ii) *The proliferation of modern weaponry*. The proliferation of medium-sized fleets increases the risks faced by interventionary forces. The potential targets are now better able to fight back. The proliferation of sophisticated weapons systems on land as well as sea means that naval powers must increasingly expect to operate in a hostile maritime environment whenever there is a crisis. As the British task force learned off the Falkland Islands in 1982, naval powers can no longer expect free rides at sea. (iii) *The growth of the Soviet Navy*. No longer do Western interventionary forces have a monopoly of 'blue water' naval capability. They now have to contemplate the complicating prospect of the presence of Soviet naval forces. (iv) *The evolution of maritime rights*. Creeping jurisdiction complicates naval planning and increases potential costs. In this way developments in the law of the sea have been confirming existing trends against intervention (MccGwire, 1977, pp. 3−25).

Many members of the international community would welcome the growth of any inhibitions on intervention. Therefore whatever further inhibitions are added by changes in the maritime environment would be welcomed. But intervention is not always illegitimate. It is possible to envisage occasions when justice as well as order might be served by military intervention, and occasions when maintaining the balance of power by intervention will be seen as more important than sticking to the letter of international law (Bull, 1977, pp. 142−5). The identity of non-intervention and international law is closer than that of non-intervention and justice. Nevertheless, there have been trends in the maritime environment as a whole, as well as secular trends in international relations, which have increased the costs which have to be faced when contemplating salt-water intervention.

Although some developments in the law of the sea promise to increase the costs of intervention, these remain marginal for the foreseeable future. The actions of governments in this regard will principally be determined by considerations other than the law of the sea, or even of international law in general. We should not forget the extent to which we still live in an 'anarchical society', an international system with only tenuous 'law'. We should not therefore underestimate the significance for the future of maritime affairs of 'the menacing interaction of trends' (Brown, 1977, ch. 21), 'the spectre of a new mercantalism' (Bull, 1976, p. 3; Kemp, 1978), the determination and will of superpowers to 'go it alone' if necessary (Kissinger, 1978, pp. 5−10) and the absence of a 'recognised and respected structure for conflict management' (IISS, 1979, p. 4). There are many sources of instability, and there will be many occasions when the intrusion of external forces will be seen to be to somebody's advantage. And although the threat is rising, one can still easily be tempted to exaggerate the extent to which 'the great equalizer' has arrived in the shape of midget navies with giant punches (Howard, 1976, p. 6).

International politics are always changing, but more kaleidoscopically than in a linear direction. 'Intervention is dead' proclaimed the war in Vietnam. 'Long live intervention' proclaimed some Africans in the second half of the 1970s, despite the rhetoric of the OAU. Colonialism had gone; but a form of tacit neo-colonialism seems to have arrived. The weak will always look for protectors; and the strong will always look for gain. Interventions will therefore continue to take place. But if they will not be as frequent as in the historic 'age of imperialism,' because of changing cost−benefit calculations, they will certainly be more frequent than was generally assumed during the anti-intervention mood which characterized Western thinking in the years following the American tragedy in Vietnam. The continuing 'agony of small nations' will provide frequent opportunities in the future for powerful states to intervene for ambitious purposes, to

intervene as a result of feelings of insecurity, to intervene in response
to requests, to intervene to pre-empt another's intervention, and to
intervene to maintain the principle of non-intervention. Intervention
in international politics seems to follow a cyclical pattern. At present
we seem to be in for a season of it, with political threats and economic
prizes existing against a background of regional instabilities in many
parts of the world. The superpowers are edgy, their field of competion
is global and their military confidence is greater than ever in the case
of the Soviet Union and greater than for a decade in the case of the
United States.

The Arms Control Dimension

One manifestation of the tense relationship between the superpowers
since the late 1970s has been that the process of arms control has
collapsed in disarray. Although it was one of the brightest and best
innovations of the 'golden age' of contemporary strategic theorizing
in the early 1960s, arms control has steadily lost its way since the mid-
1970s. SALT II did for the theory and practice of arms control what
Vietnam had done earlier for the theory and practice of limited war.

Despite its poor record, arms control remains a popular idea.
'Public opinion' supports it, because it seems to promise more security at less cost, while governments pursue it for propaganda reasons
more than any confidence that it will lead anywhere. The record
suggests that there is plenty of reason to be cynical. Nevertheless,
there is still enough substance in the idea of arms control and certainly its potential benefits, to justify further efforts, though these
efforts, if they are sensible, will be low-key and without inflated
hopes. If mutually satisfactory arms control agreements can be
reached, they could contribute incrementally to a more stable and
relaxed international community. Restraining the growth or deployment of weaponry is not a panacea for the problem of international
conflict, but it is an approach which cannot be ignored by those who
wish to ease the mistrust which exists between states. Whether such
measures are better done formally or informally, or multilaterally or
unilaterally, is too big a question to be tackled here, though it is
evident that in practice the superpowers will prefer the formal and
multilateral route.

If arms control is to prosper in future, rather than exacerbate superpower mistrust (its main role since the late 1970s), it is incumbent
upon strategists to rethink their approaches. In particular, it would
seem beneficial to try to move in small rather than in big steps, and to
try to move in nebulous and non-quantifiable areas such as 'confidence building measures' rather than to try to reach agreement about

ever-more complex 'balances' of weapons. Furthermore, in order to create momentum, there might sometimes be advantages in moving towards peripheral areas rather than remaining entangled with ICBMs and SLBMs, where the superpower strategic dialectic is at its most complex and symbolic. With these thoughts in mind, there might be some value in reopening discussion about arms control at sea, although immediate prospects for agreement do not seem any stronger than in other areas of the subject.

Elizabeth Young has described one 'unavoidable side-effect' of UNCLOS III as 'substantial new constraints on military activity at sea'. She dubbed these constraints – in a phrase commended earlier – 'a kind of de facto arms control not specifically intended or designed as such' (1974, p. 262). Hedley Bull found this insight 'hard to deny', though he added the reservation that the idea might underestimate the determination of the great powers to protect their interests by force if necessary, and that it overlooked the possibility that some regional powers might change their ideas about naval power when and if they acquired 'blue water' fleets of their own (1976, p. 9).

On first sight, the tendency to confine military activities to particular areas – the 'patchwork' implication of the law of the sea discussed in Chapter 7 – does appear to be a form of arms control, namely, 'restraint internationally exercised on . . . deployment' (Bull, 1961, p. ix). But here, as in other respects, arms control is rarely as straightforward as it appears. For one thing, although something described as 'a kind of de facto arms control' might sound self-evidently desirable, it should be noted that there has grown up a real uncertainty within the strategic community about the value and meaning of arms control. In comparison with the verities of the early 1960s, arms control is now regarded more sceptically. To many observers, the SALT negotiations stimulated mistrust and arms racing, and the agreements reached channelled procurement rather than capped arms competition. As a result, arms control is easier to define than to recognize in practice. To label something 'arms control' often begs more questions than it answers. Indeed, despite the continuing popularity of the idea of formal arms control, it may be an idea which is simply out of season in the international milieu of the 1980s.

As well as being out of season, some forms of arms control are not self-evidently desirable. In opposing the idea of a completely demilitarized seabed, for example, Laurence Martin has argued that the presence of bottom-based sensors would be an important source of confidence-building in any agreeement designed to enhance seaborne deterrence by prohibiting the trailing of SSBNs (1967, p. 36). More generally, the possibility exists of arms control agreements in which one side might secure a unilateral advantage, or arms control

183

negotiations in which both sides are tempted to engage in heavy arms racing in order to amass bargaining chips. Arms control policy can be nothing more than a continuation of the arms race by other means.

Although a more patchwork character to naval deployments would tend to support the standard definition of arms control, this would in no way diminish the essential strategic utility of warships. The sea still uniquely provides large-scale military access to distant regions, and, when the chips are down, vital interests are what count. In war and crisis arms control agreements and law of the sea conventions count for relatively litle. At that point one should recall the updated comment of Sir Charles Webster used in chapter 4 (p. 75 above).

As well as the law of the sea intruding into arms control, the opposite may sometimes be the case. Some arms control treaties have implications for the law of the sea. In addition to the Seabed Treaty, discussed earlier, there is the Nuclear Test Ban (1963), and the Latin American Nuclear Free Zone (1967)[2]. The related concept of 'zones of peace' has direct practical implications. The establishment of 'zones of peace' – though not presently likely[3] – could affect operational patterns. However, the increased range of SLBMs, together with the limited role of nuclear weapons outside the US–Soviet context, means that the establishment of zones of peace would not be of major strategic significance outside the Mediterranean, as long, that is, as any agreement was restricted to nuclear weapons and did not include nuclear propulsion.

Arms control and the law of the sea overlap at various points; most importantly, both can be conceived as extensions of naval strategy. But maritime arms control has not flourished since the 1920s, though in the 1970s both the Mediterranean and the Indian Ocean were the objects of some (albeit limited) attention. Several developments led the Carter administration to worry that the Indian Ocean might become the scene of costly and dangerous naval arms competition, comparable with the Mediterranean. This led to some consideration of naval arms control in the region (Haass, 1978, pp. 50–7). But with military build-up being the order of the day around the Indian Ocean in the early 1980s, in the aftermath of the Iranian revolution, the Soviet intervention in Afghanistan and general uncertainty in the Gulf, the prospects for any sort of maritime arms control are not good. As of 1983 there seems to be no immediate likelihood of any resumption of naval arms limitation talks on the part of the superpowers, while the local nations themselves do not appear interested in controlling or reducing their own forces by multilateral agreement. A rhetorical commitment to the idea of an 'Indian Ocean Zone of Peace' will doubtless remain, but nobody expects substantive movement in this direction within the foreseeable future.

If the possibility of further militarization justifies the consideration of arms control schemes for the Indian Ocean, the argument is already overdue with respect to the Mediterranean. In fact, over the years various ideas have been mooted for the Mediterranean, though none has come to fruition (Blechman, 1975, esp. ch. 4). The most frequently discussed scheme for the Mediterranean is one involving the disengagement of superpower naval forces. There are features in the situation which suggest that rather than maintain the cold war concept of permanent naval presence, the United States should be thinking about a reduced presence (or a mutual withdrawal by treaty) for normal times, thereby permitting a surge in the event of crisis. This would help maintain the value of the capital of naval diplomacy, by increasing in political salience what would be lost in reaction-time. In such a scheme, naval strategy, the law of the sea and arms control could usefully and effectively walk hand-in-hand (Booth, 1979b, pp. 28–35).

There is another area where maritime arms control and trends in the law of the sea could overlap and produce a yet more radical outcome: this is in the area of strategic ASW, which seeks to control those activities which threaten the stability of deterrence by the development of systems which are successfully able to track and destroy missile-firing submarines. Although the moment does not seem propitious for pursuing such a far-reaching idea, there are several good reasons for addressing ourselves to the unthinkable in this area of strategic affairs (Booth, 1981, pp. 14–18). First, experience suggests that when a chilly period of international politics gives way to a relaxation of tensions, this may be a productive time for arms control proposals, and new ideas might be more acceptable than warmed-up old ones. Secondly, the arms build-up on the part of both superpowers is presently proceeding at a pace and in directions which show that strategic rationality is outrunning political wisdom; in such circumstances it is by no means too soon to begin working to shape the decisions which might be made in the second half of this decade about the weapons with which the superpowers will confront each other at the start of the next century.

The prospect of securing international agreement to control strategic ASW appears to be limited in the immediate future. Strategic ASW is a topic on the arms control agenda, but it has a very low priority. During the later stages of SALT II it was sometimes suggested as a possible issue for negotiation in SALT III, with the aim of making deterrence more stable. But SALT III did not come to pass, and the idea dropped from sight in the anti-arms control atmosphere of the early 1980s. Nevertheless, the issue of strategic ASW did briefly resurface at the beginning of 1983, when a long leading article in *Pravda* listed a set of Soviet proposals for the START talks. These proposals included, in addition to the more obvious ones concerning the 'balance' of strategic nuclear weaponry, the idea of establishing safe zones for submarines. These would be areas in which all anti-submarine activities by the other side would be banned (*Guardian*, 3 January 1983). The Western response was cool to the whole *Pravda* package.

There are many obstacles confronting the various schemes which have been suggested over the years to control strategic ASW. Never-theless, this is an issue which is worth exploration, since a suitable scheme could curb the arms race and enhance strategic stability. One scheme which is of direct relevance to the present discussion goes under the acronym ASWEEZ and involves a close association with the law of the sea. The scheme is based on the idea of prohibiting ASW activities in the EEZs of the superpowers for all but their own and allied naval activity (Booth, 1981, pp. 14–18).

If the ASWEEZ scheme were to be put into operation, it would give an enormous boost to creeping jurisdiction. It would greatly enhance the international significance of the EEZ by closely identifying secu-rity interests with the 200-mile limit. It would also involve some concession on the part of the superpowers on the important principle of their complete freedom to deploy their warships in all the EEZs of all countries. Together with other obstacles, such as the problems of verification and enforcement, these legal implications mean that the prospects for the ASWEEZ scheme or anything similar are remote. But as the costs of submarines escalate, and as steady progress continues in the multidirectional efforts of the superpowers in ASW measures, the attractiveness of SSBN sanctuaries will grow. Sanctuaries should mean that the costs and vulnerability of submarines will be lessened, since effort could be redirected away from underwater leviathans like *Trident* towards SUMs (Shallow Underwater Mobiles), where the in-vestment is in the missile rather than in the launch vehicle. Given the potential strategic advantages of such a scheme, the price paid in law of the sea terms might come to appear to be relatively low. In any case, as the range of SLBMs increases, and as ASW techniques progress, it is already apparent that SSBN sanctuaries are developing in a de facto sense, because of the protection able to be offered against hostile ASW forces by one's own forces in one's own contiguous seas. The 'de-fended bastions' for Soviet submarines in the Barents Sea is the best example of this trend (MccGwire, 1981, pp. 149, 153).

We are moving towards the point when the next step in controlling strategic ASW will be only a short one. There might well be political as well as strategic advantages in taking that step in the years ahead, when and if the superpowers, in an ameliorating international atmos-phere, begin to look for worthwhile ways of signalling reassurance. Like deterrence, *détente* must not only be done, it must also be seen to be done.

The Law of the Sea and the Assets of Warships

Of all weapons systems, warships have usually been thought to possess special and indeed unique characteristics in terms of their diplomatic usefulness.[4] Oliver Cromwell called a man-of-war his 'best
Ambassador'. There are various ways of describing the assets of warships. One is as follows (Booth, 1977, pp. 33–6): *versatility*, their
ability to perform a variety of tasks; *controllability*, their escalatory and
de-escalatory potential; *mobility*, their ability to move between
regions with relative ease and relative independence; *projection
ability*, their efficiency as bulk carriers of manpower and firepower;
access potential, their ability to reach distant locations – 'The sea is
one', as the old Admiralty maxim had it; *symbolism*, arising from the
fact that warships are chunks of national sovereignty; and, finally,
endurance, the staying power of warships which enables them to be
adjacent to a problem but removable, but also removed but commit-
table. If these are the traditional assets of warships, it remains to
examine the possible effects on them of territorialist changes in the
law of the sea.

Versatility

This would be unchanged by a more restrictive regime. Of all the
weapons systems in a country's inventory, warships are still the most
versatile, although it is undeniable that some tasks are now better
performed by aircraft because of the need for instantaneous response.[5]
This was the case with the Western response to the crisis in Shaba
Province in 1978, but the potential versatility of warships will remain
unchanged as a result of any law of the sea developments. If the
versatility of warships does become more limited, it will be more the
result of the decision of planners to opt for 'task-specific' vessels, or
because of foreign ministries opting out of opportunities.

Controllability

For reasons discussed earlier, the escalatory aspects of naval diplomacy will be assisted by restrictive changes in the legal regime.
Increased distance will assist withdrawability, while the new boundaries will add another rung in the escalation ladder, so aiding the
flexibility of the instrument. To marry the phraseology of Francis
Bacon and Thomas Schelling, warships will still be able to take as
much or as little of the diplomacy of violence as they wish.

Mobility

There are threats of restriction here, though in practice a mixture of
diplomacy and resolution should overcome most problems at an
acceptable price. Whatever the new legal restrictions on movement,

warships will remain uniquely able to project large amounts of pre-packaged firepower to distant regions within a relatively short time.

Projection ability
When 'vital interests' are engaged, the use of the sea becomes a matter of capability rather than law. In both peace and war the payload of warships enables naval powers to be relatively independent military powers outside their own regions. Britain − for better or worse − could not remain a power to be reckoned with in the South Atlantic without the possession of surface naval forces.

Access potential
Changes in the law of the sea which may affect maritime access constitute the biggest threat to the traditional usefulness of warships. But even if there were to be new obstacles to naval mobility, it would still remain true that the movement of sizeable armed forces across the sea will always be easier than over land or in the air. Potentially, a country with a navy will remain a military neighbour to all countries with coasts. It follows therefore that if a 'superpower' is a country with global interests, a global naval capability is fundamental for protecting and enhancing those interests. Despite the new problems confronting the exercise of maritime power, those states wanting to be global or regional military actors have little alternative but to provide themselves with the offensive and defensive potential which warships provide.

Symbolism
The role of warships as visible signifiers and representatives of a country's intentions and commitments is likely to be enhanced by territorialist trends in the maritime environment. These trends will make the sea an area in which issues of legitimacy will become more important, and hence the increased symbolic potential attaching to the movement of chunks of national sovereignty. In addition, in a more general sense, the symbolic use of military instruments has grown in significance in inverse proportion to the costliness of using naked military force.

Endurance
Technology has increased the potential endurance of warships: economic considerations on the other hand have tended to work in the opposite direction. The potential staying power of warships will remain one of their advantages, but to the extent any changes in the law of the sea increase distances from and complicate access to bases, to this extent it will diminish the efficiency of men and ships.

In summary, we can conclude that changes in the law of the sea in a territorialist direction threaten some of the basic assets of warships but promise to enhance others. All the old liabilities of warships remain, but here again changes could have a two-edged effect. Some liabilities may be increased (notably the problem of timeliness) while others may be lessened (the responsiveness of potential targets to naval diplomacy would be increased as a result of the new significance of maritime affairs). As diplomatic instruments, warships will continue to be valuable, indeed unique assets. Problems of cost and usability are growing, but warships retain special characteristics which cannot be ignored by those states with the interest and economic capacity to use the sea in extensive ways. In this respect, the trend towards a *mare clausum* poses problems for navies but it also provides new opportunities.

Some of the established ideas about the utility of warships have been under scrutiny in recent years (Booth, 1977, ch. 9). The business of adjusting military means to political interests has been difficult for the traditional naval powers. Technological, political and economic changes affecting the maritime environment have left the old answers about the utility of navies in a state of flux. However, this breast-beating uncertainty has almost exclusively been a concern of the Western maritime nations. Any uncertainties in the Soviet Union have not been overt and Admiral Gorshkov's victory in the debate on resource allocation in the mid-1970s shows that the issue was resolved in favour of those who recognized the utility of naval power. Meanwhile, the increasing potential of the navies of middle and smaller powers seems so adequately to meet their needs in using the sea that there is little questioning of the costs and potential benefits of warships. The turning point in the naval histories of the former monopolist naval powers occurred because some of the foreign policy goals for which navies had always played an essential supporting role — especially those concerned with colonialist responsibilities — either changed or disappeared. This brought into question the character of naval needs. Additional complications have arisen because of the improbability of general war and the uncertainties entailed in the proposition that in the modern world, naval strategy, like other forms of strategy, is less concerned with contributing to victory in war than with furthering national interests short of war.

When considering the utility of warships, an important distinction must therefore be made between those few states wishing to use their navies in support of foreign policy in distant seas, and the majority of states interested in exercising naval power only within their 'own' waters, however defined. There is little evidence that the many small-navy countries are dissatisfied with the return they receive from the money they invest in ships. Law of the sea developments pull in two ways. On the one hand they encourage a form of mini-navalism: there are new EEZs to be patrolled, there is good order to be maintained and there is the badge of maritime sovereignty to be displayed. On the other hand, the same developments pull in the opposite direction: new norms discourage others from trampling on new-found rights, and therefore tend to alleviate some naval concerns.

Whatever type of state we are considering, the costs of military power are more obvious. Furthermore, governments tend to be more aware of a wider range of alternative instruments than in the distant past. But this does not mean that military power is without utility. For one thing, the rising cost of war increases the value of military power for deterrence. Hence the non-acquisitive utility of military power has increased rather than declined. As far as the acquisitive uses of military power are concerned, it is evident that between smaller countries there are fewer of the military inhibitions which have come to characterize relations between the great powers. For the most part their conflicts will be land-oriented, but in some cases war at sea will have a role. In future it may well be that stories about naval battles will be written by the historians of such countries as India, Iran, Iraq, Israel and Brazil rather than those of the traditional naval powers. For the major naval powers the deployment of power at sea will be more a matter of deterrence and diplomacy than of brute force, at least in their relations with each other. Interventions against smaller powers will still take place, but not as readily as in the past. And one of the reasons for the declining utility of old-style military intervention on the part of the great powers is directly related to the increasing utility of the defensive military potential of smaller countries. But as the Falklands War showed, and the shelling of parts of the Lebanon by units of the Sixth Fleet in 1983, the violent projection of force from the sea is by no means dead.

Although its effects have been rather limited, developments in the law of the sea have had some impact on the question of utility. They have served to enhance the significance and hence the utility of warships for constabulary functions of all types of states, as will be discussed in the next chapter. For the rest, regardless of developments in the law of the sea, it could be argued that navies would still have had decreasing utility for the great naval powers in an acquisitive sense, but that they would have additional utility for all states in enhancing the non-acquisitive functions of military power. Since most states are satisfied with using their navies for constabulary functions and non-acquisitive roles in regional seas, this suggests that their warships have no need to fear for future employment.

Despite the growing problems they face, the major naval nations (the producers rather than the consumers of international order at sea) cannot escape from their military responsibilities without risk. As far as their navies are concerned, this means that there will always be a pressure for them to modernize as long as they have interests in using the sea and wish to support policy in distant regions. There is no evidence to suppose that they will cease to want to do such things. While many states will be interested in a practical sense only in what happens immediately off their shores, perhaps up to 12 miles, many others will be interested in what happens beyond, up to 200 miles. Whatever a particular state's attitude to the ongoing regime at sea, whether it wants to challenge it, suffer it, defer to it, or enjoy it, its ability to threaten and use force at sea will have some bearing on the responsiveness of other states to its diplomacy on maritime-related matters. Although force may be far in the background of a particular relationship, there will be some issues, and especially those of a maritime nature, in which one country's assessment of what another can do in a naval sense will greatly affect its expectations, calculations and subsequent policies.

Notes: Chapter 8

1 Map 3 shows the major confrontations at sea between 1974 and 1982, the period covered by UNCLOS III. There were many other minor disputes and conflicts. For an overloaded but useful map covering the whole range of conflicts at sea in the post war period, see *The Times Atlas Of The Oceans*, 1983, pp. 190−1. In all, 180 incidents are identified. Between 1952 and 1958 there were 32 peacetime incidents, but these had risen to 49 between 1973 and 1979. The number of states involved in the two periods rose from 51 to 86. The greatest number of involvements by flag, as victims or assailants, were as follows: USA 73, UK 44, USSR 24, China 14, Israel 14, Egypt 12, France 12. The regional distribution incidents was: Mediterranean and Middle East 63, North-East Asia 27, South-East Asia 25, Caribbean 20.
2 In the Nuclear Test Ban Treaty the parties agreed not to carry out nuclear weapons test explosions under water, as well as in the atmosphere or in space. China and France are not parties. The Latin American Free Zone involved the parties agreeing to forbid in their territories the testing, manufacture, production and acquisition of nuclear weapons. The area covered by the agreement includes the territorial seas of the parties, which is theoretically out to 200 miles in the case of those countries such as Ecuador which have extensive claims. Argentina, Brazil, Chile and Cuba are important non-parties. In addition to these treaties with implications for the law of the sea, the only other arms control agreement with a maritime dimension is SALT I (1972). The ABM agreement ruled out sea-based anti-ballistic missiles, while the 'Interim Agreement' put limits on the numbers of sea-based ballistic missile launchers.
3 For a sophisticated analysis of the problems and prospects (not good) of the 'zone of peace' concept in one major area, that of the Indian Ocean, see Buzan, 1981, pp. 194−204. The worrying Soviet submarine activity discussed in Chapter 6 should undermine one's confidence in the idea of the Baltic as a 'sea of peace'.
4 This point is definitively made by the Appendix 'Sixty years of gunboat diplomacy' in Cable, 1981, pp. 193−258. The second edition of this book brought up to 1979 this invaluable listing of the 'political applications of limited naval force'.
5 For this reason there is something to be said for giving renewed attention to artificial islands as staging posts, and the military uses of amphibious aircraft − water being 'the only self-sealing runway material' (MccGwire 1978).

9

Naval Policy and Plans

In practice, the law of the sea has never been as complicated as international lawyers have made it appear. Had it been, then generations of merchant captains and naval officers could scarcely have been able to make a living at using the sea. That said, there is no doubt at all that the law of the sea has become both more important and complex in the course of UNCLOS III. When today's naval captains were junior officers, it usually did not matter where they placed their warships in peacetime – if they belonged to the Anglo-American monopolist powers – but this is no longer the case. The new psycho-legal boundaries and their associated regulations now impose a variety of new problems and responsibilites. As a result, the law of the sea has to be given more prominence in the formulation of naval policy and plans. But for many years to come – until a paradigm shift occurs in the peacetime use of the sea – the naval interest will have greater impact on shaping the law of the sea than the law of the sea will have on shaping the naval strategies of the great powers.

Changing Tasks

Much of the discussion about the law of the sea suggests that one effect of UNCLOS III has been and will be to promote a variety of new tasks as well as new laws for old navies. However, it can be argued that what is happening is a change of emphasis rather than the arrival of new tasks, and that a change of emphasis would have happened regardless of UNCLOS III.

Among the new law-related tasks, the main focus of attention has been on policing or constabulary responsibilities in coastal waters. 'Sovereignty protection' has become a priority mission.[1] The rationale given to this task by law of the sea developments is readily apparent, but pollution, economic exploitation and increased traffic would have pushed matters in this direction in any case; in fact, there might have been more emphasis on this task in an unregulated situation marked by determined unilateral claims. The need for good order in coastal waters would have existed independently of any change in the law of the sea. It might therefore be argued that there would have been even more trouble at sea in the absence of the EEZ concept, as a result of more disputes over rights; if this is the case then some states will have fewer requirements for naval forces than they would otherwise have had. In short, UNCLOS III let some states off the hook in a naval sense.

To a greater or lesser degree, the changing regime has affected naval requirements. The creation of new rights and responsibilities over larger areas of sea creates requirements which did not previously exist. Although these do not necessarily have to be met by new re-sources (only a re-allocation of the old), several factors do encourage at least a token effort: for warships, as was mentioned earlier, are badges of sovereignty. The most useful law, of course, is that which is self-enforcing. But such a situation normally requires a common morality among those to whom the law applies. However, this is not the situation in international politics. In some cases international law will be self-enforcing — most states do have an interest in being law-abiding — but sometimes it will be a case of 'no policeman, no law' (McConnell and Kelly, 1973, p. 451). Where this is so it is the job of governments to provide policemen, to show that there is law and that it is backed by political will. This occurred in 1977 when the EEC demonstrated firmness in support of its new licensing system for fishing by non-member states in its 200-mile zone. Without firmness, backed by a maritime policeman, who can doubt that the harvesting of the seas by Soviet and other Eastern European fleets would have continued?

The acquisition of maritime badges of sovereignty by less devel-oped countries will be assisted by the superpowers and other devel-oped countries looking for outlets for their naval armaments. At the same time, the existence of so many regional security problems will encourage those states unable to cope to call for support in the shape of naval aid, equipment, advice and even direct help. There will there-fore be plenty of scope for a maritime version of the military aid assistance already extensively employed for land and air forces, and internal security. This sort of development is already evident in the navies of some of the smaller naval powers of the Indian Ocean. There is a ten-year US-designed Saudi Naval Expansion Program, for example. It involves the development of a Naval Academy, an attempt to improve the training of Saudi naval officers and the creation of an improved logistic and servicing infrastructure. Typifying the im-provement of the skills possible in embryonic navies under the influence of developed states has been the progress which Omani officers have made. Their professionalism has developed under British tuition and they have proved capable of taking over posts in their navy hitherto filled by foreign, mainly British, personnel. In the case of the Omani Navy, as in others, foreign officers can sometimes play a big part in the improvement of professional standards. A less well known example has been the role played by Pakistani officers and petty officers in the development of navies of several of the smaller Gulf states (Booth and Dowdy, forthcoming). Any opportunity to expand influence through such forms of naval aid is likely to be welcomed by most countries, but especially the superpowers.

The trend towards the jurisdictional fragmentation of coastal seas will be strengthened not only by the developing naval skills of coastal states, but also by the punch being given by some types of small warship. Some countries will undoubtedly be too preoccupied by other matters to make more than the most token naval effort, but others will take it very seriously. Buzan has drawn attention to a very important difference of perception in this respect between developed and less developed states:

> whereas a developed state would tend to look upon enforcement as a technical problem, a less-developed state may not have that option. Where it is physically unable to police its zone ade- quately, its government may have to resort intermittently to more drastic political or military action in order to influence violators. One might therefore expect that developing countries would tend more towards extreme actions, such as violent seizures of vessels or disruptions of political and economic relations, than would more powerful developed states (1976, pp. 46–7).

If the conclusion to be drawn is that naval power encourages maritime responsibility, the important implication is that the proliferation of modern naval vessels to less developed countries can be an act of international responsibility.

Some pressures are therefore encouraging some coastal defence forces to become more like 'real' navies, for some EEZs cover consid- erable amounts of ocean. On the other hand, some wider pressures have constrained some former great navies to become more like coast- guards. These wider pressures mainly arise out of the sheer cost of maintaining sizeable 'blue water' navies, together with a decreasing need for distant water operations as a result of withdrawals from empire. While this latter process was taking place, new requirements in coastal areas were building up. The superpowers alone were able to pursue both options. On the one hand they had the will, interest and capability to contemplate extensive global efforts, while on the other hand they already maintained impressive coastal forces. New atten- tion was naturally drawn to the constabulary role, but the super- powers could not avoid having the basic shape of their naval forces fixed by general war requirements.

Although the general war missions of navies are difficult and im-

194

probable, naval forces have come under unduly heavy criticism for their alleged lack of usefulness at the highest levels of violence in major war. This is an unreasonable criticism, but one which has been badly dealt with by naval establishments. Certainly warships will find it extraordinarily difficult to carry out their missions in nuclear war, but are they any different from tanks or aircraft once nuclear weapons start flying? In nuclear war warships will fare no better or worse than anything else; they will therefore be no more or no less useful – or useless. In general war, all the traditional military missions become a nightmare. The law of the sea is essentially irrelevant at such levels of violence except to the extent that any peacetime inhibitions on ASW, oceanography, or geographical familiarization will degrade operational capabilities and skills.

The debate about the future of major navies is sometimes framed in relation to the 'hi-lo mix'. The bulk of discussion suggests that law of the sea developments are likely to confirm the trends at the 'lo' end of the spectrum. It was argued earlier that the legitimizing of coastal rights by international agreement will tend to reduce any sense of urgency at the 'lo' end (for most countries), while continuing general war requirements (together with some fairly bad scenarios regarding threats to sea lines of communication) will continue to draw much attention to the 'hi' end of the spectrum for the superpowers but few others. It was evident from the discussion of maritime disputes and conflicts that there will be plenty of problems in the middle range – arising out of such considerations as the new navalism in several parts of the world, continuing regional conflicts and increased opportunities for naval diplomacy. This suggests that the ships conceived for the 'hi' end of the spectrum should also have built-in flexibility for employment in the middle level. This inevitably implies a continuing need for aircraft carriers. The practical proof of this was fully brought out by the Falklands War. Without its remaining 'carriers' Britain would have been unable to have recovered the islands. This experience also seems to have confirmed – for the states able to afford them – the value of 'big' as opposed to 'small' carriers. Britain could have done with the former but only had the latter, and not in any number. As on so many other occasions in the past, its forces had no alternative but to make the most of what they had. They coped and improvised magnificently, and turned a costly politico-strategic failure on the part of the British government into a great military victory, albeit a costly one in view of the prize.

By pushing out the naval interests of new states, by promising to enhance naval diplomacy and by helping to create some maritime-based disputes, the present state of the law of the sea leads to the following conclusions regarding future naval tasks. It adds to complications to almost all tasks; it lets some countries off the hook; it adds renewed emphasis to existing trends at the lower end of the spectrum; it has no effect on the higher end; and finally, most interestingly, it promises to draw more attention to the 'middle' or 'grey' part of the spectrum in the 'hi-lo' debate.

Technical Requirements

If the emphasis in naval activity in the years ahead is to be on deterrence, demonstration and enforcement, there will be important implications for the shape and technical character of maritime forces. However, when we examine the problem in detail we can see that the shape of maritime forces will not be significantly changed as a result of law of the sea developments as such. All that can be said is that these developments have crystallized thinking and helped accentuate some existing trends. In the mid-1970s when coastal states began to face up to the realization that the changing law of the sea would entail the need to patrol greatly expanded areas, there was a tendency in some parts to exaggerate the quantity of warship-building which would be needed, and to overemphasize the 'small is beautiful' theory. In the course of the 1980s a better sense of proportion has been restored.

In attempting to deal with the implications of the changing law of the sea, Richard Hill in the early 1970s discussed the character of future maritime law-keeping forces according to their operational reach (1972, pp. 178–9). Since all nations with coasts have the requirement of maintaining good order in the territorial sea, he argued that at the bottom end of the scale they all required at least a few patrol craft. This will build up with the 'size, importance, and maritime bias' of the country concerned. At its biggest it will be an organization as comprehensive as the US Coast Guard. The needs of such forces are the ability to apply carefully graduated force, to keep the sea, to move rapidly when required, to gather information and to communicate. Aircraft and helicopters will be essential for some tasks, and useful for all. In the middle of the spectrum there are nations with deep-sea fishing interests, which may require vessels for administrative support, and perhaps for their regulation. Sea-keeping and endurance would be their primary needs. Finally, there are those nations which wish to employ maritime forces in the protection of their legal interests on a worldwide basis. They require vessels capable of operating independently in conditions of minimal threat, with some backing force capable of taking a tactical initiative. Combat aircraft will be necessary in many situations, submarines less so. The nearer the ships are to an area of dispute, the more essential will be the ability to deploy graduated force. This means guns, some self-defence, good data acquisition and communications, and command and control facilities. Higher-quality forces, including fleet submarines and combat aircraft, will act as deterrents to higher levels of action. Hill's conclusion was that 'It so happens that such forces are not very different from the shape of many modern navies. If there are differences, the law-keeping requirement tends to weigh the balance away from general war-fighting ability towards the capacity for low-level confrontation.' If this is the case for most navies, the superpowers and to a lesser extent their most capable allies have to build for the 'worst case', which is as far removed from law-keeping operations as we can get. This means that the shape of their naval forces will remain being primarily determined by general war tasks.

In some countries, the problem of the naval role in support of mineral extraction and other offshore activities of a fixed nature has attracted attention.[2] In view of the several economic implications of oil shortages, the problem of the protection of oil rigs has caused strong anxieties in some circles, though less so today than in the oil and hijacking scare-days of the 1970s. Nevertheless, the North Sea remains a sensitive area in this respect, and as Geoffrey Till and others have pointed out, contemporary opinion believes that navies need to be able to demonstrate a sufficient capacity to react in order to deter such military threats at the lower end of the scale as hijackings and limited harrassment, while more substantial threats would be met by a navy's general war-fighting capabilities. What can be offered is a kind of 'direct but limited' protection, and this seems best afforded by area rather than point defence, not least because the rigs themselves are only a part of the system that needs defending. The protection forces require aerial surveillance to ensure swift reaction, and associated ships with 'simple, visible weaponry, high speed, good sea-keeping and loiter characteristics, manoeuvrability and hull strength' (Till, 1982, pp. 206–7). Cheapness would obviously also be a virtue, since this would help increase the number of units, but in naval weaponry of all kinds, 'cheapness' seems more unattainable than ever.

The major powers are obliged to give attention to the 'unthinkable' in their naval planning, but this should not be at the exclusion of the probable, and here the earlier discussion pointed to the importance of flexibility in the middle of the spectrum. This means that warships should not become so specialized and sophisticated (and hence valuable) in order to be of some use in the improbable contingency of general war that they are too important to risk at lower levels where the stake is less. A strategy which is not optimized to deal with probable contingencies is irrational, and a convergence of factors suggests that confrontations at sea will focus on the middle part of the spectrum. These factors include regional conflicts, law of the sea disputes, the increasing international salience of maritime affairs, the new navalism of regional powers, superpower interests and ambitions, and problems of access to resources. The requirements needed to operate effectively in the middle of the spectrum include offensive and defensive capabilities, endurance (perhaps more so than speed), good reconnaissance capabilities, the ability to communicate with enemies as well as friends, and a willingness to accept some loss of quality in return for greater quantity and risk-taking potential (Eberle, 1976, pp. 29–32). As was mentioned earlier, aircraft carriers will continue to be invaluable for those states wanting to project power against hostile shores. They are costly and in some way vulnerable, but modern combat aircraft have proliferated even more than mininavies, and must be countered by naval task forces. Mobile airfields, which provide a range of defensive and offensive potential, can, as yet, be provided only in one unavoidably costly way: the carrier.

The surface of the ocean is not the only problem. O'Connell has argued that as a coastal state's rights in the seabed expand, either by the prolongation of the continental shelf or by the acquisition of blocks of ocean floor for exploitation, its navy's task of protection and surveillance 'spreads commensurately', with implications for fleet disposition, manning and procurement policies (O'Connell, 1975, p. 148). Seabed protection may become a task for some navies, but it is not likely one to be met out of new resources.

Some of the requirements for a modern navy cannot be easily met by many countries. Even the richest are feeling the pinch. As a result, when economic considerations are added to the wide differences of national interest in using the sea, it is apparent that the gap between the small and the mighty in the naval domain is unlikely to decrease by much. However, there may be a significant reduction in the area of usable force in the middle of the spectrum, between the naval powers of the second rank and the mighty. This would have happened regardless of law of the sea developments, although a boost will have been given by the new salience of maritime affairs for many middle powers.

For most nations the most immediate and obvious effect of the changing law of the sea as a result of UNCLOS III was the greatly expanded problems of control and enforcement as a consequence of the acquisition of EEZs, particularly since four-fifths of the world's fishing takes place in these zones. The problem this presents for many states is not only the result of the size of the area to be controlled and the complexity of the regulations involved; it is also the result of the fact that some of the likely offenders will be the vessels of major powers. The culprit will not therefore be a lone fisherman out to make a quick profit, but a group of ships with the support of their national government. There have been many disputes over fishing rights in recent years and tension has been particularly intense when small communities have had their futures endangered by the arrival of the factory fishing methods of the major fishing nations.

The regulation of fisheries is not the only problem. Although good order at sea is the norm in most parts of the world, in some regions it is a thin veneer. In parts of south-east Asia, for example, modern day 'pirates' still harass shipping, particularly coastal freighters and fishermen (*Time* magazine, 31 July 1978). Whether it is fisheries, pirates, or pollution, effective regulation requires detection capabilities and then the ability to apprehend law-breakers. Aircraft are obviously invaluable for the former task, but ships are essential for the latter. Since certainty of arrest will be a major deterrent, it is of paramount importance for coastal states to have enough aircraft and ships to carry out the task of regulation effectively. The answer to the question 'how much is enough to do the task effectively?' will depend upon the size of the sea area to be controlled, the character of the resources involved and the possibility of trouble. Obviously regulation will be costly: but against arguments about the costs of effective enforcement must be set arguments about the costs of *failing* to provide enforcement. For most states, and especially those with large EEZs, providing the aircraft and shipping necessary to rule over the new coastal waves will continue to prove something of a strain. But one thing is clear: states which do not undertake an appropriate effort can expect that others will sometimes seek to take advantage of them.

Planning

In contrast to what was said at the opening of this chapter, it is sometimes suggested that the changing law of the sea clarifies rather than complicates the job of a naval officer, by giving him a stronger set of 'do's' and 'don'ts'. There is a valid point here, but it altogether places too much emphasis on the theory of the matter as opposed to the problem of putting ideas into practice under the pressure of events. And the more complex the law, the greater the problems of decision-making. Good planning cannot guarantee that the right decision will be made, and that it will be executed properly, but it can at least maximize a country's chances of avoiding avoidable errors.

In facing up to the problems of managing their expanded and more valuable 'offshore estate' through the 1970s, naval policy-makers found little in the established literature of maritime strategy to help them make their choices. As Geoffrey Till has pointed out, even the established maritime states found their existing literature and bureaucracies unequal to the task: 'the United States has some forty overlapping agencies concerned with the offshore estate, the British over twenty. Very evidently, old patterns do not fit the new realities, which demand instead a co-ordinated maritime policy and new patterns of administration' (1982, p. 203). Clarity in naval planning should begin at home, in the offshore estate (or 'tapestry' as some have called it). But the problems involved are largely bureaucratic and technical. The more serious political and strategic problems grow with distance from the homeland.

A major requirement for the naval powers is the need to give sustained attention to pre-crisis planning (Knight, 1977, pp. 38–9). This will be the more important for states which believe that the post-Convention settling period might demand assertive naval behaviour in order to ensure that international agreements are not eroded by idiosyncratic unilateral interpretations. Steps to be taken might include the negotiation of bilateral and multilateral treaties to further naval tasks (basing agreements, joint undertakings, and so on), the threat or use of force to prevent claims which threaten naval missions, and the employment of covert operations such as emplanting ASW devices on continental shelves. Because the location of the next crisis cannot be confidently predicted, this all needs a global awareness on the part of superpower naval planners.

One important aspect of pre-crisis planning is the development of appropriate tactics and rules of engagement. International law affects the exercise of naval power in a wider sense than the narrow law of the sea as interpreted in this book. A variety of rules affect the use of weapons systems, the rights of neutrals, rules of engagement, and so on. Because these exist, and because they exist in an increasingly complex environment (including one where the war/peace distinction is less clear), it behoves naval staffs to become better equipped to handle the legal aspects of naval planning, whether it is in the drafting of rules of engagement or in their interpretation (O'Connell, 1975, p. 189; McCoy, 1977). The issue of the rules of engagement – what was or was not permitted – was one of the many subjects debated in Britain as a result of the post-Falklands War *post mortem* (*The Times*, 26 and 31 January 1983; *Guardian*, 31 January 1983).

Military manuals normally mention the 'laws of war', that is, behaviour which is permitted in time of war,[3] but they do not go far enough: one reason for this is that the distinction between 'peace' and 'war' is not always clear. We now live in an ambiguous era where tensions rise and fall, and when 'cold wars' are almost as demanding in their way as 'hot' ones. Shooting might even take place, but 'peace' is still deemed to be in existence. War is rarely declared. Consequently, and in view of the heightened dangers of employing force, it is incumbent upon military organizations to provide not only instruction on the laws of war and the rules of engagement on the war/peace boundary, but also to make officers conversant with the background to the general rules of law governing military operations short of war. As O'Connell has shown, international law in such situations impinges upon naval planning through matters such as the tactical use of

ASW in times of political tension, the choice of areas in which operations are to be mounted or the ships and devices to be deployed, or
even procurement policy in cases where weapons or their launching
vehicles would be of doubtful legality in any situation that can be
envisaged (O'Connell, 1973). The traditional strategy of blockade is
obviously one area with an important legal dimension.[4]

It would clearly be impossible to give naval officers specific guidance for every possible situation which might be faced: but what can
be done is to give commanders a thorough grounding in the legal
dimension of their profession, to help them exercise their 'best judgement' in different circumstances in order that their conduct may
remain within the rules of law (McCoy, 1977, pp. 8–9). Administrative
and training arrangements have to be developed to meet the problem,
so that 'the lawyers and the seamen' can work closely together, and,
ideally, come to understand each other's outlooks better. O'Connell
has pointed out that some progress along these lines was made in the
1970s in the US Navy and the Royal Australian Navy. But even in these
exceptions, 'it is evident that any crisis would immediately reveal
areas of confusion and indecision because the forward thinking about
legal policy and rules of the game was lacking'.[5] For some British naval
officers, the experience of 'Confrontation' between Indonesia and
Malaysia in the mid-1960s provided direct experience of the importance of proper legal training in effective naval planning (O'Connell,
1975, p. 137). It is not evident that this lesson has percolated into the
officer training process.

Pre-crisis planning of the one sort or another is all the more important because naval powers have no longer to worry simply about other
established 'naval powers'; they also have to worry about the growing
sea-denial capabilities of smaller navies as a result of the diffusion of
modern naval forces to South American states, some nations bordering the Indian Ocean and elsewhere. This is an aspect of the emerging maritime environment which cannot be ignored. Some of these
smaller naval powers are now equipping themselves with a range of
cost-effective technology. Particularly popular in many regions have
been one or more of the range of Fast Attack Craft (FAC) available.
These ships come armed with missiles, guns, or torpedoes – or some
combination of these – and they are in the 100–500 ton range. Especially when armed with powerful surface-to-surface missiles such as
Exocet, these small ships can pack a powerful punch. Higher up the
scale, some developing navies have been acquiring frigates or corvettes. Among the latter, the Italian *Lupo* class has proved to be popular in several navies in countries bordering the Indian Ocean (Booth
and Dowdy, forthcoming).

The acquisition of such weaponry is one sign of the modernisation
of naval assets which has been taking place in various parts of the

world. In many cases the new warships are additions to rather than replacements of existing warships. There is a step-up in capability taking place; a navy with one frigate will order more, or move from corvettes to frigates, or a FAC-armed navy will develop corvettes. This trend does not justify the label 'naval arms race', at least yet. It is rather a sign that in many parts of the world there is no suplus of capability over requirement, and that navies are struggling to modernize and build up their strength in order to fulfil their basic tasks.

In addition to having to face the prospect of intrusion by the larger maritime powers, the smaller navies (like their big brothers) need to attend to their day-to-day surveillance and enforcement procedures within their zones of expanded maritime jurisdiction. This will particularly be the case where lines of demarcation are in dispute, or where there are suspicions about illegal fishing or other contraventions of international law or the national legislation of the coastal state. There is a particular requirement to work out enforcement procedures, in order to assist naval officers in carrying out their duties, and in order to minimize misunderstandings from those being dealt with.

Clearly, surveillance and enforcement duties will pose a heavy strain on some of the less capable Third World navies. Hence a variety of stop-gaps and quick-fixes has been suggested (Dowdy, 1981, pp. 147–8). Some of these measures are technical, such as making better use of shore-based radar for surveillance: others involve political co-ordination – sharing assets – between neighbouring coastal states. The prospects for such developments would presently appear to be low, since most if not all the potential co-ordinators are themselves overstretched, and neighbouring states are not invariably the most trustful. A more likely way by which less-developed states will seek to overcome weaknesses involves the seeking of greater assistance from developed naval powers. This is something the latter might well be keen to grasp, for as was discussed earlier, they are always keen to develop potential channels of influence.

When navies are discharging law of the sea tasks there is always a need for effective two-way communication. If law, strategy and diplomacy are to work together and with minimum violence in the unsettled period ahead, it is important that those involved can communicate quickly and effectively with each other. The *Mayaguez* incident was interesting for many reasons, not least because it revealed the poverty of the communications between the United States and Cambodia. At one critical stage the US President could only communicate quickly to Phnom Penh through the press (Rowan, 1975, pp. 204–5). If it be glibly assumed that this was a matter mainly for the naval power concerned, it should be added that it was of even greater importance for the weaker target country. After all, the Cambodians suffered most from the confusion, and inability to communicate. Effective communication is not only a question of technology: it is also a question of political and cultural awareness. As it happens, while electronic and other methods of communication increase in speed, political and cultural obstacles remain as great as ever.

Better planning and the meeting of the necessary technical requirements will help navies to achieve their objectives, but only if the training of officers also keeps in step. As Lieutenant Commander Regan of the US Coast Guard has put it, 'It is essential that naval line officers be sufficiently knowledgeable in international law to prevent unwitting violations and to enable them to use the law positively to enhance the effectiveness of naval actions' (1983, p. 52). It is important in situations of peace and war — and near war — that officers do not find themselves faced by predicaments in which they do not know the law. The implications can be serious for a whole range of issues, from failing to know the rights of those seeking refuge to failing to understand the rules of engagement. Used badly, the law can degrade the national interest: used well it can limit the number of one's enemies at the political level while helping in tactical situations. 'In sum', Lieutenant Commander Regan's words again,

> international law is of importance to the naval commander because it is also domestic law, because violations have potential major and political repercussions, and because when used skilfully it may be used as an effective weapon in the commander's arsenal. More importantly, law is one of man's few ways of preserving his humanity and should be obeyed for that reason alone. But obedience requires knowledge. It is time to upgrade the international law training program for the officer corps (1983, p. 56).

The problem is identified: the solution is in the hands of naval establishments.

Running through many of the requirements for an effective naval policy discussed earlier is the need for careful and continued coordination in planning between relevant government departments. The convergence of problems at the intersection of developments in naval strategy, foreign policy and international law calls for the coordination at a policy-making level of specialists in each field; it is important for each specialist, in turn, to attempt to become literate in the language and concepts of the specialists in other fields. This, in turn, will help the furtherance of one of the central concerns of strategy, namely, the attempt to ensure a proper relationship between instrument and aim, between power and purpose and between context and capability. A sophisticated approach to strategy requires generalists as well as specialists, and intellectuals as well as technicians. Shared knowledge can sometimes prevent avoidable errors. George Walker has written:

> Not many military commanders can or should make policy or practice law: not many lawyers can or should make policy or make war; not many policy scientists or decision theorists wage war or practice law. All three disciplines, and other professions as well can, however, learn from the processes of others and appreciate the multi-faceted issues of seapower and ocean law (1978, p. 99).

International law will affect naval planning, for almost all governments − at least for most of the time − are predisposed to observe it. But if this object is to be achieved, naval commanders need more guidelines, advice and information about their roles in the current period of international relations. And simply giving attention to the laws of war is not enough (McCoy, 1977, pp. 8−15). Living as we do in an ambiguous era of 'neither war nor peace', and with naval officers no longer being able to deploy their ships in the seas of the world with the freedom of the past, the intellectual make-up of naval commanders must include an understanding of the theory and practice of limited war, the theory and practice of crisis management and the development of the law of the sea.

Law-making activities require relevant technology and relevant behaviour. Relevant technology means flexibility and moderation rather than simply destructiveness. The pressure for faster and more destructive weaponry, which characterizes research and development for major 'shooting wars', is not appropriate for law-making activities, nor are actions which favour getting in the first hard blow rather than providing the opportunity for gradual escalation. In law-making activities it is important to have the capability to stop a ship, and not simply blow it up, and it is important to be able to communicate, and not simply engage in a fight.

International law is a useful tool of statecraft, and navies and naval officers can play their part in strengthening its norms. This means that rights must be upheld, for in an 'anarchial society' they tend to lapse if they are not exercised. It is for the law-abiding, and the majority whose security is enhanced by observance of law, to strengthen the norms of international law. This not only means being willing to fight to uphold the law, it also means refusing to take actions which weaken the law. Western states must vigorously uphold the law. If they do not, they cannot legitimately call others to account, when they transgress.

Notes: Chapter 9

1   'Sovereignty protection', in one form or another, had always been particularly important to Canadian naval forces, for example. In the Canadian National Services Act of 1910 the St Laurent government thought that it was important that Canada should assume control of Canadian waters from the Royal Navy, for reasons of nation-building and sovereignty. In the course of time this task metamorphosed into that of patrolling the country's EEZ; this includes the seas in the inhospitable north (Best, 1979). In 1980 Canadian air units carried out numerous missions in northern latitudes to establish a Canadian presence and to ensure that foreign vessels were operating in accordance with national regulations. As a whole, Tracker aircraft expended over 3,400 flying hours in aid of the Department of Fisheries and Oceans Canada. Ships of Maritime Command were also at sea on the east and west coasts, patrolling the EEZ. Foreign fishing vessels were located, identified and sometimes boarded. Of the over 200 vessels identified, forty-five were boarded. Three were found to be in violation of fisheries agreements (Department of National Defence, 1981, pp. 41−2).

2   For a comprehensive analysis of the threat of 'offshore maritime terrorism', the legal dimension of the problem and some policy-oriented recommendations for 'premeditated prevention', see Joyner, 1983, pp. 16−31. Joyner's verdict, confirming those of many other commentators, is that many coastal states today may be ill prepared to deal efficaciously with a terrorist attack against an off-shore facility. However, in practice the terrorist threat seems − so far − to have been exaggerated. For a sceptical view, see Guida, 1980, pp. 22−3.

3   There is no comprehensive book on the laws of war in so far as they relate specifically to war at sea. Some of the main laws, with a general introduction and notes, are included in Roberts and Guelff, 1982.

4   International law recognizes various types of blockade. They can be classified into three. First, the blockade of the enemy coast in war. Secondly, blockades in 'peacetime' for self-defence or as a reprisal against the wrongful act of another state. Finally, blockades authorized by the United Nations to maintain or restore international peace and security. (O'Connell, 1975, pp. 101−13, 110−12, 114−18; Till, 1982, pp. 122−8.)

5   Major Hays Parks has shown that even in the US Navy, probably the institution which gives most attention to this subject, progress has been limited. He argued in the late 1970s that required training in the Geneva Conventions was slighted throughout the chain of command. He also pointed to the fact that foreign officers at the Naval Staff College receive almost three times as much international law training as their US counterparts (Parks, 1977, pp. 26−32).

10
Policy at Sea?

It is too early to draw up a 'Conclusion' on UNCLOS III. As was made evident in earlier chapters, this glacier conference, and its long Convention, represent not so much an end-result as a stage in a developing process; it is not so much an end in itself, as the end of the beginning. Historically speaking, UNCLOS III will come to be seen as the start of a new era in the international politics of the sea. We cannot yet predict whether the traditional naval powers will respond wisely to the immediate challenge, and imaginatively to the possibilities of the longer term.

In the first half-year following the signing of the UN Convention in December 1982, the warnings of those who for some years had been saying that we had entered a grim period of international politics seemed to be coming to pass. These months saw the continuing 'agony of small nations', superpower rivalry, regional instabilities, war and confrontation, intervention and pressure, the dangers of ambition and of incapacity, and the continuing arms build-up and 'perfection' of weaponry at the highest levels while below these levels there was a steady diffusion of sophisticated military power. Added to this brew was some uncertainty regarding the future of the maritime environment, whose political, strategic, economic and legal significance has been increasingly perceived by the international community. Faced by the grim situation of contemporary international politics, it is easy to feel weighed down by the press of problems. Strong countries continue to exert their power, and weak countries continue to give them the opportunities they can exploit. Competition and conflict remain the norm of international politics, with the operational 'realities' being power and national interest. The international system is no nearer than ever to being ruled by morality and reason. But more than ever in this tinderbox, policy-makers must seek ways of moderating the processes of competition and conflict. International law can help towards this end, somewhat, and so can a controlled and moderate military (including naval) policy.

The immediate overriding task for world statesmanship is, and will remain, the avoidance of nuclear war. This will be more difficult in the

1980s and 1990s than it was in the 1960s and 1970s, because both superpowers are likely to be edgy and under pressure, and have in their possession weapons and strategies which do not encourage relaxed feelings about security. Furthermore, both superpowers will find their relations with their allies more difficult to manage, in part because their allies will be more than ever troubled by the behaviour of their superpower 'protector'. Further afield, the superpowers will find world affairs in general ever more difficult to control.

In this setting, the use and threat of force cannot be wished away. It is therefore important that those responsible for managing the West's military power approach the task in a Clausewitzian fashion, and not with the accountant's mentality, which knows the price of everything but the value of nothing, is familiar with thinking about techniques rather than ends, and tends to equate money with effectiveness. Three per cent additional spending on 'defence' does not necessarily buy 3 per cent additional 'security'. Security is much more complex than that. Furthermore, an effective defence posture does not only require the provisioning of armed forces with the necessary hardware and manpower, but it also requires that those forces be consistently directed, and confidently used when required. The effective use, and non-use, of military power will be one of the main tests of leadership. In the dangerous years ahead it is certain that there will be occasions when it will be necessary for the Western powers to demonstrate military toughness (which is not to be confused with a Pavlovian arms build-up). A wise leader will be selective when choosing the ground (or sea) on which to act. But when action is called for, it should be discharged decisively. There is no value, to paraphrase Theodore Roosevelt, in meaning well feebly.

The 1982 Falklands War offered many lessons for policy-makers and commentators in this area. It reminded us of the importance of decisiveness. It showed that diplomacy and military power are not mutually exclusive but are complementary aspects of policy. It proved yet again that surface ships are essential for the projection of military force over great distances for a sustained period. And, more important than anything, it emphasized that deterrence must not only be done, but it must also be seen to be done: however professional one's war-fighting capability, an effective deterrent policy is preferable. To turn General MacArthur's famous maxim on its head: there is no substitute for deterrence.

For some countries, particularly the superpowers and emerging regional powers, there will be an important naval dimension to their security problems. But the managers of the naval instrument will face more complex times, and earlier chapters have shown that some of the problems will result from the changing law of the sea. In particular, naval establishments have become concerned that creeping jurisdiction will add important legal inhibitions to the already growing political and economic costs involved in the exercise of naval power in a post-imperial money-conscious world. Legal constraints, it is believed, will add further burdens to the debit side of the political calculation about the procurement and employment of warships. Consequently, the threat of creeping jurisdiction is something which the naval establishments of the major powers have steadfastly sought to resist. In this light, the 1982 UN Convention represented a success for them. It met the security interests of the naval powers almost all the way down the line. But will the Convention be allowed to work effectively? If it is not, the naval interest will have been put at some risk as a result of the priority given by the Reagan administration to free enterprise dogmas and by its antipathies towards the Third World. The US change of policy on the Draft Convention was followed loyally, which is not the same as wisely, by Mrs Thatcher's government in Britain, and by several other members of the industrialized world.

Through the process of UNCLOS III, the major naval establishments favoured the most permissive legal regime possible. However, several chapters in this book have argued that even a more restrictive regime at sea need not be as threatening to the utility of the naval interest as has been generally assumed. A more restrictive regime would obviously increase the problem facing warship movement and aircraft overflight, as was brought out in Chapters 5 and 7, but the obstacles would not be insurmountable. If that is recognized, there might be less resistance from naval establishments to a law of the sea policy which sees an interest in harmonizing with any trends in a territorialist direction in the middle and long term.

If one's foreign policy leads one to think that a more restrictive regime is desirable, in order to identify with the majority of the international community and to bring about a saner management of the oceans, then one should resist granting an absolute veto to to the naval interest. Navies, after all, must adapt to changing circumstances, and in this respect Chapter 7 showed that the focus of naval concern — the proliferation of psycho-legal boundaries — represents opportunities as well as obstacles. The explanation for this apparent paradox lies in the nature of naval diplomacy, which seeks to use warships to transmit political and military signals without firing a shot. The more the sea becomes impregnated with the legal and political character of the land, the more will it become the object of national feelings as well as of commercial ambitions. The proliferation of psycho-legal boundaries indicates the new stake which many states have in the sea, but also, by the same token, it increases the scope which naval strategists will have to manipulate their military power to show displeasure or demonstrate support. The boundaries represent new political thresholds at sea. They are never likely to have the same significance as land frontiers, but they will have sufficient salience that they will assist in the maturation of Scheilling's concept of 'the diplomacy of violence' in the maritime arena.

As identified earlier, the implications for naval strategy which may arise out of possible changes in the legal character of the sea are somewhat different from those which have been presented by those who, for want of better terms, can be called the 'hawks' and 'doves' in the subject. The hawks tend simply to see the legal manifestations of the territorialization of the oceans as a threat to the usefulness of a traditional and important instrument of policy. On the other hand the doves tend to interpret the development of the law of the sea as a process which promises to consign 'gunboat diplomacy' to the rubbish heap of strategic history.

This book has offered an alternative viewpoint. Unlike the hawks, it has not seen creeping jurisdiction as simply a threat to naval mobility: it has also foreseen the possibility that the proliferation of psycho-legal boundaries will provide new opportunities for the exploitation of warships in their signalling role. Unlike the dovish perspective, on the other hand, this book has not assumed that naval power either is or should be going out of business. Instead, it has been argued that the revival of a more selective but salient form of naval diplomacy will be one of the more desirable evil necessities in a highly militarized world of diffused power and widespread instability. Great or regional powers need, on the one hand, the ability to transmit signals by means of the movement of their strategic assets, and, on the other hand, they (and the international community at large) need control and restraint. The spread of new psycho-legal boundaries at sea should assist in the achievement of both these objectives. They should affect the psychodynamics of naval strategy, by encouraging calculation before the employment of warships, and by intensifying the degree to which the political atmosphere is charged during employment. In these ways the territorialization of the oceans should help naval powers to turn military potential into diplomatic impact.

The periodic explosion of international conflict is one of the few things which can be taken for granted in an unpredictable world. And when crises occur, or when fighting breaks out, nobody can guarantee that the relatively powerful members of the international community will deny themselves the opportunities presented for political, military, or economic gain. External powers might become involved in local conflicts because they feel that their prestige cannot allow them to stand aside. Or they may intervene to pre-empt an adversary's intervention. Responsibilites to allies and associates will have to be faced, and interests will have to be furthered. In such circumstances, as was discussed in Chapter 8, warships can be particularly valuable because of their special assets — their flexibility, their mobility and the fact that they are efficient bulk carriers of manpower and firepower.

Now that both superpowers have global reach in a military sense, and a new or renewed confidence about using their military power, it is unlikely in the years ahead that either will allow the other a completely free ride in a crisis. Apart from some special areas, such as the Caribbean or eastern Baltic, we might expect that if the warships of one superpower are present in a crisis, then the other will also be there in at least some strength — to show interest, to challenge calculations and to impose some constraints on behaviour. Furthermore, with the diffusion of military power across the globe, including the growth of regional navies, middle-power confrontations at sea can be expected — certainly less apocalyptic in their potential violence than war between the superpowers, but potentially more likely to result in shooting. Warships will remain in business because naval diplomacy is 'action language', even when force is not contemplated. Actions still speak louder than words, and it is a foolish government which denies itself affordable options.

It should be clear, therefore, that whatever the legal problems which may arise and affect naval mobility, warships will remain essential as long as states have a significant interest in using the area. There is no evidence to suggest that such an interest is waning: indeed the opposite is the case. And while 'mastery of the seas' is no longer possible in the Mahanist sense, it does not follow that naval strategy is futile. Many important national objectives can be furthered by navies unable to 'sweep' the seas. Warships — and only warships — of the right type and in the right number can give the nations which possess them almost guaranteed access to those distant places, resources and allies — in short, *interests* — which may be thought necessary to further a country's foreign policy. And, it should go without saying, warships of the right type and in the right number will be even more important for many more members of the international community as badges of sovereignty over their own seas in an era when the maritime territorial imperative will be much in evidence.

But will the requisite warships be available? For the medium future there is no doubt, since both superpowers have large navies projected to the end of the century, and there is an expansion of maritime power elsewhere. This latter phenomenon, the growth of middle-power navies, itself has major implications, for while a considerable gap in capability will continue to exist between the mightiest and the majority, the balance between extra-regional and local naval forces (including relevant air forces) has and will continue to change. The gap is slowly closing to the advantage of the local countries. And the technological sophistication of the naval powers cannot entirely abolish the geographical advantage of the local country, particularly when budgets increasingly constrain numbers. As the balance of capability changes, the requirement for numbers on the part of the extra-regional forces will grow, as well as the requirements for quality. A superpower cannot, with confidence, operate a three-ocean naval responsibility with a one-and-a-half ocean navy. Even regional powers will need commensurate numerical strength. Without doubt, it will be costly to operate a distant water naval force in the decades ahead, but politicians should contemplate not only the direct costs of warships, but they should also be conscious of the costs of not having them when needed.[1] The British government learned that lesson, the hard way, in the spring of 1982. It was almost caught out, with too few warships too far away.

All states with coasts need some sort of naval strategy, however minimal. Its scope will depend upon its power potential and its interest in using the sea. And the latter demands consideration of the way adversaries might use the sea in hostile ways. In this respect, the late 1980s and 1990s do not appear likely to be periods when many states will be able to take their security for granted. We seem to have entered one of those seasons when power politics has come back into fashion. When such a prospect presents itself it is not a time for rolling over and playing dead, for by rejecting the military dimension of policy one might well bring about the threat one had feared. Making 'impotence a declaration of policy', as Henry Kissinger once put it (*Time* magazine, 26 November 1979), can invite trouble just as much as an over-militarized policy can provoke that very trouble it was designed to deter. A delicate balance must be struck in policy-making. More than ever security demands leaders who are both realists and utopians, men and women who can both manipulate military power and do so with a sense of purpose which helps to build a moderate international society. Mindless arms-building and an attitude of every-man-for-himself are not helpful: nor do they justify being called a 'security' policy. The delicate balance between realism and utopianism must be achieved with respect to national policy towards the sea, as elsewhere. And the good news is that it may be achievable, if the chance is grasped.

It was argued earlier that the territorialization of the oceans appears to be irresistible, because of a variety of economic and political pressures and technological possibilities. If it is indeed irresistible, then it is obviously sensible that the process be carried out in as orderly and just a fashion as is humanly possible. This would place a premium on the development of the law of the sea in any circumstances, but when, as at present, there is a sense of fragility in the fabric of international society, the potential role of international law is all the more important. The sea itself, for the most part, does not promise to be a particularly dangerous or disorderly place. The overwhelming majority of the international community continues to have an interest in stability at sea. But Chapter 8 showed that there are abundant occasions for local conflicts and disputes of a maritime nature, or with a maritime dimension. Order at sea could erode if there is no agreed legal regime and if politics among nations slide further into the troubled times which so many have foretold and feared.

The future maritime regime will depend in part upon the naval factor. The naval interest will help to shape the norms at sea, and naval practice will help to determine whether they come into operation. With regard to the latter, navies will be particularly important when claims are contested. The development of a workable law of the sea will require a judicious combination of naval power and diplomacy. Neither can be neglected by those who would seek to produce security across the world. But security lies not simply in military power: it lies also in movement towards a fairer world order.

National security is a multi-layered phenomenon, binding together individuals, states and the international system. These are so closely entangled that security demands to be treated in what Barry Buzan has called a 'holistic' perspective (1983, *passim*). At this juncture in international history it should be more evident than it seemingly is that 'security policy' and 'defence policy' are not necessarily synonymous. A 'holistic' conception of security would ensure their re-integration. This can be seen nowhere more clearly than in the development of the law of the sea, where a sensible security policy for the maritime environment requires not only the provision of warships of the right type and in the right number, but also some sense of what kind of world is desired. The outlook of those who place the unilaterally asserted rights of deep seabed mining companies before all else, including the opportunity to nudge international affairs in the direction of a fairer world order, is depressingly reactionary from this point of view.

It should be apparent from the discussion in earlier chapters that the maritime dimension of a 'holistic' security policy should lead all states, including the naval powers, towards signing and ratifying the Convention which was cobbled together so laboriously by UNCLOS III. Chapters 3 and 4 showed conclusively that there are no significant naval reasons for rejecting the Convention. Indeed, the Convention was seen as a triumph for the naval interest. The law of the sea upheld naval mobility against the claims of those who would restrain it. The only negative security interest is possibly that of access to 'strategic minerals', and this factor, it seems, is both easily exaggerated and offset by positive aspects of the Convention. While details of the text can be criticized, for the most part the Convention is fair and workable. From the naval, and indeed wider security viewpoint, it was therefore irrational on the part of the Reagan administration to risk

jeopardizing the advantages of the Convention for the sake of indulg-
ing the visceral instincts of 'America First' supporters at home. What
is bad for the Third World is not necessarily good for America. And
what is good for deep seabed mining companies is not necessarily
good for US foreign policy.

In both the United States and Britain, a majority of close observers of
UNCLOS III have spoken out in favour of the Convention and against
the narrow perspective of their governments. Before President
Reagan's election the leading Western naval powers supported the
Draft Convention. After the Reagan rethink improvements were made
in the text to try to meet some of the dissatisfactions expressed: but
they did not go far enough to inspire another rethink. Nor did the
signing ceremony in December 1982. Even now, although time has
been lost and momentum has slowed, it is not too late for the United
States to change course and allow policy to be guided by enlightened
self-interest. Nor is it too late for Britain to change. Unfortunately, the
times do not appear propitious. The two major Western naval powers
have many domestic and foreign problems requiring urgent attention,
and they also have at their heads two leaders who stubbornly pride
themselves on their resolution; the cultivation of their self-images and
political repute for toughness is unlikely to be modified by the mere
appeal of enlightened national self-interest. Narrow unilateralism on
the part of the Reagan and Thatcher governments looks like winning
the day, although the shortcomings of the Convention are now few.
Nobody got everything in the 1982 Convention but everybody got
something. A U-turn would therefore be welcome on the part of the
major Western naval powers, but it probably remains for more enlightened leaders than President Reagan and Prime Minister Thatcher
to readjust their country's policies away from short-term unilateralism
and towards a constructive engagement with almost all the rest of the
international community.

It is generally agreed that a universal law of the sea treaty would be
better than no treaty at all, and the consequent uncertain development
of customary law. Without doubt, those states wanting to use the sea
have interest in a universally accepted body of law governing the
multiple and complex uses of the oceans. These interests include
everything from reliable access, through rules of navigation, to agreements to prevent pollution. In all these respects the Western naval
powers have little to lose and plenty to gain from adhering to the
Convention which is now on the table. The door is open; it is for the
unilateralist states to show the statesmanship to take the opportunity
to enter. And they should contemplate doing so for the strongest of
motives – national self-interest – let alone the interests of the wider
international community. A universally agreed Convention will give
order, precision and predictability to maritime affairs; it will

strengthen global norms and cement common interests in the orderly use of the sea. All these possibilties may be undermined in the absence of a universal Convention.

'Chaos' at sea is unlikely, even without a Convention, but if the Western industrialized states fail to support the Convention, its effect will be badly diluted, and the risks of disorder, imprecision and unpredictability will be somewhat higher. And one very undesirable consequence of this from the Western viewpoint, and particularly the viewpoint of Western naval establishments, might be the encouragement of just that creeping jurisdiction which they have hitherto been so keen to avoid. Such a possibility is all the more likely if the more radical coastal states are provoked or are tempted into shifting their major attention from resource questions to those of naval mobility. In this case, the strategic interests of the naval powers might be seen as a lever to gain concessions elsewhere. Some coastal states would favour restrictions on naval mobility for its own sake. Chapters 3 and 4 suggested the directions in which pressure might occur, and the naval powers cannot assume that the consensus on military mobility will last indefinitely, especially if the Convention merely limps into action. Chaos is not the inevitable outcome of a less than universally ratified Convention, but neither is perfect peace the inevitable outcome of a change of policy on the part of the Western naval powers. If the latter did do a U-turn, and decided to adhere to the Convention at the eleventh hour, the benefits would not come overnight. There would inevitably be difficulties to be worked through before the troubled common could settle down. The lawyer's dream throughout UNCLOS III of a universal and multi-purpose treaty for two-thirds of the earth's surface has not yet turned into a nightmare, but there is still plenty of reason for us to feel restless.

Whatever happens to the Convention in the short run, UNCLOS III will be seen in historical perspective to have been a major milestone in the history of the law of the sea, and therefore in the maritime dimension of international affairs in general. UNCLOS III sensitized many states to the scope of maritime affairs, even those which had not been particularly maritime-minded in the past. UNCLOS III itself was both an effect and a catalyst of the fact that traditional norms relating to the sea have been under pressure. It will be many years before the detailed effects of UNCLOS III will be worked out, but its one general and lasting result will be to ensure that to a greater extent than ever before the sea will be thought about as an extension to the land.

UNCLOS III helped both to legitimize and generate the maritime territorial imperative. The process will continue: the technology is increasingly permissive and commercially it is unavoidable. But it remains to be seen how these changes will be manifest in the strategic domain: will the results of the Convention lead to a paradigm shift in the peacetime deployment of warships, or will the compromise reached during UNCLOS III solidify into historical concrete? The answer cannot be confidently predicted, but at present it seems that, sooner or later, in one way or another, there will be pressure for change: the spirit of UNCLOS III has become part of the national interests of many states. Despite the natural tendency of those closely associated with the conference to see its Convention as an end, historically speaking it was only a beginning.

We are at the doorstep of a special stage in the history of international politics: many members of the international community recognize that they have a greater stake in maritime developments than ever before; a tactical setting is evolving which offers new opportunities for naval diplomacy as a result of the proliferation of new psycho-legal frontiers; there is a continuing and modernizing set of relevant naval capabilities; and we face the prospect of a fragile international order in which there will be many occasions for both regional and extra-regional powers to try to intrude their military power into a local trouble-spot. The use of warships to support foreign policy is therefore here to stay. The optimum national policy for the sea which emerges from this would be one which includes a foreign policy which seeks to strengthen the structure of international society, and a military posture which would meet with restraint the violence which occasionally erupts; such an approach would typify any 'strategy' worth its name. This book has argued that signing and ratifying the 1982 Convention would meet the needs of the foreign policy aspect of an optimum policy for the sea, while naval diplomacy, as a form of ritualized violence, is an essential element of the military posture.

Since we cannot abolish international conflict, we can only hope to house-train it. It is therefore imperative that we follow policies which seek to minimize the occasions and consequences of international conflict, but, being realists, we must also recognize the likelihood of violence. We must therefore seek to make the world as safe as possible for the struggles between nations. A wise policy for the sea can help in all respects. An imaginative and sensible naval strategy can make a contribution to a restrained national strategy, while the implementation and development of the 1982 UN Convention On The Law Of The Sea can make a contribution to ensuring that the structure of international society is strengthened. In the 1930s somebody said that 'wars don't start nowadays because people want them, but because the world order has failed' (Hynes, 1976, p. 102). If this was true then, it is even more true fifty years later, given the potential destructiveness of modern war. At the end of the 1930s the world order failed with disastrous consequences. In the 1980s a policy for the sea which seeks to ensure that the work of UNCLOS III will not have been in vain is one small step which we can take to help to ensure that the world order will not fail us again.

Note: Chapter 10

1   Though sometimes forgotten, this important point has generally been well recognized by a traditional seapower like Britain. At the beginning of the century a Foreign Office document put the case with admirable clarity. It noted that there were important British interests 'in distant seas where the opportune presence of a British ship of war may avert a disaster which can only be remedied later at much inconvenience and considerable sacrifice' (quoted by Marder, 1961, p. 53). However valid this point remains, it should nevertheless be read against the warning in Chapter 7 that warships can provoke trouble, shape the will to use them and provide options which are better left uncontemplated. Warships give choice. Without surface warships the British government could hardly have contemplated the retaking of the Falkland Islands in 1982: whether having the luxury of such a choice was in Britain's interests is another question.

Appendix

Table 1   Territorial Sea Claims (1 January 1983)

Three nautical miles (24)

Antigua and Barbuda	German Dem. Rep.	St Vincent and
Australia	Germany, Fed. Rep.	the Grenadines
Bahamas, The	Ireland	Singapore
Bahrain	Jordan	Solomon Islands
Belgium	Kiribati	Tuvalu
Belize	Netherlands	United Arab
Chile	Qatar	Emirates
Denmark	Saint Lucia	United Kingdom
Dominica		United States

Four nautical miles (2)
Finland
Norway

Six nautical miles (4)

Dominican Republic	Israel
Greece	Turkey (12 in the Black Sea)

Twelve nautical miles (77)

Algeria	Guatemala	Libya
Bangladesh	Guinea	Malaysia
Barbados	Guinea-Bissau	Malta
Bulgaria	Guyana	Mauritius
Burma	Haiti	Mexico
Canada	Honduras	Monaco
Cape Verde	Iceland	Morocco
China	India	Mozambique
Colombia	Indonesia	Nauru
Comoros	Iran	New Zealand
Costa Rica	Iraq	Oman
Cuba	Italy	Pakistan
Cyprus	Ivory Coast	Papua New Guinea
Djibouti	Jamaica	Poland
Egypt	Japan	Portugal
Equatorial Guinea	Kampuchea	Romania
Ethiopia	Kenya	São Tomé and Príncipe
Fiji	Korea, North	Saudi Arabia
France	Korea, South	Seychelles
Grenada	Kuwait	South Africa

217

Soviet Union	Thailand	Western Samoa
Spain	Trinidad and Tobago	Yemen (Aden)
Sri Lanka	Tunisia	Yemen (Sana)
Sudan	Vanuatu	Yugoslavia
Suriname	Venezuela	Zaïre
Sweden	Vietnam	

Fifteen nautical miles (1)
Albania

Twenty nautical miles (1)
Angola

Thirty nautical miles (2)
Nigeria
Togo

Thirty-Five nautical miles (1)
Syria

Fifty nautical miles (4)

Cameroon	Madagascar
Gambia, The	Tanzania

Seventy nautical miles (1)
Senegal

Two hundred nautical miles (4)

Argentina*	El Salvador	Panama
Benin	Ghana	Peru
Brazil	Liberia	Sierra Leone
Congo	Nicaragua	Somalia
Ecuador		Uruguay*

Rectangular/polygonal claim (3)

Maldives	Philippines	Tonga

---

*Overflight and navigation permitted beyond 12 nautical miles.

Table 2   *States with 200-Mile Exclusive Economic Zones*

Bangladesh	Cuba	Guatemala
Barbados	Djibouti	Guinea
Burma	Dominica	Guinea-Bissau
Cape Verde	Dominican Republic	Guyana
Colombia	Fiji	Haiti
Comoros	France	Honduras
Costa Rica	Grenada	Iceland

218

India
Indonesia
Ivory Coast
Kampuchea
Kenya
Korea, North
Madagascar
Maldives
Malaysia
Mauritiana
Mauritius
Mexico

Morocco
Mozambique
Nauru
New Zealand
Nigeria
Norway
Oman
Pakistan
Papua New Guinea
Philippines
Portugal
São Tomé and Príncipe

Seychelles
Spain
Sri Lanka
Suriname
Thailand
Togo
United Arab Emirates
Vanuatu
Venezuela
Vietnam
Yemen (Aden)

Table 3   *States with 200-Mile Exclusive Fisheries Zones*

Angola
Argentina
Australia
Bahamas, The
Benin
Brazil
Canada
Chile
Congo
Denmark
Ecuador
El Salvador
Gambia
German Democratic
   Republic
Germany, Federal
   Republic
Ghana
Iran

Ireland
Japan
Kiribati
Liberia
Netherlands
Nicaragua
Panama
Peru
Poland
Sierra Leone
Solomon Islands
Somalia
South Africa
Soviet Union
Sweden
Tuvalu
United Kingdom
United States
Uruguay

Table 4   *Broad Margin States*

Argentina
Australia
Brazil
Canada
France
India
Indonesia

Ireland
Madagascar
Mauritius
Namibia*
New Zealand
Oman
Somalia

South Africa
Soviet Union
Spain
Sri Lanka
United Kingdom
United States

*not yet independent

Table 5   *States with Archipelagic Claims*

Cape Verde Islands	Philippines
Fiji*	São Tomé and Príncipe
Indonesia	Solomon Islands***
Papua New Guinea**	

Archipelagic Claims to Non-Independent Areas

Danlac Archipelago (Ethiopia)	Faeroe Islands (Denmark)
Galapagos Archipelago (Ecuador)	Svalbard (Norway)

*no closing lines yet determined
**interim delimitation arrangement
***five separate areas enclosed

Table 6   *Important Historic Bays and Other Closed Water Bodies*

Argentina	Gulf of Matias
	Gulf of San Jorge
Australia	St Vincent Gulf
	Shark Bay
	Spencer Gulf
Burma	Gulf of Martaban
Canada	Hudson Bay
China	Gulf of Pohai
Italy	Gulf of Taranto
Libya	Gulf of Sirte
Panama	Gulf of Panama
Soviet Union	Cheshskaya Gulf
	Sea of Okhotsk

Table 7   *Land-Locked States*

Afghanistan	Hungary	Paraguay
Andorra	Laos	Rwanda
Austria	Lesotho	San Marino
Bhutan	Liechtenstein	Swaziland
Bolivia	Luxembourg	Switzerland
Botswana	Malawi	Uganda
Burundi	Mali	Upper Volta
Central African Republic	Mongolia	Vatican City
Chad	Nepal	Zambia
Czechoslovakia	Niger	Zimbabwe

References

Adelman, Kenneth L. (1981), 'Japan's security dilemma: an American View', *Survival*, vol. 23, no. 2 (March/April), pp. 72–9.

Alexander, Lewis M. (1983), 'The ocean enclosure movement: inventory and prospect', *San Diego Law Review*, vol. 20, no. 3, pp. 561–94.

Alexandersson, Gunnar (1982), *The Baltic Straits* (The Hague: Sijthoff & Noordhoff International Publishers).

Allen, Scott (1983), *'Mare Liberum'*, *United States Naval Institute Proceedings*, vol. 109/7/965 (July), pp. 45–49.

Ardrey, Robert (1967), *The Territorial Imperative* (London: Collins).

Barry, James A. (1972), 'The seabed arms control issue, 1967–1971: Superpower Symbiosis?', *Naval War College Review*, vol. 25, no. 5 (September–October, pp. 87–101.

Bell, Coral (1971), *The Conventions of Crisis: A Study in Diplomatic Management* (London: Oxford University Press).

Best, John (1979), 'Sovereignty in the North gets renewed attention', *Ottawa Journal*, 25 September.

Bildt, Carl (1983), 'Sweden and the Soviet submarines', *Survival*, vol. 25, no. 4 (July/August), pp. 165–9.

Blechman, Barry (1975), *The Control of Naval Armaments, Prospects and Possibilities* (Washington, DC: The Brookings Institution).

Blechman, Barry M., and Berman, Robert P. (eds) (1979), *Guide to Far Eastern Navies* (London: Seeley, Service).

Booth, Ken (1976), 'Foreign policies at risk: some problems of managing naval power', *Naval War College Review*, vol. 29, no. 1 (Summer), pp. 3–15.

Booth, Ken (1977), *Navies and Foreign Policy* (London: Croom Helm).

Booth, Ken (1978), 'US naval strategy: problems of survivability, usability, and credibility', *Naval War College Review*, vol. 31, no. 1 (Summer), pp. 11–28.

Booth, Ken (1979a), *Strategy and Ethnocentrism* (London: Croom Helm).

Booth, Ken (1979b), 'Superpower naval disengagement in the Mediterranean', *RUSI Journal*, vol. 124, no. 2 (June), pp. 28–35.

Booth, Ken (1980), *Las Armadas y la Politica Exterior* (Buenos Aires: Instituto De Publicaciones Navales).

Booth, Ken (1981), 'Law and strategy in northern waters', *Naval War College Review*, vol. 34 no. 4 (July–August), pp. 3–21.

Booth, Ken (1983), 'Naval strategy and the spread of psycho-legal boundaries at sea', *International Journal*, vol. 38 no. 3 (Summer), pp. 373–96.

Booth, Ken, and Dowdy, Lee (forthcoming), 'Structure and strategy in Indian Ocean naval developments: a stocktaking', in Lee Dowdy and Russell B. Trood, *The Indian Ocean: Perspectives on a Strategic Arena* (Chapel Hill, NC: Duke University Press).

Bracken, Paul (1983), *The Command and Control of Nuclear Forces* (New Haven, Conn: Yale University Press).

Brodie, Bernard (1973), *War and Politics* (London: Cassell).

221

Brown, E. D. (1983), 'Freedom of the seas versus the common heritage of mankind: fundamental principles in conflict', *San Diego Law Review*, vol. 20, no. 3, pp. 521–60.

Brown, Neville (1977), *The Future Global Challenge* (London: Royal United Services Institute).

Brownlie, Ian (1973), *Principles of Public International Law* (Oxford: Clarendon Press).

Bull, Hedley (1961), *The Control of the Arms Race, Disarmament and Arms Control in the Missile Age* (London: Weidenfield & Nicolson for the ISS).

Bull, Hedley (1976), 'Sea power and political influence', in *Power at Sea, I The New Environment* (London: IISS, Adelphi Papers no. 122, Spring), pp. 1–9.

Bull, Hedley (1977), *The Anarchical Society. A Study of Order in World Politics* (London: Macmillan).

Burns, Thomas (1978), *The Secret War for the Ocean Depths* (New York: Rawson Associates).

Butler, W. E. (1971), *The Soviet Union and the Law of the Sea* (Baltimore, Md: Johns Hopkins University Press).

Buzan, Barry (1978), *A Sea of Troubles? Sources of Dispute in the New Ocean Regime* (London: IISS, Adelphi Papers no. 143, Spring).

Buzan, Barry (1981), 'Naval power, the law of the sea, and the Indian Ocean as a zone of peace', *Marine Policy*, vol. 5 (July), pp. 194–204.

Buzan, Barry (1983), *People, States, & Fear. The National Security Problem in International Relations* (Brighton: Wheatsheaf Books).

Cable, James (1971), *Gunboat Diplomacy: Political Applications of Limited Naval Force* (London: Chatto & Windus for the IISS; 2nd edn., 1981).

Cable, Sir James (1982), 'The fashion for island grabbing', *Daily Telegraph*, 5 May.

Calder, Ritchie (1976), 'The lawless sea', *New Statesman*, 14 May.

Clingan, Thomas A. (1980), 'The next twenty years of naval mobility', *United States Naval Institute Proceedings*, vol. 106/5/927 (May), pp. 82–93.

Coleman, Terry (1982), 'Nott: If our losses were doubled we would have gone on', *Guardian*, 13 September.

Colombos, C. John (1967), *The International Law of the Sea* (London: Longman).

Connell, Jon (1982), 'Nott – "badly misunderstood"', *Sunday Times*, 5 September.

Craven, John P. (1966), 'Sea power and the sea bed', *United States Naval Institute Proceedings*, vol. 92/4/750 (April), pp. 36–52.

Darman, Richard G. (1978), 'The Law of the Sea: Rethinking US interests', *Foreign Affairs*, vol. 56, no. 2 (January), pp. 373–95.

Delaney, Captain Robert F., and Townsend, Major Patrick (1979), 'Defense of the depths', *United States Naval Institute Proceedings*, vol. 105/11/921 (November), pp. 37–41.

Department of National Defence (1981), *Defence 1980* (Ottawa: Department of National Defence).

Dismukes, Bradford, and McConnell, James M. (eds) (1979), *Soviet Naval Diplomacy* (New York: Pergamon).

Dowden, Richard (1983), 'Why the Swedes must sink a sub', *The Times*, 13 October.

Dowdy, W. L. (1981), 'Third World navies: new responsibilities, old problems', *Marine Policy*, vol. 5 (April), pp. 147–8.

Eberle, Rear-Admiral J. H. F. (1976), 'Designing a modern navy: a workshop discussion', in *Power at Sea, II Superpowers and Navies* (London: IISS,

Adelphi Papers no. 122, Spring), pp. 29–32.

Eddy, Paul, Linklater, Magnus, and Gillman, Peter (1982), *The Falklands War* (London: Sphere).

Fairhall, David (1983), 'MoD says Argentine trawlers were not in Falklands Sound', *Guardian*, 4 August.

Ferreira, Dominigos, P. C. B. (1983), *The Naval Power of Brazil: An Emerging Power at Sea*, National Security Affairs Issue Paper Series, 83-1 (Washington DC: National Defense University Press).

Fields, Donald (1983), 'Sweden protests over Russian spy-subs', *Guardian*, 27 April.

Fisher, Roger (1971), *Basic Negotiating Strategy* (Harmondsworth: Penguin).

Friedman, Norman (1980), 'SOSUS and US ASW Tactics', *United States Naval Institute Proceedings*, vol. 106/3/925 (March), pp. 120–3.

Froman, F. D. (1977), 'Kiev and the Montreux Convention: the aircraft carrier that became a cruiser to squeeze through the Turkish Straits', *San Diego Law Review*, vol. 14, pp. 681–717.

Gamble, John King (ed.) (1979), *Law of the Sea: Neglected Issues* (Honolulu: Law of the Sea Institute, University of Hawaii).

Garnett, J. C. (1976), 'The concept of war', in *The Year Book of World Affairs 1976* (London: Stevens & Stevens), pp. 133–149.

George, James L. (ed.) (1978), *Problems of Sea Power as We Approach the Twenty-First Century* (Washington, DC: American Enterprise, Institute for Public Policy Research).

Gold, Edgar, and Johnston, Douglas (1979), 'Ship-generated maritime pollution: the creator of regulated navigation', a paper presented at the 13th Annual Conference of the Law of the Sea Institute, Mexico City, October.

Gorshkov, Admiral S. G. (1979), *The Sea Power of the State* (Annapolis, Md: Naval Institute Press).

Gretton, Vice-Admiral Sir Peter (1965), *Maritime Strategy: a Study of British Defence Problems* (London: Cassell).

Guest, Ian (1981), 'Sea law experts ponder Tripoli's claim', *Guardian*, 21 August.

Guida, Richard A. (1980), 'International terrorism and the defense of offshore facilities', *United States Naval Institute Proceedings*, vol. 106/1/923 (January), pp. 22–3.

Haass, Richard (1978), 'Naval arms limitation in the Indian Ocean' *Survival*, vol. 20, no. 2 (March/April), pp. 50–7.

Halloran, Richard (1983), 'Soviet warships sail within 50 miles of US coastline', *The Times*, 16 February.

Hastings, Max, and Jenkins, Simon (1983), *The Battle for the Falklands* (London: Michael Joseph).

Heikal, Mohamed (1975), *The Road to Ramadan* (London: Collins).

Henkin, Louis (1968), *How Nations Behave: Law and Foreign Policy* (London: Pall Mall).

Hill, Captain J. R. (1972), 'Maritime forces in confrontation', *Brassey's Annual 1972* (London: Clowes), pp. 23–6.

Hollick, Ann L. (1981), *US Foreign Policy and the Law of the Sea* (Princeton, NJ: Princeton University Press).

Hoopes, Townsend (1969), *The Limits of Intervention* (New York: McKay).

Howard, Michael (1976), 'Order and conflict at sea in the 1980s', in *Power at Sea, III Competition and Conflict* (London: IISS Adelphi Papers no. 124, Spring), pp. 1–6.

Hynes, Samuel (1979), *The Auden Generation. Literature and Politics in England in the 1930s* (London: Faber).

IISS (1979), *Strategic Survey 1978* (London: IISS).

IISS (1981), *Strategic Survey 1980–1981)* (London: IISS).

Jackson, Robert (1975), *South Asian Crisis. India-Pakistan-Bangladesh* (London: Chatto & Windus).

Janis, Mark W. (1976), *Sea Power and the Law of the Sea* (Lexington, Mass.: Lexington Books).

Janis, Mark W., and Daniel, Donald C. F. (1974), 'The USSR: ocean use and ocean law', *Maritime Studies Management* (2), pp. 71–87.

Jenkins, Simon (1983), 'The truth about the Belgrano', *Spectator*, 11 June.

John, Ieuan G. (1975), *EEC Policy towards Eastern Europe* (Westmead, Hants: Saxon House).

Joyner, Christopher C. (1983), 'Offshore maritime terrorism: international implications and the legal response', *Naval War College Review*, vol. 36, no. 4 (July–August), pp. 16–31.

Kemp, Geoffrey (1978), 'Scarcity and strategy', *Foreign Affairs*, vol. 56, no. 2 (January), pp. 396–414.

Kissinger, Henry A. (1978), The Admiral Raymond A. Spruance Lecture, 8 March 1978, *Naval War College Review*, vol. 31, no. 1 (Summer), pp. 4–10.

Knight, H. Gary (1977), 'The law of the sea and naval missions', *United States Naval Institute Proceedings*, vol. 103/6/889 (June), pp. 34–43.

Knorr, Klaus (1966), *On the Uses of Military Power in the Nuclear Age* (Princeton, NJ: Princeton University Press).

Knorr, Klaus (1977), 'On the international uses of military force in the contemporary world', *Orbis*, vol. 21, no. 1 (Spring), pp. 5–27.

Knorr, Klaus and Morgenstern, Oskar (1968), *Political Conjecture in Military Planning*, Princeton University Policy Memorandum no. 35 (Princeton, NJ: Princeton University Press, November).

Lapidoth-Eschelbacher, Ruth (1982), *The Red Sea and the Gulf of Aden* (The Hague: Sijthoff & Noordhoff International Publishers).

Larus, Joel (1981), 'India: the neglected service faces the future', *United States Naval Institute Proceedings*, vol. 107/3/935 (March), pp. 77–83.

Laughton, J. K. (1866), 'The sovereignty of the sea', *Fortnightly Review*, 15 May–1 August, pp. 718–25.

Laursen, Finn (1982), 'Security versus access to resources: explaining a decade of US ocean policy', *World Politics*, vol. 34, no. 2 (January), pp. 197–229.

Leifer, M. (1978), *Malacca, Singapore and Indonesia* (The Hague: Sijthoff & Noordhoff International Publishers).

Luard, Evan (1974), *The Control of the Sea-bed. A New International Issue* (London: Heinemann).

Luttwak, Edward (1974), *The Political Uses of Sea Power* (Baltimore, Md: Johns Hopkins University Press).

MccGwire, Michael (1975), 'The geopolitical importance of strategic waterways in the Asian-Pacific region', *Orbis*, vol. 19, no. 3 (Fall), pp. 1058–76.

MccGwire, Michael (1977), 'Changing naval operations and military intervention', *Naval War College Review*, vol. 19, no. 4 (Spring), pp. 3–25.

MccGwire, Michael (1978), 'A navy for all seasons: fleet structure circa 2000', unpublished paper, April.

MccGwire, Michael (1981), 'Soviet naval doctrine and strategy', in Derek Leebaert (ed.), *Soviet Military Thinking* (London: Allen & Unwin), p. 125–81.

References

McConnell, James M., and Kelly, Anne M. (1973), 'Superpower naval diplomacy in the Indo-Pakistani crisis', in Michael MccGwire (ed.), *Soviet Naval Developments: Capability and Context* (New York: Praeger), pp. 442–55.

McCoy, Cdr Dennis F. (1977), *International Law and Naval Operations* (Newport, RI: US Naval War College).

Mann Borgese, Elisabeth (1982), 'Law of the sea: the next phase'. *Third World Quarterly*, vol. 4, no. 3 (October), pp. 698–718.

Marder, A. J. (1961), *From the Dreadnought to Scapa Flow*, Vol. I (London: Oxford University Press).

Martin, L. W. (1967), *The Sea in Modern Strategy* (London: Chatto & Windus for the ISS).

Moore, John Norton (1980), 'The regime of straits and the Third United Nations Conference on the Law of the Sea', *American Journal of International Law*, vol. 74, pp. 77–121.

Myrdal, Alva (1976), *The Game of Disarmament* (New York: Pantheon).

Neutze, Cdr Dennis R. (1982), 'The Gulf of Sidra incident: a legal perspective', *United States Naval Institute Proceedings*, vol. 108/1/947 (January), pp. 26–31.

Neutze, Cdr Dennis R. (1983), 'Whose law of whose sea?', *United States Naval Institute Proceedings*, vol. 109/1/959 (January), pp. 43–8.

Njenga, Francis X. (1975), 'Africa', in R. E. Osgood *et al.*, *Perspectives on Ocean Policy* (Washington, DC: Johns Hopkins University Press), pp. 87–105.

O'Connell, D. P. (1973), 'Naval policy and international law and international relations', in *Britain and the Sea*, The Collected Papers and Records of the Conference held at the Royal Naval College Greenwich, 12–14 September, pp. 30–1. Extracts were printed in the *New Scientist*, 25 October 1973.

O'Connell, D. P. (1975), *The Influence of Law on Sea Power* (Manchester: Manchester University Press).

O'Connell, D. P. (1978), 'Transit rights and maritime strategy', *RUSI Journal*, June, pp. 11–18.

Oliver, Captain E. F. (1973), 'Malacca: dire straits', *United States Naval Institute Proceedings*, vol. 99/6/824 (June) pp. 27–33.

Osgood, R. E. (1974), 'US security interests in ocean law', *Ocean Development and International Law Journal*, vol. 2 (Spring), pp. 1–36.

Osgood, Robert E. (1976), 'Military implications of the new ocean politics', in *Power at Sea I. The New Environment* (London: IISS Adelphi Papers no. 122, Spring), pp. 10–16.

Osgood, R. E., Hollick, A. L., Pearson, C. S., and Orr, J. C. (1975), *Toward a National Ocean Policy: 1976 and Beyond* (Washington, D.C.: USGPO).

O'Shaughnessy, Hugh (1983), 'Falklands: US to back Argentina', *Observer*, 7 August.

Ottoway, David B. (1981), 'In God they trust – and a low profile', *Manchester Guardian Weekly*, 8 March.

Painton, Frederick, (1983), 'Those mystery subs', *Time*, 11 July, pp. 6–9.

Pardo, Arvid (1983), 'The Convention on the Law of the Sea: a preliminary appraisal', *San Diego Law Review*, vol. 20, no. 3, pp. 489–503.

Parks, Major Hays (1977), 'Law of war training in the navy and marine corps', *United States Naval Institute Proceedings* vol. 103/12/894 (December), pp. 26–32.

Poulantzas, Nicholas M. (1970), 'The problem of "peaceful purposes" revisited', *Nederlands Junsten blad*, afl. 10, pp. 265–9.

Ramazani, R. K. (1979), *The Persian Gulf and the Strait of Hormuz* (The Hague: Sijthoff & Noordhoff).

Rapoport, Anatol (1960), *Fights, Games and Debates* (Ann Arbor, Mich.: University of Michigan Press).

Ratiner, Leigh S. (1982), 'The law of the sea: a crossroads for American foreign policy', *Foreign Affairs*, vol. 60, no. 2 (Summer), pp. 1006–21.

Regan, Lt Comm. Paul M. (1981), 'International law and the naval commander', *United States Naval Institute Proceedings* vol. 107/8/942 (August), pp. 51–56.

Reisman, W. Michael (1980), 'The regime of straits and national security: an appraisal of international lawmaking', *American Journal of International Law*, vol. 74, pp. 48–76.

Richardson, Elliot L. (1980), 'Power, mobility, and the law of the sea', *Foreign Affairs*, vol. 58, no. 4 (Spring), pp. 902–19.

Richardson, Elliot L. (1983), 'The United States posture toward the Law of the Sea Convention: awkward but not irreparable', *San Diego Law Review*, vol. 20, no. 3, pp. 505–19.

Roberts, Adam, and Guelff, Richard (1982), *Documents on the Laws of War* (Oxford: Clarendon).

Robertson, G. David, and Vasaturo, Gaylene (1983), 'Recent developments in the law of the sea 1981–1982', *San Diego Law Review*, vol. 20, no. 3, pp. 679–711.

Rosen, Jane (1981), 'US blocks law of sea treaty', *Manchester Guardian Weekly*, 15 March.

Rowan, Roy (1975), *The Four Days of Mayaguez* (New York: Norton).

Schelling, Thomas C. (1960), *The Strategy of Conflict* (Cambridge, Mass.: Harvard University Press).

Schelling, Thomas C. (1966), *Arms and Influence* (New Haven, Conn.: Yale University Press).

Sebek, V. (1977), *The Eastern European States and the Development of the Law of the Sea* (New York: Oceana).

Smith, George P. (1980), *Restricting the Concept of Free Seas. Modern Maritime Law Re-Evaluated* (New York: Krieger).

Swayze, Cdr Frank B. (1980), 'Negotiating a law of the sea', *United States Naval Institute Proceedings*, vol. 106/7/929 (July), pp. 33–9.

Till, Geoffrey (1982), *Maritime Strategy and the Nuclear Age* (London: Macmillan).

Truver, S. G. (1980), *The Strait of Gibralter and the Mediterranean* (The Hague: Sijthoff & Noordhoff International Publishers).

Vayrynen, Raimo (1978), 'The sea-bed treaty reviewed', *World Today*, vol. 34, no. 6 (June), pp. 236–44.

Vigor, Peter (1975), *The Soviet View of War, Peace, and Neutrality* (London: Routledge & Kegan Paul).

Walker, George K. (1978), 'Sea power and the law of the sea: the need for a contextual approach', *Naval War College Review*, vol. 30, no. 4 (Spring), pp. 88–101.

Watt, D. Cameron (1982), 'Beating the US under the sea', *The Times*, 28 September.

Webley, Simon (1982), *The Law of the Sea Treaty: Some Crucial Questions for the UK* (London: Institute for European Defence and Strategic Studies).

Whymant, Robert (1978), Soviet war games anger Japan', *Guardian*, 8 June.

Will, George (1980), 'Vietnam complex lives on', *Manchester Guardian Weekly*, 6 January.

References

Winchester, Simon (1981), Why Reagan set the tomcats on "the world's most dangerous man"', *Sunday Times*, 23 August.

Wylie, J. C. (1969), 'The Sixth Fleet and American diplomacy' in J. C. Hurewitz (ed.), *Soviet-American Rivalry in the Middle East* (New York: Praeger), pp. 56–9.

Young, Elizabeth (1974), 'New laws for old navies: military implications of the law of the sea', *Survival*, vol. 16, no. 6 (November/December), pp. 262–7.

Young, Elizabeth (1978), 'Jurisdiction at Sea', *World Today*, vol. 34, no. 6 (June), pp. 199–201.

Young, Elizabeth, and Sebek, Viktor (1978), 'Red seas and blue seas: Soviet uses of ocean law', *Survival*, vol. 20, no. 6 (November/December), pp. 255–62.

Zuleta, Bernard (1983), 'The law of the sea after Montego Bay', *San Diego Law Review*, vol. 20, no. 3, pp. 475–88.

Zumwalt, Elmo (1976), *On Watch* (New York: Quadrangle/The New York Times Book Co.).

Index

Index